Mark Allen Debra Powell Dickie Dolby

rechecked

IELTS Graduation

Student's Book

C153650964

Contents

Unit and topic	Reading skills	Listening skills	Speaking skills	Writing skills	Language focus and Vocabulary	Study skills
7 The world of work	Prediction True, False, Not Given Flow chart completion Matching information and sections Short answer questions Note completion Yes, No, Not Given Matching details to paragraphs	**Section 2** Prediction Short answer questions Sentence completion Table completion	Predicting the future Expressing certainty Pronunciation Connected speech	**Task 1** Multiple diagrams Ways of describing data Determiners	*that*-clauses Synonyms for people	Editing your writing
8 Art and the city	Distinguishing fact and opinion Matching: People and descriptions Summary completion (No list) Sentence completion (From a list)	**Section 3** Analysing multiple-choice options Short answer questions Note completion **Section 4** Discourse markers Multiple choice Sentence completion Short answer questions	Structuring what you say	**Task 2** Review: Balanced argument and opinion essays Refuting opposing arguments Giving and refuting opinions Writing conclusions	Linking expressions Types of buildings, furniture vocabulary	Improving your spelling
9 Tomorrow's world	Identifying the writer's purpose Yes, No, Not Given Matching: identification of arguments	**Section 2** Listening for dates and numbers Sentence completion Note completion **Section 4** Prediction Summary completion Diagram completion	Expressing likes and dislikes Pronunciation Sentence stress: Weak forms	**Task 1** Describing illustrations Maps	Academic vocabulary Expressing the future:probability Prefixes	Understanding question task words
10 From me to you	Identification of main idea and supporting information Multiple-choice questions Summary completion (from a list) Sentence completion Yes, No, Not Given	**Section 1** Multiple-choice: Diagrams Sentence completion Multiple choice **Section 3** Multiple options Table completion Summary completion	**Parts 1, 2 and 3**	**Task 2** Keeping your focus Different question tasks Expecting the unexpected Stating your view	Articles Media vocabulary	Idiomatic expressions

Introduction

Overview of the book

Welcome to IELTS Graduation, a course book which is designed to help you prepare for the IELTS academic test.

This book contains a wide range of activities to help you develop the academic language and exam skills necessary to achieve an IELTS band score of between 5.5 and 7.5. If your IELTS level is lower than this, you might prefer to study IELTS Foundation first.

Each unit contains practice in Reading, Writing, Speaking and Listening with each part of the test broken down and explained, and exam skills practised. The units also contain Language Focus sections, which analyse the main grammatical areas relevant to a higher IELTS level, together with Vocabulary sections focused on common IELTS topics. There are also regular Pronunciation sections as well as pages developing your Study Skills.

The back of the book contains further grammatical explanations and exercises along with extra vocabulary work. There are also complete model answers for all the Writing questions accompanied by useful comments. Complete scripts for all the Listening exercises are in the back of the book.

Overview of the IELTS test

IELTS consists of four modules. Further information on how IELTS is assessed can be found on the IELTS website: **www.ielts.org**

THE LISTENING MODULE (40 minutes)

There are four sections in the Listening test. The first two sections are general listening situations, whereas the last two sections are academic situations. Section 4 is usually a lecture. The listening test lasts for 30 minutes plus 10 minutes at the end of the test to write your answers on the answer sheet. There are about 40 questions in total. You only hear each section of the test **once** so you need to keep up with the tape.

Question types

Completion of sentences, notes, summaries, tables, diagrams or flow charts
Short answer questions
Multiple-choice questions
Labelling parts of a diagram

Advice

- Be prepared for varying speaker speeds and different accents (American, Australian, Canadian, American, New Zealand, British)
- Prepare yourself before you listen by reading the questions carefully and trying to imagine what the situation is about. Think about the type of vocabulary you may hear.
- Answer all the questions. If you miss a question, guess the answer.
- Spelling counts, so make a note of your common spelling mistakes and work on reducing them.
- Practise your listening by listening to the radio and watching English films and television. Don't try to understand every word. Just pick out the main points in what is being said.

THE READING MODULE (60 minutes)

There are 40 questions in the reading module. The module consists of three passages which total about 2000–2200 words and become progressively more difficult. The passages are on topics of general interest and are intended for non-specialist readers. At least one passage will contain detailed, logical argument. Passages come from magazines and journals, books and newspapers.

Question types

Completion of sentences, notes, summaries, tables, diagrams or flow charts
Short answer questions
Multiple-choice questions
Matching headings to paragraphs or sections of the passage
Locating information in a paragraph or section
Matching lists / phrases
True / False / Not Given: identifying information in the passage
Yes / No / Not Given: identifying the writer's view or opinion

Advice

- Skim read the passage (1–3 minutes) for general understanding.
- Read the questions (11–15 per passage) and underline key words.
- Scan the passage for key words or synonyms or parallel expressions for these.
- Identify the sentence or paragraph which contains the answer to the question and read it intensively.
- **Write answers directly onto the answer paper. You do not have extra time at the end of the examination to transfer your answers**

THE WRITING MODULE (60 minutes)

There are two compulsory writing tasks which should be answered using a formal, academic style of English. Task 2 is worth more so it is suggested that this is written first.

Task 1

20 minutes	150 words	Write a factual description of a diagram

Advice

- Summarize the main features of the diagram in 2/3 paragraphs.
- Don't attempt to describe every detail.
- Describe changes and/or make comparisons where relevant.
- Don't speculate about possible causes or reasons for trends.
- Support your points with figures from the diagram.
- Be prepared for a range of different diagrams (graphs, tables, bar charts, pie charts, processes, illustrations or maps).
- Organize your time: Think and Plan (2–3 mins) → Write (12–15mins) → Check (2–3 mins)

Task 2

40 minutes	250 words	Write an essay in response to a given opinion or problem

Advice

- Take time to understand the question and keep every sentence focused on it.
- Introduce, develop and conclude your essay.
- Support your points with explanation, evidence or examples.
- Make your own opinion clear.
- Aim for 2 or 3 main points – with each in a separate paragraph.
- Be flexible – different questions will require different approaches so read the question carefully.
- Organize your time: Think and Plan (5–10 mins) → Write (25–30mins) → Check (5 mins)

The IELTS Writing paper is assessed using the following four criteria:

Task 1

1 **Task Achievement** – This assesses how well you have understood the diagram and if you have summarized and highlighted the main patterns and differences.
2 **Coherence and Cohesion** – This assesses how clear your summary is and whether or not you have used paragraphs. It also assesses your use of linking and reference words.
3 **Lexical Resource** – This assesses your vocabulary and spelling and also looks at your word formation.
4 **Grammatical Range and Accuracy** – This assesses whether or not you have used a wide range of sentence types, both simple and complex. It also tests your punctuation.

Task 2

1 **Task Response** – This assesses how well you have understood the question and whether or not you have answered all the different parts of the question. It tests your ability to make clear and logical arguments.

2 **Coherence and Cohesion** – This assesses how logically and clearly you have linked your ideas together and whether or not you have used paragraphs. It also assesses your use of linking and reference words.
3 **Lexical Resource** – This assesses your vocabulary and spelling and also looks at your word formation. You need to show a wide range of topic vocabulary linked to the question.
4 **Grammatical Range and Accuracy** – This assesses whether or not you have used a wide range of sentence types, both simple and complex. It also tests your punctuation.

THE SPEAKING MODULE (11–15 minutes)

There are three parts to the speaking test.

SPEAKING PART 1

4–5 minutes	**You will be given three topics and asked questions about each one. You will be speaking about your personal life and hobbies.**

SPEAKING PART 2

3–4 minutes	**You will speak about a given topic for about 1–2 minutes. You will be asked 1–2 follow-up questions related to the topic.**

SPEAKING PART 3

3–4 minutes	**You will be asked some general more abstract questions linked to the Part 2 topic.**

Advice

- Listen carefully to the questions.
- Be prepared for a range of different topics.
- Remember that it is your grammar mistakes and pronunciation that can seriously affect your level.
- Speak as clearly and naturally as possible. Don't use expressions unless you know how to use them correctly.

The IELTS Speaking module is assessed using the following four criteria:

1 **Fluency and Coherence** – This assesses how well you can carry on speaking without hesitating or correcting yourself. It also tests your use of discourse markers.
2 **Lexical Resource** – This assesses how wide your vocabulary range is. It also assesses your use of collocation and idiomatic language.
3 **Grammatical Range and Accuracy** – This assesses how regularly you can speak without making mistakes. It also looks at how often you use complex sentences in your speech.
4 **Pronunciation** – This assesses your ability to pronounce the sounds of English accurately and whether or not most of what you say can be clearly understood.

1 Learn to succeed

Which subjects did you study at school?

Which did you like the most / least? Why?

Would you like to study another subject in the future?

Are there any subjects in your country which are traditionally 'male' or 'female'? If so, why do you think this is?

Reading

Exam strategy

Timing

You won't have time in the examination to read all three passages intensively. Therefore, you need to develop strategies for reading each passage and for answering each question type.

1 Skim read the whole passage for a general idea of the meaning and purpose of the text.

2 Read the first set of questions.

3 Scan read the text to find the section of the text that will answer each question.

4 Read that part of the text intensively to find the answer.

Skim and scan reading

TIP

Use the title, subtitle and illustrations in a reading text to help you to predict what the text is about.

Reading strategy

Skim reading for a general idea

Read the introduction, the first sentence of each paragraph and the conclusion quickly to understand the gist or main idea of the text. Do NOT worry about vocabulary for this first reading. Spend about 2–3 minutes for this reading.

1 Look at the title and subtitle for the passage on page 10 and answer questions **1** and **2**.
Circle the appropriate letter **A–D**.

1 The main idea in the passage is a discussion of

A differences between male and female brains.
B differing male and female ability in math.
C why men are more successful in math and science careers.
D the effect of cultural conditioning on mathematical ability.

2 The purpose of the passage is to present

A a problem and a solution.
B one side of an argument.
C cause and effect.
D both sides of an argument.

2 Skim read the passage quickly (**2–3** minutes) to check your predictions.

Reading strategy

Scan reading

Scan reading involves reading a text quickly to **locate** a number, date, name, place, etc. You do not need to understand the text to scan read successfully.

3 Scan the passage (**1–2** minutes) to find the following:

3 a year in which the OECD administered a test
4 the average difference in the size of male and female brains (%)
5 the name of a professor at Yale university
6 the university which employs Dr. Elizabeth Spelke

Battle of Sexes Whirls Above the Science Gap

The debate continues over whether physiological differences between men and women or cultural attitudes help men dominate in scientific and mathematical careers.

A When Lawrence H. Summers, the president of Harvard, suggested recently that one factor in women's lagging progress in science and mathematics might be innate differences between the sexes, his comment elicited so many fierce reactions that he quickly apologized. But many people were left to wonder: Did he have a point?

Researchers say there are many discrepancies between men and women – in their attitudes towards math and science, in the architecture of their brains, in the way they metabolize medications. Yet researchers warn that a difference in form does not necessarily mean a difference in function. 'We can't get anywhere denying that there are neurological and hormonal differences between males and females, because clearly there are,' said Virginia Valian, a psychology professor. 'The trouble we have as scientists is in assessing their significance to real-life performance.'

B For example, neuroscientists have shown that women's brains are about 10% smaller than men's, on average, even after accounting for women's comparatively smaller body size. But throughout history, people have cited such anatomical distinctions to support hypotheses that merely reflect the prejudices of the time. A century ago the French scientist Gustav Le Bon pointed to the smaller brains of women and said that explained the 'fickleness, inconstancy, absence of thought and logic, and incapacity to reason' in women.

Overall size aside, some evidence suggests that female brains are relatively more endowed with the prized neurons, the grey matter, thought to do the bulk of the brain's thinking while men's brains have more white matter, the tissue between neurons. And they use the grey and white matter in different proportions when solving problems. What such discrepancies may or may not mean is anyone's conjecture. 'It is cognition that counts, not the physical matter that does the cognition,' argued Nancy Kanwisher, a professor of neuroscience at the Massachusetts Institute of Technology.

C When they do study cognitive prowess, many researchers have been impressed with how similarly young boys and girls, ranging from 5 months through 7 years, master new tasks. 'We adults may think very different things about boys and girls, and treat them accordingly, but when we measure their capacities, they're remarkably alike,' said Elizabeth Spelke, a professor of psychology at Harvard. In adolescence, though, some differences in aptitude begin to emerge, especially when it comes to performance on standardized tests. While average verbal scores are very similar, boys have outscored girls on math for the past three decades or so.

D Nor is the masculine edge in math unique to the United States. In an international standardized test administered in 2003 by the international research group Organization for Economic Cooperation and Development (OECD) to 250,000 15-year-olds in 41 countries, boys did moderately better on the math portion in just half the nations. For nearly all the other countries, there were no significant differences found between the sexes.

But average scores varied wildly from place to place and from one subcategory of math to the next. Japanese girls, for example, were on par with Japanese boys on every math section save that of 'uncertainty' which measures probabilistic skills, and Japanese girls scored higher over all than did the boys of many other nations, including the United States. In Iceland, girls did better than Icelandic boys by a significant margin on all parts of the test, as they habitually do on their national maths exams. Interestingly, in Iceland and everywhere else, girls participating in the survey expressed more negative attitudes toward math.

E As a result of these findings, many researchers are convinced that neither sex has a monopoly on basic math ability and that culture rather than chromosomes explains any gap in math scores. According to Yu Xie, a sociologist at the University of Michigan, among Asians people rarely talk about having a gift for math or anything else. If a student comes home with a poor grade in math, he said, the parents push the child to work harder. He adds that there is good survey data showing that this disbelief in innate ability, along with the conviction that math ability can be improved through practice, is a tremendous cultural asset in Asian society and among Asian-Americans.

F Many people argue that it is unnecessary to invoke 'innate differences' to explain the gap that persists in fields like physics, engineering, mathematics and chemistry. C. Megan Urry, a professor of physics and astronomy at Yale, said there was clear evidence that societal and cultural factors still hindered women in science. Dr. Urry cited a 1983 study in which 360 people – half men, half women – rated mathematics papers. On average, the men rated them higher when the author had a masculine name than when the author had a feminine name. There was a similar, but smaller, disparity in the scores women gave. Dr. Elizabeth Spelke, said: 'It's hard for me to get excited about small differences in biology when the evidence shows that women in science are still discriminated against every step of the way.'

The debate is sure to go on. Sandra F. Witelson, a professor or psychiatry and behavioural neurosciences at McMaster University in Hamilton, Ontario, said biology might yet be found to play some part. 'People have to have an open mind,' Dr. Witelson said.

TIP

The words in the question will usually not be exactly the same as the words in the passage. Look for parallel expressions in the passage and the headings. Parallel expressions are words or phrases with similar meanings to those in the passage.

Matching: Headings to sections

Exam information

For this question type you must choose the heading that best summarizes the main idea of a section or paragraph of the passage. There will usually be more headings than paragraphs or sections.

4 The correct heading for Section **A** is **iii**. Find synonyms in the subtitle and Section A for *controversy* and *inborn*.

5 Read the passage and answer questions **1–5**.

The reading passage has six sections, **A–F**. Choose the correct heading for sections **B–F** from the list of headings below.

List of headings

i Discrimination based on gender
ii Importance of physical differences between men and women
iii Controversy surrounding inborn differences between the sexes
iv Comparison of performance of Japanese and Icelandic schoolchildren
v Comparison of abilities of male and female children
vi Proposed reasons for success of Asian children
vii Effects of environment on performance
viii Differences in how males and females rate math papers
ix International comparison of math results
x Differences in how men and women solve problems

0 Section A **iii**
1 Section B ____
2 Section C ____
3 Section D ____
4 Section E ____
5 Section F ____

TIP

There may be some letters (names) you do not need to use.

Matching: Opinions and people

6 Scan the passage to find the people in **A–G**. Then answer questions **6–11**.

Match the opinions to the people that express them.

6 The ability to think is more important than brain anatomy. ____
7 Attitude is the most important factor in a successful performance. ____
8, 9 Men and women are not given the same respect. ____, ____
10, 11 There may be a link between ability and gender. ____, ____

A Lawrence Summers
B Gustav Le Bon
C Nancy Kanwisher
D Elizabeth Spelke
E Yu Xie
F Megan Urry
G Sandra Witelson

Sentence completion (from a list)

Exam information

Use words from a list or from the passage to complete the sentences. The correct answer must complete the sentence grammatically and agree with what is said in the text. The answers to the questions will follow the order of information in the passage.

Question strategy

1 Read the questions and guess the missing information from what comes before and after the gap.

2 Use key words in the question to help you to locate the paragraph which answers the question. Look for parallel expressions in the questions and passage, ie words or phrases with similar meanings to those in the passage.

7 Answer questions **12–16**. The words <u>underlined</u> in the questions are synonyms for words used in the passage.

Complete the sentences using words from the box.

12 There appears to be little difference in the <u>learning capacity</u> of ________ .
13 Tests show little difference in the <u>language</u> abilities of ________ .
14 Japanese girls <u>got better results in math</u> than ________ .
15 The <u>worst opinion</u> of math was held by ________ .
16 The importance of <u>effort</u> has been demonstrated by ________ .

A Icelandic boys
B teenage girls
C American teenagers
D Asian children
E American boys
F young boys and girls
G Japanese boys
H adolescents
I Icelandic girls

Vocabulary

TIP

Sometimes questions repeat the same words that are used in the passage. However, more often questions contain words or phrases with similar meanings to those used in the passage. Finding these parallel expressions in the text will help you to locate the answer to the question.

Synonyms and parallel expressions

1 Match the expressions taken from the passage in **A** with parallel expressions in **B**.

A	**B**
0 innate _e_ (A)	a at the same level as
1 discrepancy / disparity (A)	b treated unfairly
2 anatomical distinctions (B)	c difference
3 cognition (B)	d teenage years
4 prowess / aptitude (C)	e inborn
5 adolescence (C)	f (ability with) words
6 verbal (ability) (C)	g physical differences
7 on a par (with) (D)	h the ability to think and understand
8 discriminated (against) (F)	i ability

TIP

Prefixes usually give information about the meaning of a word. If you understand the meaning of the prefix, it can help you to guess the meaning of a new word.

Word formation: Prefixes

1 These examples come from the reading passage:

eg '**neuro**scientists have shown that ... ' (Section B)
eg ' ... from one **sub**category of math to the next.' (Section D)
'**neuro**-' is a prefix referring to anything to do with nerves or the nervous system.
'**sub**-' can refer to a small part of a larger thing.

What do you think *neuroscientist* and *subcategory* refer to in the reading passage?

2 Match these common prefixes to their meanings.

1	**anti-**war; **pro**-war	a	again
2	**cyber**space	b	former
3	**non-**smoker	c	not enough; below
4	**re**organization	d	bad(ly); wrong(ly)
5	**ex**-wife	e	half; partly
6	**mal**practice; **mis**behaviour	f	distant; involving the phone or television
7	**under**ground	g	against; in favour of
8	**semi-**circle	h	relating to computers / the Internet
9	**tele**communication	i	false; not real
10	**pseudo-**science	j	ahead; before
11	**fore**cast	k	relating to yourself or itself
12	**eco**-friendly	l	two or twice
13	**bi**lingual	m	relating to the environment
14	**auto**biography; **self-**discipline	n	not

3 Complete these sentences using the prefix in the sentence and one of the words in the box.

ability annual ~~café~~ esteem final graduate
information president profit write

0 A cyber café is a popular place for tourists and travellers to send and receive e-mails.
1 A charity is a non-________ organization which gives help or money to people who are ill or poor.
2 Tickets were sold out months before the semi________ was due to be played.
3 It's much easier to re________ work that has been done on a computer.
4 Most under________ courses at British universities take three years to complete.
5 The ex-________ of the United States was present at the ceremony.
6 The government was accused of deliberately deceiving the public by giving it mis________ about the threat of war.
7 A bi________ event takes place twice a year.
8 He was suffering from depression and low self-________
9 After the accident he was left with a severe physical dis________ .

Language focus

Unreal sentence subjects
There is/was …

See Grammar reference, page 169.

We use ***there*** + the verb 'to be' to say that something 'is' or exists. In these sentences, ***there*** is the grammatical subject. The real subject, or the focus of the sentence, comes after the verb 'to be'.

Compare: There are many discrepancies between men and women.

The real subject of the sentence is 'many discrepancies', which comes after the verb 'are'.

1 Underline the correct verb in 1–3 and then complete the rules in a and b.

1 **There is/are** neurological and hormonal **differences** between men and women.
2 **There is/are** clear **evidence** that cultural factors still hindered women in science.
3 **There was/were** a smaller **disparity** in the scores women gave.

a If the noun after 'be' is singular or uncountable, the verb is ________ .
b If the noun after 'be' is plural, the verb is ________ .

2 We can use 'there' with all tenses of 'to be'. Complete each sentence with the best form of the verb 'be'.

1 Throughout history, there ________ scientists who have suggested that women are less intelligent because their brains are smaller.
2 Test results show that there ________ little difference in the abilities of boys and girls under 7 years of age.
3 There ________ 250,000 teenagers involved in the OECD test administered in 2003.
4 There ________ no significant difference in the results for boys and girls in half the countries tested.
5 There ________ undoubtedly ________ further studies into the learning abilities of males and females.

3 Note what happens to the word order of the sentence when 'to be' is followed by a past or present participle. Tick the correct form of the sentence, a or b. Then study the reading passage Sections **D** and **E** on page 10 to check your answers.

1 a There **were found** no significant differences between the sexes.
  b There **were** no significant differences **found** between the sexes.
2 a There **is** good survey data **showing** that disbelief in innate ability … is a(n) … asset.
  b There **is showing** good survey data that disbelief in innate ability … is a(n) … asset.

4 Improve these sentences. Use 'There + to be … '

0 Did you know a bank on campus is?
  Did you know there's a bank on campus?

1 Something unusual about the test results was.
2 A loud noise outside the classroom was.
3 No reason to believe that men are more capable than women is.

4 Someone is waiting to meet you.
5 Similar results were obtained by Japanese boys and girls.

Listening

Exam strategy

Learning to predict

To answer the questions as effectively as possible, it is important to:

1 Keep up with the CD.
2 Use the time you are given to read the questions before you listen to predict what the conversation will be about.

Section 1

Form completion

1 1.1 You are going to hear a conversation between a tutor and a student. Before you listen:

1 Underline keywords in the instructions. Pay careful attention to any words in **BOLD** in **CAPITAL LETTERS**.
2 Underline keywords in questions **1–6**. The first word has been done for you as an example.

Now listen to the first part of the recording and answer questions **1–6**.

Write **NO MORE THAN ONE WORD** for each answer.

1 What year is the student in?
2 How is the student feeling?

2 Fill in the form below and answer questions **3–6**.

Personal Information Form

Sex: Female

Name: **3** ....

Address: Bramble House

Room No **4** ....

Type of Accommodation: Shared

Nationality: **5** ....

Emergency Contact Number: **6**....................

Exam strategy

Maps and diagrams

Look at the map or diagram carefully and make sure you understand what direction you need to be following. Is it right or left? North or South? Circle or underline any keywords or areas. Find the starting point once the CD begins.

Map completion

3 Look at the map on page 16 and discuss the following questions. Use the Useful language box to help you.

0 Where is Chemistry Lab B?
It is in University Lane, next to Chemistry Lab A.
1 Where is Dalton House?
2 Which building is immediately opposite the cafeteria?
3 How do you get to Lecture Hall A from Dalton House?

Useful language: prepositions of place and location

at the top of ... at the bottom of ... next to ...
immediately opposite ... in (a street, town) ... near ...
on the corner of ...

4 1.2 You are going to hear the rest of the conversation. Before you listen, look at the instruction below and the map. Read question **12**. Now listen to the recording and answer questions **7–12**.

Find the location of the buildings in the box by writing a letter (**A–G**) for questions **7–11**. There are more letters than buildings.

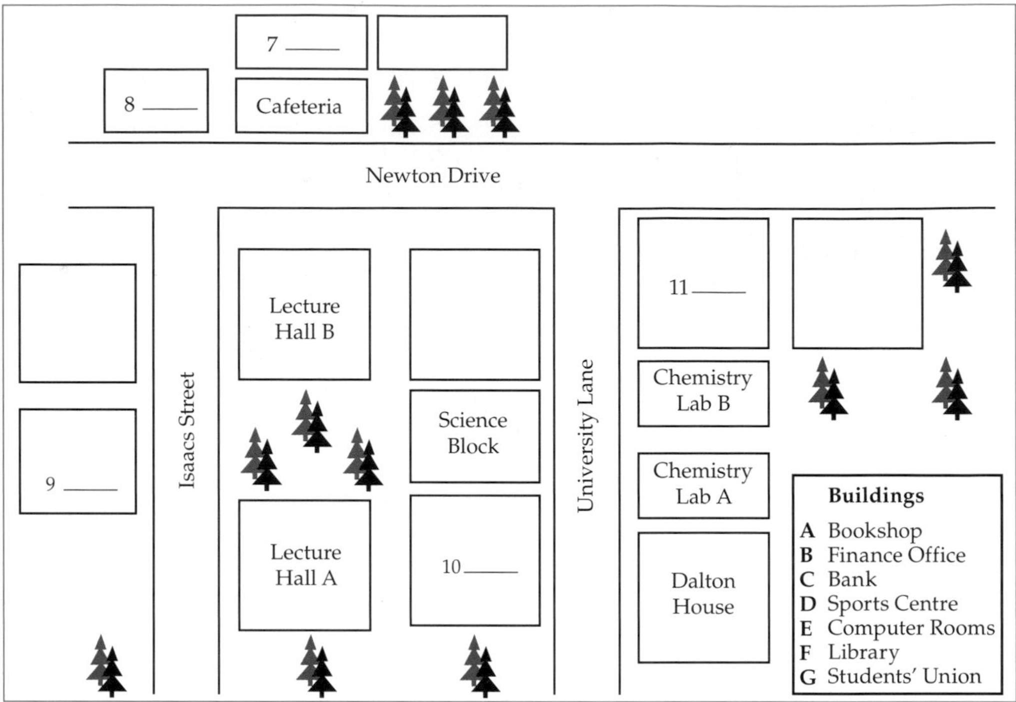

12 Circle the correct answer.
The tutor is available on:
A Thursday afternoon
B Monday evening
C Wednesday all day
D Thursday morning
E Friday mornings only

Speaking

Exam strategy

Make sure that your language changes with the test. It should become more formal and impersonal as the test progresses.

In Parts 1 and 2 the topics will be more personal and you will talk more about yourself. In Part 3 the topics will be more academic and you will talk more about local and global issues.

Understanding the test

1 Work in pairs. Discuss the following Part 1 questions.

1 How often do you read books?
2 Do you think it's important for children to learn by visiting exhibitions and museums?
3 Are libraries in your country more popular now than 10 years ago?
4 What are the characteristics of a good writer?

Exam strategy

Keep to the topic.
Keep talking.
Develop your answer.

Exam information

In Part 2 you will be given a topic to speak about. Before you speak, you will be given 1 minute to think and prepare and you will be given a pencil and paper to make notes.

2 Work in pairs. Make notes about the topics below. Discuss the topics for 1 minute.

A

Describe a subject you really enjoy studying.

You should say:
What it is
Why you like it
How long you have been studying it for

You should also explain how this subject will help you in your future career.

B

Describe a teacher you really admire.

You should say:
Who it is
Why you like them
How long you have known them

You should also explain what this person has taught you.

3 Discuss the following Part 3 questions with your partner.

1 Do you agree or disagree with the idea that, in the future, teachers will play a smaller role in education and students will rely more on internet resources?
2 How would you compare single sex education with co-educational environments?
3 In your country, are subjects like physics and chemistry more important than subjects like art and music?
4 Do you agree or disagree with the idea that students learn far more outside the classroom than inside it?
5 Evaluate whether or not there are any real differences in the approaches of men and women to learning.

Writing 1

Task 1

1 What can you remember about Writing Task 1 from the Introduction to IELTS section at the front of the book?

1 How long should you spend on Task 1 and how should you use this time?
2 How many words should you write and in how many paragraphs?
3 What four areas of your writing does the examiner look at?
4 Should you express your own views and give reasons explaining the information in the diagram?
5 Should you try to write about every detail?

2 All Writing Task 1 questions give you a diagram or illustration and ask you to select and report the main features and make comparisons where relevant. There are a range of possible diagram types.

1 Make a simple drawing to illustrate each of the following:

A Graph
B Bar chart
C Pie chart
D Table
E Multiple diagram (eg two or more diagrams about the same topic)
F Process or cycle (eg flow chart showing the greenhouse effect)
G Illustration (eg how two different cameras work)
H Map

2 Use the words below to label the correct parts of your drawings.

vertical axis column/bar key row stages locations
horizontal axis segment parts figures line

Task 1: Changes over time

Exam strategy

It is important to identify whether a diagram shows changes over time or differences in one fixed time, as they require different vocabulary and grammatical structures.

3 Look at the following diagrams.

1 For each diagram, decide if you need to: write about changes over time, make comparisons or both?

1 **Highest qualification of school leavers (%)**

	Level 3	Level 2	No exam
2004	28	45	13
2005	30	50	8
2006	30	49	4
2007	32	55	5

2

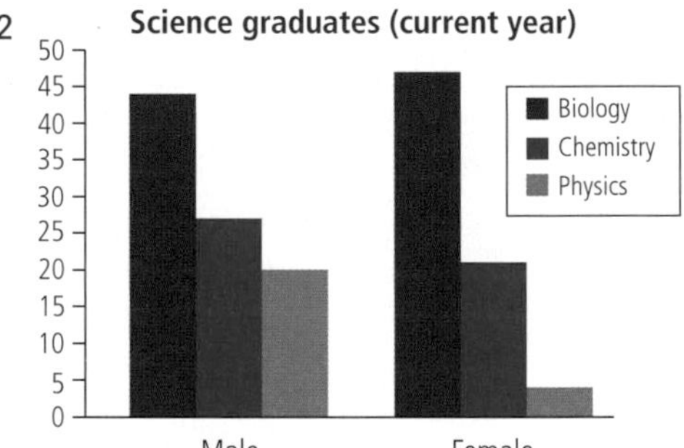

3

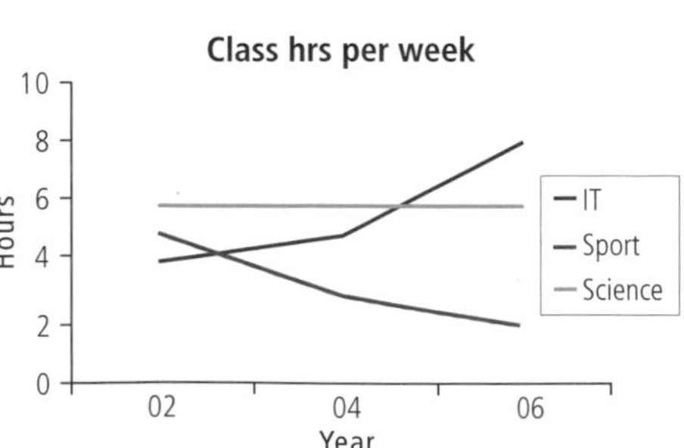

4

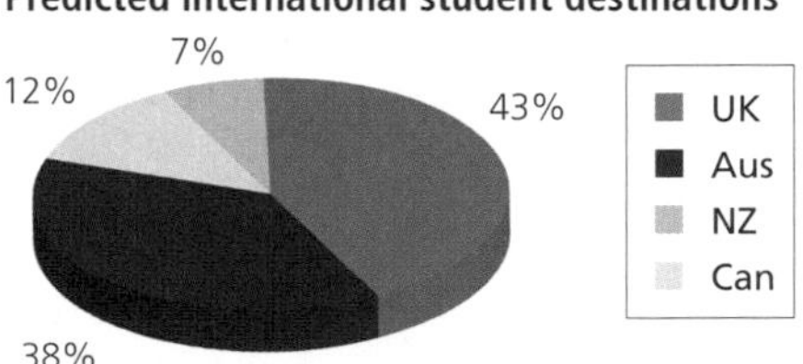

Question strategy

Study the diagram carefully to check you understand what period(s) of time the diagram describes and use appropriate tenses. See page 168 for a review of tenses.

2 Which tenses would you use for each diagram? Why?
3 Write an appropriate introductory sentence that describes what each diagram shows.

0 (Diagram 1) The table shows school leavers' highest qualifications for the categories level 3, level 2 and no exam as a percentage for the years 2004 to 2007.

4 Look at the Useful language table below for describing changes over time.

1 Work in pairs. Find suitable words from the table to describe the main changes in diagrams 1 and 3.
2 Use these words to add two further sentences to the descriptions below.

Diagram 1

Regarding level 3 qualifications, the percentage increased steadily from 28% in 2004 to 32% in 2007. ____________________

____

____

____

Diagram 3

The class hours for sport fell significantly throughout the five year period dropping to two hours per week in 2006.

Useful language: describing trends

Meaning	VERB	NOUN
go down	decrease fall drop decline plunge (big change) plummet (big change)	*same* *same* *same* *same* / /
go up	increase rise grow double treble rocket (big change)	*same* *same* growth doubling in + n trebling in + n /
no change	level off remain the same remain stable stabilize	a levelling off at / / /
constant change	fluctuate	fluctuation in + n
position	reach a high / peak of reach a low of stood at	a high of a low of /

Meaning	ADJ/ADV
small change	steady(ily) slight(ly) gradual(ly)
large change	considerable (ly) sharp(ly) dramatic(ally) significant(ly) substantial(ly)

ADJ & ADV PATTERNS	TIME PHRASES
Sb + v + **ADJ + N** *There was a* ***substantial increase*** *in students in 2006.*	from *2000* to *2005* from *150* to *200 units* in *2006*
Sb + **V + ADV** *The number of students* ***increased substantially*** *throughout the period from 2002 to 2006.*	for *5 years* between *2000* and *2005* during / throughout the period from *2000* to *2005*

5 Look at the following simplified diagrams, showing applications for different courses by month in various colleges.

1 Write a description of the main changes using language from the table above.

Accounting
Economics
Business Studies

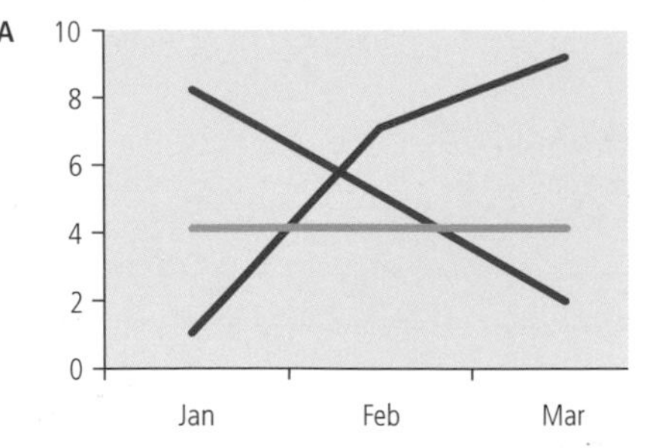

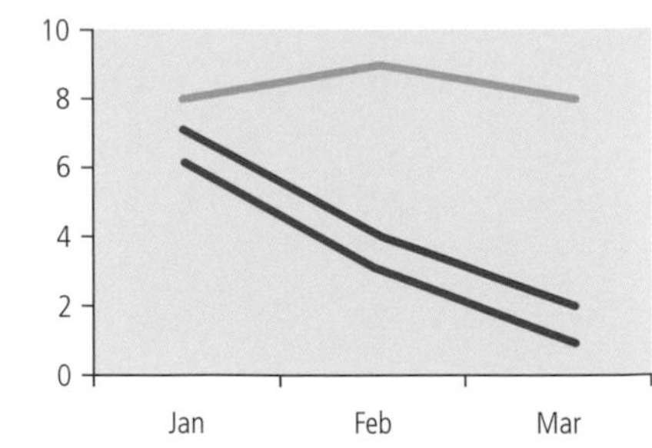

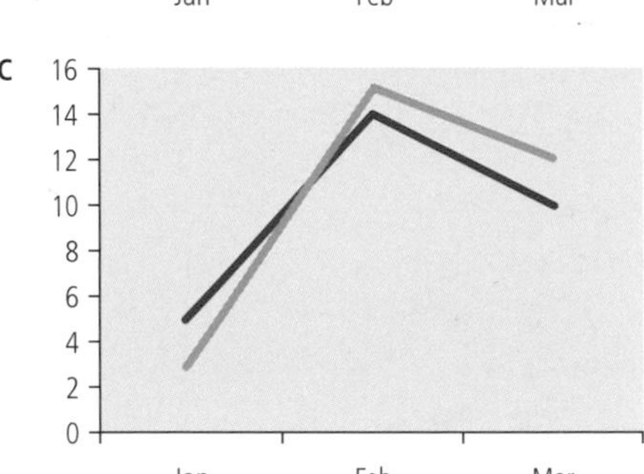

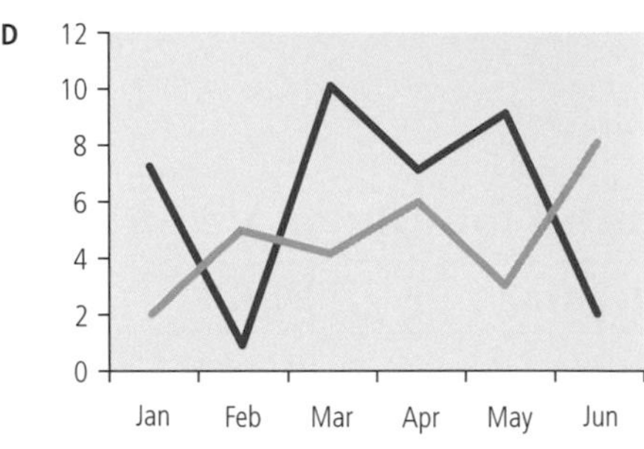

0 *The three subjects all reveal completely different trends with only applications for Accounting remaining stable throughout the three months. Applicants for Economics and Business Studies showed opposite trends with the former falling steadily and the latter rising sharply.*

2 Which diagrams show:
(a) similar trends (eg all elements increasing)?
(b) different trends (eg some elements increase but others decrease)?
(c) fluctuating trends (eg constant changing)?

3 How might a pencil help you to identify the main trend in a graph, bar chart, pie chart or table?

TIP

To find the main trends of graphs, bar charts and tables it helps to compare the beginning and end of the diagram.

Exam strategy

Task 1 Paragraph plan

Paragraph 1 – Say what the diagram shows in your own words (you will lose marks if you copy the question). Follow this with several sentences describing the main features supported by reference to the diagram (eg include dates and figures).

Paragraph 2 – Give further details – describe other features, significant differences and make comparisons where relevant. Support with figures from the diagram.

Summarizing sentence – End with one or two sentences that give an overall summary of the main features. No explanation, reasons or conclusion should be given.

6 Study the following example of a typical Task 1 question and answer the questions.

1 Does this diagram show changes over time?
2 Should your writing be formal or informal?
3 What tenses would be required?
4 Do you need to write about changes over time, make comparisons or both?
5 What is being described?
6 What significant points would you mention?

This graph illustrates the number of Chinese, Japanese and Indian students who enrolled at North Dean University over a five-year period.

Summarize the information by selecting and reporting the main features, and make comparisons where relevant.

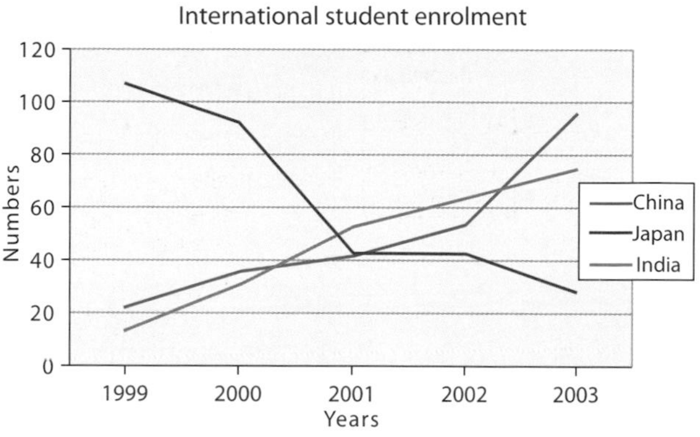

7 Read this extract from a student's answer and discuss in pairs what is wrong.

Well, first of all the blue line starts low then has a steadily rise. After a bit more it then rises sharp. This is probably because of the strong Chinese economy.

Exam information

A formal writing style is required. Sentences should be regularly supported by data from the diagram.

8 Read the model answer below to the question on international student enrolment and complete the following tasks.

1 Find four synonyms for 'student enrolment'.
2 What language does the writer use to show that exact numbers are not known?
3 Complete the gaps with language from the Useful language table on page 19?

Paragraph 1

The diagram shows the enrolment of Chinese, Japanese and Indian students at North Dean University from 1999 to 2003. During this period, enrolment of both Chinese and Indian students more than trebled. However, Japanese admissions (0) fell substantially with numbers being almost the reverse of those for Chinese students.

Paragraph 2

*Chinese numbers (**1**) ______________ up to 2002 followed by a (**2**) ______________ reaching almost 100 students (**3**) ______________ . Similarly, numbers of Indian students showed (**4**) ______________ throughout the period from about 10 in 1999 to over 70 in 2003. In contrast, enrolments of Japanese students (**5**) ______________ from (**6**) ______________ of over 100 students in 1999 to just over 40 in 2001. Numbers then (**7**) ______________ throughout 2001 finally dropping again to a low of around 30 in 2003. A further point of interest is that (**8**) ______________ , enrolments from all three countries were very similar, the average difference being approximately 10 students.*

Summarizing sentence

Overall, the graph highlights a considerable difference between growth in Chinese and Indian enrolments but reduction in Japanese enrolments.

164 words

4 Does this answer follow the paragraph plan given on page 20?

9 Read this Task 1 question and answer the questions.

1 Does the diagram show amounts or percentages?
2 Compare the beginning and the end of the diagram. What changes are there?
3 What other significant changes can you see?

10 Write the answer using the paragraph plan below.

The graph shows the percentage of staff trained by four different companies between 2003 and 2006.

Summarize the information by selecting and reporting the main features, and make comparisons where relevant.

You should write at least 150 words.

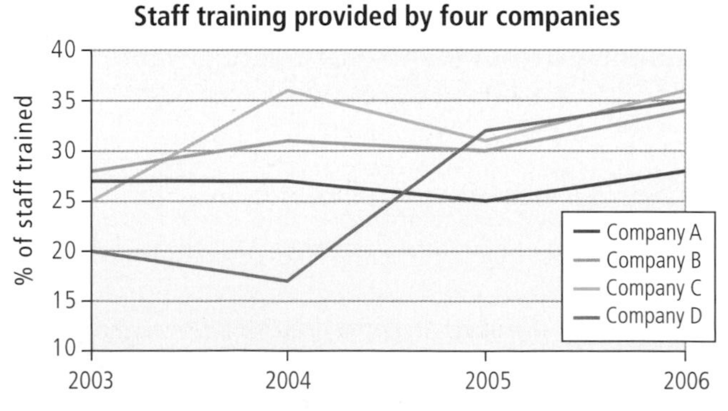

Paragraph 1

Introduce diagram

Describe main trends – compare beginning and end

Paragraph 2

Describe other details – note similarity between A and B, and difference between C and D

Summarizing sentence

Summarize overall pattern

Study skills

1 Read about the study habits of two students and fill in the table.

Write the student name in the appropriate column if the student has the study skill.

Paolo: There's so much to think about so I'm keeping a study diary now so I have a record of when my classes are and dates when homework and assignments must be handed in.

Yuan: To help me find what I'm looking for when I'm reading, I photocopy important sections so I can underline what I think is important.

Paolo: I don't always understand everything in lectures, but I make sure my notes are clear. I write the date, lecturer's name and what the lecture was about. I also try and look at my notes when I get home and write a short summary of the main ideas of each lecture.

Yuan: Well, I've got a special notebook just for vocabulary so when I learn new words I write them down with a translation and a little example. I also write down the pronunciation for words I know I pronounce incorrectly.

Making notes during lectures	Selecting key information when reading	Learning new vocabulary	Time organization

2 Think about your own study skills then look at the statements below. Decide which are true for you (✔) and which ones you are less confident about (**?**).

1 I can organize my time effectively.
2 I am always prepared when I come to class.
3 I can make useful, well-organized notes.
4 I can write clearly and accurately.
5 I work on building my vocabulary all the time.
6 I know my reading speed.

3 How could you develop those study skills you are less confident about.

Dictionary focus

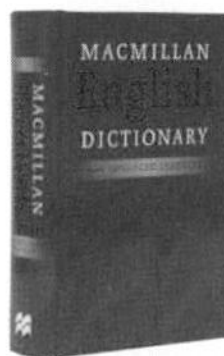

It is essential that you start to build vocabulary banks of words and expressions to help improve your IELTS band.

1 Find the following words in this unit and look them up in your dictionary.

1 Find a synonym for each word.
2 The words marked with an asterisk have several other meanings. What are they?
3 Record all the words and meanings in your IELTS vocabulary bank.

discrepancies (n) p.10	stabilize (v) p.19	amount (n) p.22
data * (n) p.10	element * (n) p.20	converge (v) p.189
figure * (n) p.18	trends * (n) p.20 & 22	

2 Living together

Look at these pictures and answer these questions.

Work in groups. Discuss these questions.

1 Which of these activities do people in your country do?
2 Which do you think are acceptable / unacceptable?

Listening 1

Section 2

Exam strategy

Finding keywords

You are given time before you listen to read the questions. Use this time effectively. Find the keywords in the questions. This will help you:

1 Listen out for the answers which could come BEFORE or AFTER the keyword.
2 Keep up with the tape.

Note completion

1 Look at this extract from a listening text and the related question.

> Unless you are a smoker yourself, you probably won't find it a particularly pleasant or enjoyable experience. More to the point is the harm smoking does to others. I'm thinking of passive smokers, in particular, those who happen to be around smokers and are forced to inhale their cigarette smoke. And this is mostly why more people today see smoking as being rather anti-social.

TIP

Read the questions carefully. Do not use more words than the question requires for each answer. You will lose marks if you do.

Complete the notes below using **NO MORE THAN THREE WORDS** for each answer.

1 ______________________ can be harmful.

Which of the following answers is correct? (**A**, **B** or **C**?)

A Passive smokers
B Passive smoking
C Passive smoking in particular

2 1.3 You are going to hear a talk given by Peter Powell. He is speaking to a group of smokers on how to give up smoking.

Before you listen, read questions **1–6** and decide which part of speech (eg noun? verb?) could go in each space.

Now listen to the first part of the recording and answer questions **1–6**. Complete the notes below using **NO MORE THAN THREE WORDS** for each answer.

Ways to give up smoking

1 To stop smoking, it is important to remember that there ....
2 Having willpower means having the determination to ....
3 Starting a hobby or .... a friend can help take your mind off smoking.
4 Another way to keep on track is to find suitable .... such as nicotine patches.
5 You may experience .... as your body becomes accustomed to less nicotine.
6 You can buy smoking aids from supermarkets or ....

Matching

Exam information

For this question type you must match one of the given choices to each statement.

3 1.4 Now listen to the second part of the recording and answer questions **7–10**.

Write Y if the statement is true
N if the statement is false

Which of the following effects of acupuncture are mentioned?

7 Lasts 15–19 minutes
8 Makes you put on weight
9 Gets rid of dangerous toxins
10 Works internally

Speaking

Part 2: Making notes

Exam information

In Part 2, you have to speak for 1–2 minutes about a topic. The topics cover a wide range of personal experiences, so you will be speaking about yourself. You will be given 1 minute before you speak to prepare and you will be given a pencil and paper to make notes. You can use this time to think about what you are going to say.

Exam strategy

On the topic card, you are given prompts to help you. Think of something to say about each of these. You can also use your own ideas. It is important to:

Keep to the topic.

Keep talking.

1 Read the topic card and complete the notes.

Describe an older person who has had an influence on your life.

You should say:
Who this person was
When you met them
What they did that was special

You should also say why they were important to your life.

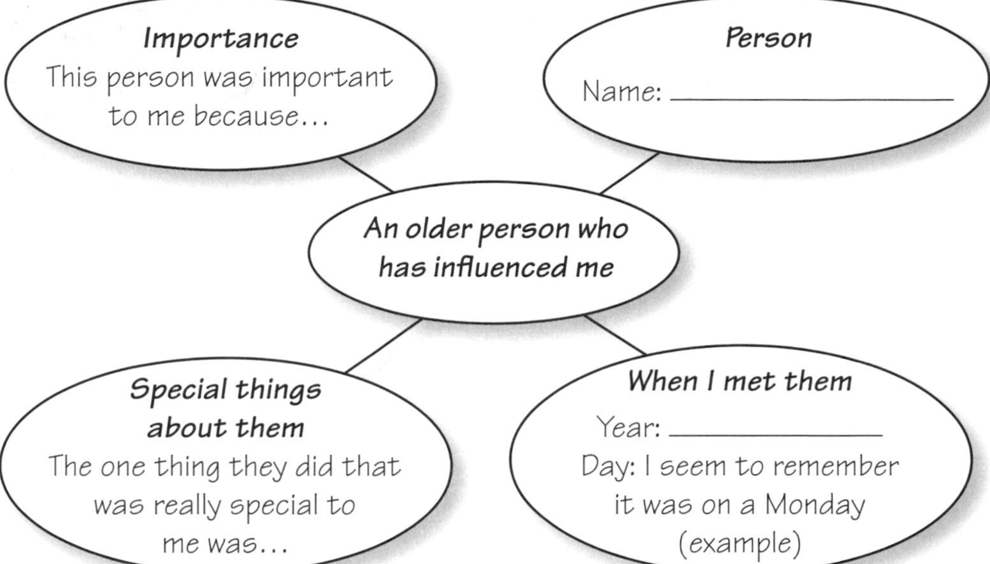

2 1.5 Listen to a student answer the topic from question 1 and answer the following questions.

1 Does the student use the prompts to help her?
2 Does she keep to the topic?
3 Is her answer long enough?
4 What did she do well?
5 How could she have improved her answer?

3 Work in pairs. Talk to each other for at least one minute about the topic in exercise 1 and the topic below. Check that your partner:

1 Speaks for 1 minute.
2 Keeps to the topic.

Describe the place where you grew up.

You should say:
Where it was
How long you lived there
What you liked about it

You should also say if you think this is a good place for children to grow up in.

Listening 2

Section 3

Work in pairs. Discuss the following questions. Give reasons for your answers.

1 What do you like to spend your money on?
2 What do teenagers in your country usually spend their money on?

Exam information

Multiple-choice questions

There will not be more than three possible answers to choose from.

Listening strategy

Keywords in listening may be exactly the same as the question words or they may be synonyms or parallel expressions.

Multiple choice

1 1.6 You are going to hear three students talking about research done on student spending. Listen carefully to the first part of the conversation and circle the appropriate answer for questions **1–4**.

TIP

Some choices seem to be the answer, but only answer half the question. The choices you make must answer the whole question.

1 The students spend the majority of their money on
A paying rent and bills.
B living expenses.
C course fees.

2 How much money does one of the students spend on books?
A £120
B under £100
C around £150

3 The interviews were attempting to highlight
A student credit card use.
B student credit card management.
C the number of credit cards an average student has.

4 What was the aim of the research?
A To analyse cause and effects
B To compare and contrast data
C To look at negative aspects

Table completion

TIP

Read the questions carefully and pay attention to instructions written in **CAPITAL LETTERS**. In the instructions on the right you have been told not to use more than three words.

2 1.7 You are now going to hear the rest of the conversation. Read and answer questions **5–12**. Complete the table using **NO MORE THAN THREE WORDS** for each answer.

Allowance	7	**Buying**
5 Despite the difficulties, parents must .... to give in to their children's demands.	**8** Children need an introduction	**10** Children should be allowed to ....
6 A .... will show them the difference between needs and wants.	**9** Parents could help their children open a	**11** Parents can encourage children to save some of ....
		12 If a child does not have enough money, the parent could promise to pay ....

Reading

1 Discuss these questions in pairs.

1 What problems do teenagers face today?
2 How has teenage life changed over the last 10 years?

2 Skim read the passage about teenagers (2–3 minutes) and answer questions **1** and **2**.

1 The passage is taken from a / an
A textbook.
B official report.
C newspaper article.
D guide on parenting.

2 The aim of the passage is to compare the
A the health of different age groups.
B health of teenage boys and teenage girls.
C physical and mental health of teenagers in Britain.
D health of teenagers in Britain and that of teenagers in other countries.

3 Scan the passage (1–2 minutes) to find what the following numbers refer to:
1 11, 13, 15
2 90%
3 35
4 120,000
5 60%

Unhealthy, unhappy, with no self-esteem: British teenagers lag behind world's young

They smoke too much, feel under massive work pressures and don't even really like each other – British children are among the unhealthiest and unhappiest in the world, according to a report published today.

A The World Health Organisation (WHO) study of more than 150,000 young people in 35 countries found that the physical and mental health of children in the UK is more like that of adolescents in former communist nations than that of their western European neighbours. Teenagers in England, in particular, but also their counterparts in Scotland and Wales have some of the highest rates of drinking, smoking and drug use – and the lowest levels of life satisfaction, fruit consumption and feelings of physical well-being.

B The WHO survey on Health Behaviour in School-aged Children (HBSC) is conducted every four years and interviews 11, 13 and 15-year-olds from the United States, Canada and nearly all eastern and western European countries. It is the largest international study of adolescent attitudes and provides an intriguing – and worrying – snapshot into the lives of British teenagers compared with their peers across the world.

C English 13-year-olds are the least likely in the world to believe their peers are 'kind and helpful', while only Russian 11-year-olds and Czech 15-year-olds had a lower opinion of their generation than the same age groups in England. Less than half of all the English adolescents saw each other as kind and helpful, compared with the study's average of 60 per cent. A third of English, Scottish and Welsh girls rated their health as only fair or poor, with only their peers in Ukraine, Lithuania and Latvia feeling worse off. Fewer than one in five girls in Spain, Italy and Switzerland feel the same way.

D When the children were asked about quality of life, England was in the bottom half of the league, while Dutch, Swedish and Greek young people were the happiest. English children struggle with a wide range of factors which reduce their quality of life. One in seven 11-year-olds, one in five 13-year-olds and one in four 15-year-olds are unhappy with their lives. A spokeswoman for the national children's charity *Childline* said: 'We counselled more than 120,000 children last year and the main reason for this was bullying. I think there is more that could be done to protect young people. Things like exam stress are also a big problem – children need to know that exams are not the only measure of success.'

E While English youngsters have below average hours of homework, with only a quarter of 15-year-olds spending more than three hours a day on after-school assignments, they feel under greater stress. Six out of ten boys and seven out of ten girls aged 15 in England say they feel pressured by schoolwork, with only Lithuanian and Welsh peers reporting greater stress.

F Campaigners said the failure to tackle public health problems affecting young people was causing a self-perpetuating cycle of abuse. One in five girls and one in seven boys aged 15 in England smoke every day. The average 15-year-old picked up the habit at the age of 12. A spokeswoman for the pressure group Action on smoking and Health said: 'We are puzzled by the Government's reluctance to introduce a smoking ban in public places because it would help reduce tobacco use among young people. It would also help to have a ban on the portrayal of smoking in films. The image of a Hollywood role model smoking on the big screen has a big impact on teenagers.'

G Throughout the survey, English children rated alongside children in Central Europe rather than with nations such as France, Germany, Italy and Spain. One in three children from all the age groups in England watches more than four hours of television per weekday, compared with the WHO average of one in five. A third of 11-year-old children from this country go without breakfast on school days, while 90 per cent of their Portuguese peers start every day with a morning meal. Only children from Lithuania, Latvia, Estonia and Finland eat less fruit than English and Welsh youngsters. More than half of teenage boys and a third of teenage girls in England admitted that they had been involved in a fight in the past 12 months – double the rate of German children.

H Health experts said the study should help countries to develop long-term policies to improve the health of young people. Marc Danzon, the WHO regional director, said: 'Looking after the health of young people is of vital importance. We know that attitudes, behaviour and lifestyle patterns strongly influence well-being and are shaped at an early age. It is important to know what factors determine these life-long patterns.'

Summary completion: From a list

Exam information

Summary completion (from a list)

Use words from a list or from the passage to complete a summary of part or all of a text. The information in the summary may not be in the same order as the information in the text. The correct answer must complete the summary grammatically and must agree with what is said in the text.

Question strategy

1. Read the summary through quickly.
2. Read the words before and after each gap to predict the part of speech and the meaning of the missing word(s).
3. Scan read the passage to find the section which answers the question. Look for synonyms and parallel expressions in the passage and in the summary. These will help you to locate the section of the passage which answers the questions.
4. Read the finished summary through to be sure it makes sense.

4 Read the summary in exercise 6 below. Study the first sentence.

1. Find three answers to question 1 in the list in exercise 6 which would be grammatically correct and could complete the meaning of the sentence.
2. Now scan read the passage on page 29 to find the paragraph which introduces the WHO survey. Read that paragraph to choose the answer to question 1 from the three possible answers.

5 Read the rest of the summary. For each question think about the part of speech and the meaning of the missing information.

6 Read the passage on page 29 and answer questions **1–10**.

Complete the summary using words from the list.

health	middle	peers	oldest
a quarter	affect	parents	less
appearance	study	studies	youngest
better than	half	more	comparable to
a fifth	find	three-quarters	grow
improve	worse than		

The results of the WHO survey show that the health of adolescents in Britain is not as good as that of children from other Western European countries and **1** ________________ the health of children from Central Europe. Less than **2** ________________ of girls from Spain, Italy and Switzerland said their health was average or poor, while one in three British children said the same. One in seven children from the **3** ________________ group and as many as **4** ________________ of 15-year-olds report that they are not happy. According to a national charity, sources of stress include their **5** ________________ and their **6** ________________. More than **7** ________________ of the English teenagers interviewed reported that they worry about the latter, despite spending **8** ________________ time than average working on this out of school hours. According to Marc Danzon, we need to **9** ________________ ways to help young people because habits which **10** ________________ health are formed when we are young.

Exam information

True, False, Not Given

There must be information in the text which agrees with or contradicts the statement. If there is no such information, then the answer is Not Given.

True, False, Not Given

7 Do the following statements agree with the information given in the passage?

Write:
TRUE if the statement agrees with the information
FALSE if the statement contradicts the information
NOT GIVEN if there is no information on this

11 Scottish adolescents report lower levels of life satisfaction than English teenagers.
12 There are many reasons why English children are unhappy.
13 English children need more protection from aggressive peers.
14 A ban on showing smoking in films has helped to change the behaviour of teenagers.
15 One in three British children eat breakfast at the weekends.

Language focus

TIP

Statements and questions in English must have a grammatical subject. This may not be true in your own language.

Sentence subjects

See Grammar reference, page 170.

1 Underline the subjects and circle the verbs in these sentences.

0 The study (found) that …
1 The survey is conducted every four years.
2 It is the largest international study of adolescent attitudes.
3 The children were asked about quality of life.
4 Childline counselled more than 120,000 children last year.
5 English youngsters have below average hours of homework.
6 Attitudes, behaviour and lifestyle strongly influence well-being.

Sentence subjects in academic writing are often long and may contain a great deal of information. For 0 and 1 above the original sentences in the text were:

1 The World Health Organisation (WHO) study of more than 150,000 young people in 35 countries *found* that …

2 The WHO survey on Health Behaviour in School-aged Children (HBSC) *is conducted* every four years.

2 Put the phrases of each sentence subject in the correct order.

0 (in the UK / and mental health / The physical / of children) is poor.
The physical and mental health of children in the UK is poor.
1 (children need / The most / from their parents / important thing) is love.
2 (parenting strategies / Many / at one age / that work) stop working with adolescents.
3 (from parents / love / Physical affection, / and praise) are important.
4 (learned / Behaviours / at an early age / and attitudes) can have a lifelong effect.

Sentence subjects reporting numerical information and comparisons

In academic writing it is common to report numerical information, like statistics and survey results, in sentence form. This information is often the subject of the sentence.

A third of English, Scottish and Welsh girls (rated) their health as poor.

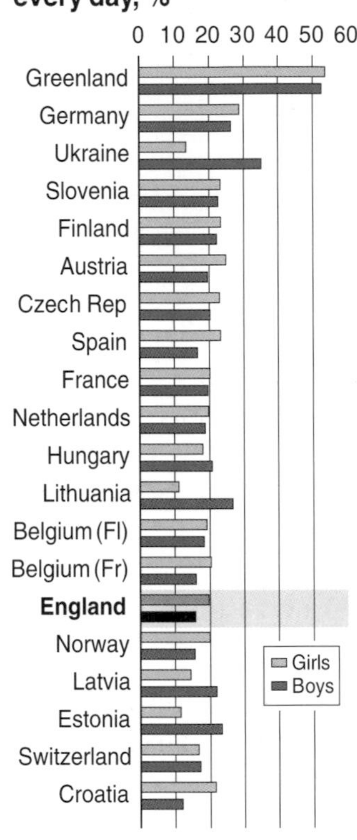

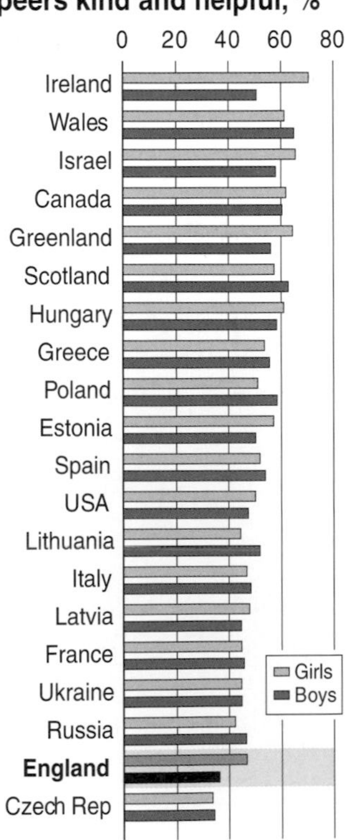

3 Write each of the fractions in Column A as a percentage. Then match the fraction in Column A with the expression in Column B.

	A		B
1	$^{1}/_{3}$	a	two thirds
2	$^{2}/_{3}$	b	three fifths
3	$^{1}/_{2}$	c	(a / one) half
4	$^{1}/_{4}$	d	three-quarters
5	$^{3}/_{4}$	e	seven out of ten
6	$^{3}/_{5}$	f	one in three
7	$^{7}/_{10}$	g	a / one quarter

4 Work in pairs. Make sentences using the information about 15-year-olds who smoke every day in the bar chart on the left. Use a numerical expression like the ones in exercise 3 and these expressions: more / less / fewer than, (just) over / under, about / approximately / roughly, nearly / almost, exactly.

eg In the Czech Republic **more than 20% of** girls and **2 in 10** boys smoke every day.

5 Make comparisons between countries and between boys and girls. Use an expression form Box **A** and one from Box **B** to complete the sentences.

A	B
more/less/fewer than (just) over/under/about/ approximately/roughly	half as many twice as many five times as many the same double

1 ______________________ Estonian girls as boys smoke.

2 There are ______________________ girls who smoke in Greenland as (there are) in Lithuania.

3 The number of boys who smoke in Greenland is ______________________ that in Estonia.

4 In France, ______________________ number of boys and girls smoke.

5 ______________________ teenagers smoke in Greenland as do in Finland.

6 Write sentences reporting numerical information and making comparisons. Use the information from the bar chart on the left about 15-year-olds who find their peers kind.

Vocabulary 1

Social issues

1 Match a word in Column A with a word in Column B to form a collocation, or word partnership.

A	B
0 drug _d_	a discrimination
1 spread of ___	b trap
2 divorce ___	c debt
3 single ___	d abuse
4 mounting ___	e rate
5 poverty ___	f smoking
6 race ___	g disease
7 sexual ___	h relations
8 underage ___	i parents
9 passive ___	j drinking

2 Match each of the expressions above with one of the problem categories below. Add one or two issues to each of the categories.

1 Money 2 Health 3 Family 4 Social groups

3 Choose two issues from exercise 2 that are problems in your country. Tell your partner what you know about these problems as they exist in your country. Describe the problems and suggest solutions.

Vocabulary 2

Word formation: Nouns and verbs

TIP

One way to increase your vocabulary is to add suffixes, eg -tion, -al, -ment, and prefixes, eg un-, il-, anti- to root words. Suffixes usually change the **form** of a word, like the part of speech or tense, of a word. Prefixes usually change the **meaning** of a word.

The most common noun ending in academic writing is -tion, followed by -ity (necessity), -er (teacher), -ness (happiness), -ism (communism) and -ment (government).

Example:
According to the text, British teenagers report low levels of fruit consumption (n).

That is, they eat, or consume (v) little fruit.

1 Write the verbs for these regularly occurring nouns ending in -tion.

0 action (example: *act*)
1 application
2 association
3 communication
4 concentration
5 direction
6 education
7 examination
8 formation
9 information
10 instruction
11 operation
12 organization
13 population
14 production
15 reaction
16 relation
17 situation
18 variation

2 Underline the stressed syllable in the nouns and verbs in exercise 1.

3 1.8 Work in pairs. Take turns saying the nouns and verbs in exercise 1 with the stress on the correct syllable. Listen to the CD to check your answers.

4 Complete these sentences with a noun or verb form of one of the words from exercise 1 on page 33.

0 Great Britain has a _population_ of over 60 million.
1 Shock is a natural ____________ to bad news.
2 The ____________ of lifestyle and behaviour patterns happens at an early age.
3 With more efficient farming methods it is possible to increase food ____________.
4 World powers recognize the importance of maintaining good ____________ with one another.
5 Parents, as well as schools, have a responsibility in the ____________ of their children.
6 This machinery should only be ____________ by someone one who is properly trained.
7 The company headquarters are ____________ in central London.
8 He was advised by the doctor to have a full medical ____________.
9 Universities are seeking to attract ____________ from international students.

Writing

Task 2

1 What can you remember about Writing Task 2 from the Introduction to IELTS section at the front of the book?

1 What is the required word length, and how many lines of writing would that be for you?
2 How long should you spend on Task 2 and how important is it?
3 What four areas of your writing does the examiner look at?
4 What style of writing should you produce?
5 What is the suggested essay structure and what are the four steps involved in writing an essay?

Understanding the question

An IELTS Task 2 question contains three different types of information.

(i) Instructions – These are fairly standard and ask you to give reasons for your answer supported by examples.
(ii) Topic Statement – The statement outlines a view or problem. It gives you the topic or subject of your essay. It is important to read this part carefully so your essay fully answers the question. For example, is the question shown in exercise 2 about teenagers or teenage stress compared with earlier generations?
(iii) Task – This is the part that tells you which type of essay you should write. For example, you may be asked to give your views, discuss both sides of an argument or suggest solutions to a problem.

2 Look at the following Task 2 question and decide which part(s) give the instructions, the statement and the task.

1 Write about the following topic:
2 *Today's teenagers have more stressful lives than previous generations.*
3 *Discuss this view and give your own opinion.*
4 Give reasons for your answer and include any relevant examples from your own knowledge or experience.

3 In your essay should you:

1 explain what a teenager is?
2 talk about common teenage habits?
3 talk in detail about your own teenage experiences?
4 describe the problem of stress and offer possible solutions?
5 give your views?
6 discuss different points of view relating to the topic?

4 Study the three Task 2 questions below. For each question, identify the topic and the task.

1 *The age at which children are allowed to work for money varies from country to country. While some people believe it is wrong, others regard it as a valuable opportunity to gain experience of the work environment.*

Discuss the arguments for and against children participating in paid work.

2 *These days, the wealthy in society often throw away perfectly good products in order to replace them with more up-to-date models.*

Do the environmental disadvantages of this development outweigh the economic advantages?

3 *Many governments state that they value equal opportunities for all but do not provide adequate support for the disabled.*

Discuss this view and give your own opinion.

Argument/Opinion Questions 1: The Balanced Argument Approach

There are two approaches to an argument/opinion question. The first is to consider ideas on both sides of an issue. This is called a balanced argument essay – you look at both sides then make a judgement at the end. The second approach involves making a judgement at the beginning and then supporting it (see Unit 4). In both essay types you need to make your own opinion clear.

5 Look at the Task 2 question about teenagers from exercise 2 again.

1 Think of two arguments supporting the topic statement and one that contradicts it.
2 Compare your ideas with a partner.

Question strategy

For questions that ask you to 'discuss' a topic or look at 'advantages and disadvantages' or points 'for and against' you can use a balanced argument approach.

6 Complete the following tasks.

1 Look at the statements below and think of three ideas for each one – two that support the idea, and one that contradicts it, or vice versa.
   (i) Smoking should be banned in all public places.
   (ii) Parents should teach children not to hit back at bullies.
   (iii) Prison sentences do not reduce crime.
   (iv) Modern teenagers are given too much freedom.
   (v) Disabled people are treated in society as second class citizens.
2 Compare your ideas with a partner.
3 In which section of the essay should you explain these ideas?
4 Should you include every idea that you have in your essay?
5 How many ideas should there be in each paragraph?

Exam strategy

To produce a clear and organized piece of writing under time pressure, you need to learn how to:

1 organize your time

2 organize your ideas

3 quickly identify the topic and the task

This will then give you more time for thinking about ideas, words and grammar.

7 The essay on page 37 answers the Task 2 question on teenage stress from exercise 2. Quickly read the essay to identify the writer's three main ideas.

1 What evidence is used to support each idea?
2 Note the five paragraph structure of the essay.

8 To achieve a good mark in Writing Task 2 it is vital to link your ideas together in different ways.

1 Add the linking words from the box below to the correct place in the essay.

Expressing contrast or concession	**Providing reasons**	**Adding further support**	**Giving examples**	**Stating results or consequences**	**Stating purpose**
despite, nevertheless, on the other hand	as a result of	in addition,	for example	so, consequently	in order to

Structure	Writing Task 2 – Balanced Argument Essay
INTRODUCTION Introduces the topic (paraphrases the question) and makes it clear that both sides of the argument will be examined.	(0) Despite a continuing improvement in standard of living, many people believe that young people suffer more stress than older generations. In this essay, the arguments surrounding the issue of teenage stress will be discussed.
BODY 1 Introduces the first idea and supports with reasons and examples. Mentions an opposing view then concludes the paragraph by refuting it with your opinion.	Firstly, teenagers are exposed to more products than earlier generations (1)____________ living in a modern consumer society. Through films and the media, they see celebrities with expensive jewellery, clothes and cars. (2)____________ youth-oriented advertising gives them an awareness of the latest technology such as digital music formats and mobile phones. (3)____________ teenagers feel pressure to acquire these items. Some might argue that these pressures are not new. However, I believe that such stresses were not so strong during earlier times.
BODY 2 Introduces the second idea and supports with reasons and examples.	It could also be argued that pressures at school are stronger than before. (4) ____________ achieve the lifestyle they see in the media, teenagers must succeed in their studies (5)____________ they can compete for the best jobs. Parental pressure, examinations and homework are all reported as causing increased levels of strain.
BODY 3 Introduces the opposing argument and supports with examples. Concludes the paragraph at the end with your view.	(6)____________ although it may be true to say that modern society produces certain stresses it does not necessarily mean that stress was previously absent. In earlier times, hunger and physical discomfort would undoubtedly have caused high levels of anxiety, as would hard physical labour, (7)____________ working down a mine. Any balanced view must take into account these alternative factors.
CONCLUSION Summarizes main points and concludes with the writer's opinion based on the arguments in the essay. No new ideas are expressed.	To sum up, consumerism and academic pressures are powerful causes of stress on today's teenagers. (8)____________ it is my view that these stresses are no greater than those experienced by earlier generations of teenagers.

9 Place the following words and phrases in the appropriate place in the box in exercise 8, and then add them to your IELTS vocabulary writing bank.

furthermore because therefore
such as to + infinitive although while due to
moreover for instance thus in spite

10 Find examples of words or phrases in the essay that link

1 between paragraphs.
2 between sentences.
3 within sentences.

11 Answer the following questions which refer back to the Language focus section

1 Find examples of long sentence subjects in the model answer. Which is the longest sentence subject in the essay?
2 Find examples of nouns formed with the suffixes *-tion, -ity, -er, -ness, -ism,* and *-ment.*

Task 2: Further practice

12 Use the ideas presented in this unit to write a balanced argument essay to answer the following question.

Write about the following topic:

Violence in playgrounds is increasing. However, it is important that parents should teach children not to hit back at bullies.

Discuss this view and give your own opinion.

Give reasons for your answer and include any relevant examples from your own knowledge or experience.

Exam strategy

Every sentence of your essay needs to connect to the question. An essay written in perfect English that doesn't relate to the question will get a low mark. Keep looking back to the question to check you are still answering the question.

Study skills

Using a dictionary

1 How can a good monolingual dictionary help your language? Give reasons.

2 All dictionaries use a system of abbreviations. Check the key in your own dictionary and give an example for each of the following.

1	adv	6	[T]
2	conj	7	sb
3	prep	8	[+ that]
4	inf	9	.... to do sth
5	[U]	10	.... doing sth

3 Look at this dictionary extract and label it with the information underneath.

> **justice** /ˈdʒʌstɪs / noun ★★★
> **1** [uncount] treatment of people that is fair and morally right: *the struggle for freedom and justice*
> **social justice**: *a society based on democracy, peace, and social justice* **1a**. the fact that something is reasonable and fair: *He appealed to their sense of justice. Campaigners are convinced of the justice of their cause.* – opposite INJUSTICE

0 High frequency word ***

1 Syllable stress and pronunciation
2 Derived word
3 Collocation
4 Example
5 Closely related meaning

Dictionary focus

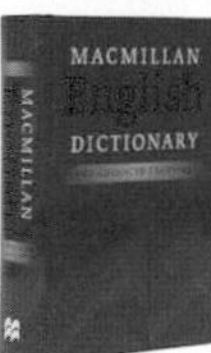

1 The words on the left have been used in this unit. Match them with the most suitable collocation on the right. Check in your dictionary and record them.

0	**addicted** + to something eg addicted to smoking	(express / give / offer)
1	**participate** + ____________	(of + sth)
2	**a product** + ____________	(in + sth)
3	**practical** + ____________	(annoying / bad)
4	**an influence** + ____________	*(to + sth)*
5	____________ + **consumerism**	(on + sth / sb)
6	____________ + **habits**	(advice / solution / use)
7	____________ + **an opinion**	(uncontrolled)

2 Using suffixes, make as many derived words as you can from the words above. Record them together in word families.

0 product (n), producer (n–person), production (n–process), produce (v), produce (n–thing), productive (adj), productively (adv)

3 Costing the earth

Look at these pictures and answer these questions.

Work in groups. Describe the differences between these vehicles. Would one of these be your 'dream car'? Which vehicles are the most/least environmentally friendly? Why?

Reading

1 Look at the title and subtitle of the article. What do you think is the main problem discussed in the text?

Circle the appropriate letter **A–D**.

1 The main problem discussed in the article is

A the rise in oil prices.
B decreasing supplies of oil.
C the need for alternative energy sources.
D the effect of oil prices on alternative fuel technology.

2 Read the article quickly and check your answer to exercise 1.

3 Do you think the writer of the article is British or American? How do you know?

The end of the Oil Age?

The wells aren't about to run dry, but high oil prices might delay the adoption of alternative fuels

1 Don't panic and don't sell the SUV just yet; the world is not running out of oil. Despite this year's 30 per cent price increase (and a 40 per cent rise in the past 12 months), no serious analyst is suggesting that we have even reached peak production, which might imply a steady increase in scarcity and price.

2 We will, of course, run out eventually, as you might expect with a finite resource that the world is burning up at the rate of 76 million barrels a day (2.8 billion imperial gallons), but it's going to take a while. Even at 2002's rate of consumption, conventional oil reserves will last more than 30 years; more fields have been discovered and are being discovered, and that's before you add fuel derived from coal, ore emulsion and oil-rich shales, or the eking out of stocks with renewable bio fuels.

3 Experts working for Ford have claimed that at present rates of consumption the world has about 600 years' worth of fossil fuels left, although we are unlikely to use them all up as some are very expensive to source and dirty to burn. Besides, as Byron McCormick, General Motors' executive head of hydrogen fuel-cell activities, says: 'The Stone Age didn't end because we ran out of stones.'

4 There might be a shortage of petrol, however, because of a lack of refining capacity, particularly in America. 'The US has so many different fuel types,' said one expert, 'that it is difficult to balance out refining capacity.' Furthermore, US environmental legislation means it's extremely hard to get permission to build new oil refineries.

5 While American's demand for oil varies seasonally, the UK's seasonal petrol demand is much steadier, although Heathrow's status as a European hub airport means we are quite low on jet fuel and a short-sighted policy on refining capacity means we are also short of automotive diesel; we are having to import both. In the long term, to the worrying detriment of our balance of payments, the UK is running out of oil, as North Sea stocks have reached their peak and are now dwindling.

6 There are many other factors driving the oil market, including geopolitics, speculators and the US market. Indeed, one of the main reasons that the price of oil has been rising is the breakdown of relations between the world's leading consumer of oil, America, and some of the world's leading producers of oil. Add to this the influence of speculation on the oil market, the massive expansion of oil consumption in China (now the world's second largest consumer) and burgeoning demand in India and it's no wonder that OPEC members are predicting petrol prices could soar.

7 Would a sustained increase in prices trigger the long-awaited adoption of alternative fuels and alternative energy technology? The answer is 'yes' and 'no'. To answer the question, you have to divide new technology into what is already or very nearly on sale, such as petrol/electric hybrid cars, liquid petroleum gas, bio fuels and diesel, and what's a long way off yet, such as fully synthetic fuels and hydrogen fuel-cell power.

8 Certainly there is some reason to suppose that higher pump prices will prompt consumers to search for wallet-friendly alternatives, particularly if that doesn't involve high initial spending. Therefore, we can expect the diesel market (currently more than 50% of European sales) to expand further. Diesel sales in the US might best be described as nascent, but those can be expected to grow as well. In the UK, liquid petroleum gas and diesel are to maintain their tax-friendly status for the next three years at least.

9 In the long term, the big worry among car makers is that sustained high fuel prices will mean higher interest rates, higher inflation and a worldwide recession. A recession would delay the development of fuel-efficient cars like Honda's Insight, Ford's Escape 4x4 and Toyota's Prius. It would also delay the development of hydrogen power and more heavily refined fuels that could lead to cleaner-burning petrol and diesel engines. 'I'm spending a lot of GM's risk capital here,' says Brian McCormick, 'and higher fuel prices are disheartening on one level, but encouraging on another.'

10 The irony is that US car companies need the revenue from high fuel-consumption but profitable vehicles like trucks and SUVs to fund the advanced research departments that are working on bringing the first generation of fuel-cell vehicles to the showrooms. These new-generation vehicles will run on hydrogen steamed out of natural gas, which is currently the cheapest and most convenient source of the fuel of the future.

11 'The technology is near at hand and we are working on it,' says McCormick. Unfortunately, governments will need to provide grants and subsidies for the massive investment required for a hydrogen fuel infrastructure, and in a worldwide recession that's not a realistic prospect. His boss GM director Larry Burns says, 'There's concern about the real risk that the high oil price will cause negative growth.'

12 Fuel isn't going to run out in the near future, but it's going to cost you more whatever you drive. It's probably not a good idea to sell your SUV right now, but whether you actually need two tons of off-road capability is likely to weigh more heavily on your mind in the long term.

Multiple-choice questions

Exam information

The most common multiple-choice question is one in which you choose one answer from four options. Other questions ask you to choose more than one correct answer from a list.

Question strategy

1 Read the **question** carefully and eliminate any answers which are obviously wrong.

2 Scan read for parallel expressions in the questions and passage and underline them.

3 Remember: (a) the correct answer to the question is the one given in the passage, and not your opinion; (b) words from an incorrect option may appear in the passage.

4 Underline key words in questions **1–4** and eliminate any answers you are sure are incorrect. Use the questions in italics to help you.

5 Circle the appropriate letter **A–D**.

1 The most probable cause of a petrol shortage in the near future would be

A high fuel consumption.
B lack of conventional oil reserves.
C oil reserves which are difficult to access.
D American laws concerning the environment.

*Which paragraph describes a **likely** cause of a petrol shortage? Only one option could cause a shortage in the **near future**.*

2 The graph which best illustrates changes to North Sea oil supplies is:

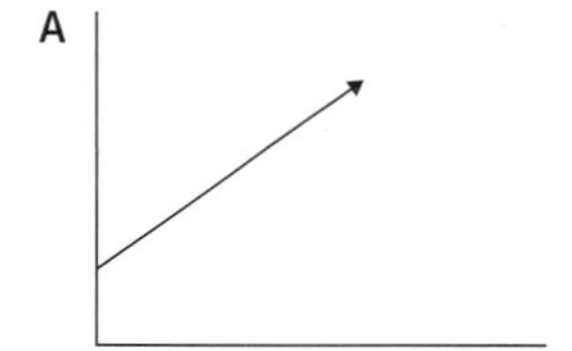

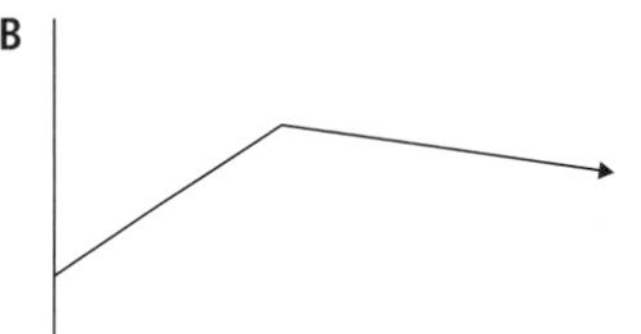

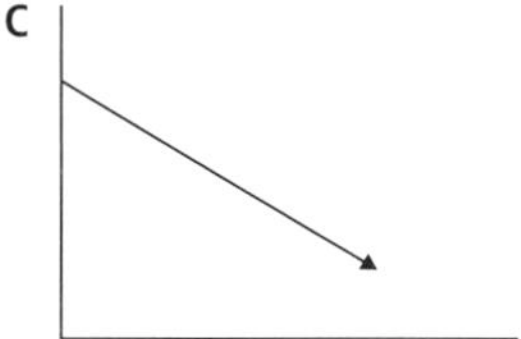

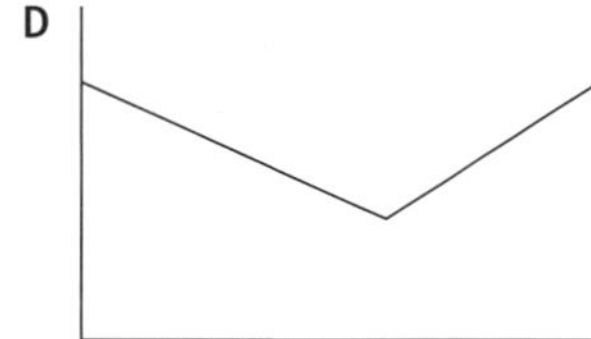

*Scan read the passage to find mention of **North Sea** oil. What happens to something after it **reaches a peak**?*

3 Which of these does **not** affect the price of oil?

A use of alternative fuels
B increase in demand
C stock market activity
D international relations

*In the passage find references to or parallel expressions for **increase in demand, stock market activity** and **international relations**. Section 6 mentions three of the options which **do** affect the price of oil.*

4 Higher fuel prices would eventually bring about

A a global economic downturn.
B lower interest rates.
C an increase in sales of large vehicles.
D development of environmentally friendly engines.

Option C is an unlikely answer. So look at A, B, and D more carefully.

Remember

Scan read the text for references to the different fuels.

Matching

6 Match each description to the fuel it describes.

Fuels
Oil (O)
Petrol (P)
Diesel (D)
Hydrogen (H)

5 The UK is not refining enough of this fuel to meet its needs.
6 The British government is encouraging people to buy this fuel.
7 An economic recession would affect the development of this fuel.
8 America buys more of this fuel than any other country.
9, 10 Less polluting versions of this fuel are being developed.
11 This could become the preferred fuel in the future.
12 China and India are using increasing amounts of this fuel.

TIP

When you meet a word you don't know in a reading passage, don't panic! Instead, use the language around the word to help you to guess the meaning or ignore the word and keep reading. Your aim is to understand the whole sentence. Don't let unknown words slow down your search for the answer.

Dealing with unknown vocabulary in a reading passage

7 One way to deal with new vocabulary is to try to guess the meaning from the context. Study the extract from the reading passage. What do you think 'nascent' means?

> Therefore, we can expect the diesel market (currently more than 50% of European sales) to expand further. Diesel sales in the US might best be described as ***nascent***, but those can be expected to grow as well.

We know that diesel sales in Europe are expanding and that the market in the US is also expected to grow. Therefore, *nascent* sales are probably sales which are not large at present.

8 Guess the meanings of the words in italics from the way they are used in the passage. Then use a dictionary to check your answers.

1 a *finite* resource (2)
2 *derived from* (2)
3 a *shortage* of petrol (4)
4 *dwindling* (5)
5 *massive* expansion (6)
6 *burgeoning* demand (6)
7 high *initial* spending (8)
8 *sustained* fuel prices (9)

Remember

Scan reading involves reading a text quickly to **locate** a word, phrase, number, etc. You do not need to understand the text to scan read successfully.

9 There may be technical vocabulary which is linked to the topic in a passage. You probably won't need to know the meaning of these words to answer the questions. Scan read the text to locate these expressions in the text. How many of them do you know the meaning of?

1 ore emulsion (Para. 2)
2 shales (Para. 2)
3 balance of payments (Para. 5)
4 geopolitics (Para. 6)
5 petrol/electric hybrid (Para. 7)
6 bio fuels (Para. 7)

The words in exercise 9 are all technical words which you may not know. You **did not** need to know the meaning of any of these words to answer the reading comprehension questions.

Language focus

Compound adjectives used in place of relative clauses

See Grammar reference, page 171.

We often use compound adjectives in academic and journalistic writing to replace lengthier relative clauses.

Example: a ten-mile journey = a journey which is ten miles long

1 These expressions are taken from the reading text. Replace the relative clauses in *italics* with a compound adjective and noun. Do **NOT** look back at the text before you answer questions **1–6**.

0 … fuel derived from coal, ore emulsion and shales *which are rich in oil* (Para. 2) — oil-rich shales

1 Would a sustained increase in prices trigger the adoption *which has been awaited for a long time* of alternative fuels … (Para. 7) — ________-________ adoption

2 … higher pump prices will prompt consumers to search for alternatives *which are friendly to the wallet* … (Para. 8) — ________-________ alternatives

3 A recession would delay the development of cars *which use fuel efficiently* … (Para. 9) — ________-________ cars

4 (A recession) would also delay the development of hydrogen power and special fuels that could lead to petrol and diesel engines *which burn more cleanly.* (Para. 9) — ________-________ petrol and diesel engines

5 … US car companies need the revenue from vehicles *which are high in fuel consumption* (Para. 10) — high ________-________ vehicles

6 These vehicles *which belong to a new generation* will … (Para. 10) — ________-________ vehicles

2 Refer back to the text on page 41 to check your answers.

3 Re-write each sentence but keep the meaning the same. Replace the relative clause in italics with a phrase containing a compound adjective. Use a word from **A** and a word from **B** to form the adjective.

A	**B**
closed high long low (x2) ~~old~~ short well (x2)	balanced circuit established ~~fashioned~~ lying paid performance standing term

0 They have ideas about raising children *which are outdated.*

They have old-fashioned ideas about raising children.

1 Areas *which are close to the level of the sea* are more likely to flood.
2 It is recommended to eat a diet *which contains a variety of foods.*
3 Ford have produced an estate car *which is designed to be fast and powerful.*
4 People entering and leaving the building are monitored on television *which allows you to watch what is happening in different parts of the building.*
5 In spite of his qualifications and experience, he was offered only employment *which lasted for a short period of time* and not a permanent post.
6 Teaching and nursing have traditionally been jobs *which did not offer much pay.*
7 Fox hunting is a British tradition *which has existed for a long time.*
8 We prefer to do business with companies *which have been successful for a long time.*

Vocabulary

Collocations

1 Divide these words into those which:

1 could come **before** the word *energy* (**b**) eg alternative energy
2 could come **after** the word *energy* (**a**) eg energy requirement

alternative (adj) **b** atomic (adj) ~~conserve~~ (v) consumption (n) conventional (adj) costs (n) efficiency (n) generate (v) harness (v) nuclear (adj) policy (n) production (n) provide (v) renewable (adj) requirement (n) **a** shortage (n) solar (adj) sustainable (adj) wave (adj) wind (adj)

2 Use one of the words from the box to complete the explanations.

0 to save energy: to conserve energy
1 plans or actions agreed on by a government or business: an energy ____________
2 to get control of a source of energy to use it for a particular purpose: to ____________ (solar) energy
3 energy obtained using methods that do not harm the environment: ____________ energy
4 the amount of energy which people use: energy ____________
5 the amount of energy which people need: energy ____________
6 the act of producing usable energy: to ____________ energy, eg electricity
7 sources of energy which replace themselves by natural processes, eg wind, waves: ____________ energy (sources)
8 traditional sources of energy, eg fossil fuels: ____________ (sources of) energy

3 Complete the gaps using the vocabulary from exercise 2. You may need to change the form of the word.

The Department of Energy denied claims that a change in its energy policy **0** is being debated in light of fresh evidence of global warming. A government Minister denied that a decision has been taken to back technologies for ____________ **1** the power of ____________ **2** and ____________ **3** sources of energy such as wind and solar power. The Department claims that renewables are unable to ____________ **4** enough power to meet growing energy ____________ **5** economically. Campaigners for the environment point out that given the predicted steep rise in energy ____________ **6** it is more important than ever that the Government takes steps to reduce demands for ____________ **7** sources of energy, like fossil fuels, which are damaging to the environment.

4 1.9 Listen and check your answers.

Listening

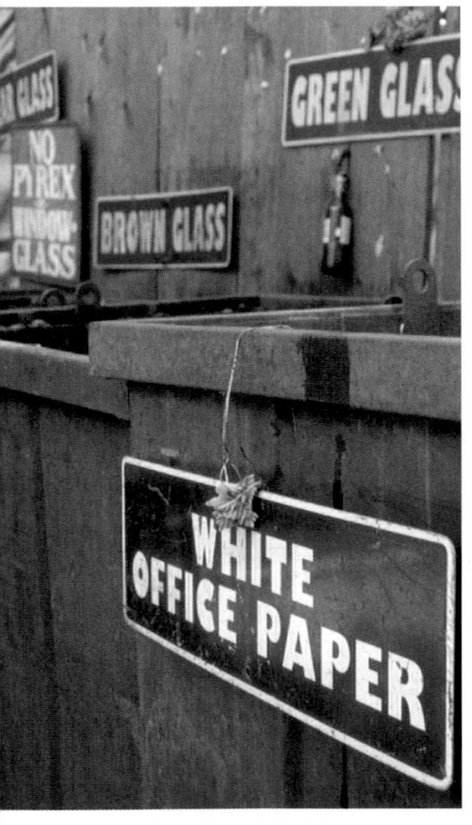

Section 3: Multiple choice

1 When you hear a recording, check if you can hear a synonym or parallel expression that matches one of the choices.

1 Match the underlined keywords in the following questions to a synonym or parallel expression in the box.

1 What is Miranda concerned about?
2 Should governments control how much waste factories produce?
3 What is likely to happen unless local councils improve their waste disposal procedures?
4 Which country is not keeping up with the rest of Europe?

a keeping pace with b worried
c how waste is disposed of d emit

2 Read the following multiple-choice question. The answer has been circled.

The student is concerned about

A missing the lecture.
B her knowledge of the subject.
(C) giving a presentation.

Now read the recording script and answer questions **1–6**.

Student: I missed yesterday's lecture on waste disposal in multi-national companies and I really wish I hadn't. I have to do a presentation on this topic next week and I'm really worried about it. I always get stressed when I have to speak in front of other people. I know the subject fairly well, but I'm scared I'll forget everything. You couldn't lend me your notes so I could just check I didn't miss anything really important?

1 Does the student speak about missing a lecture?
2 Does the student mention being worried about missing the lecture?
3 Why is A not the correct answer?
4 What does the student say about her subject knowledge?
5 Why is B not the correct answer?
6 How does the student feel about giving a presentation?

3 1.10 Listen to the first part of the conversation and circle the correct answers for questions **1–4**.

1 Miranda is concerned about

A not understanding the essay title.
B missing out on vital information.
C feeling too ill to come to college.

2 Where does Dr Dartford claim that around 8 percent of waste is recycled?

A Businesses
B Homes
C Factories

3 According to Dr Dartford, at the moment the UK

A recycles only household waste.
B recycles more than other European countries.
C is not keeping up with its growing household waste.

4 One way to bring about key changes in waste recycling is

A the separation of household waste.
B for targets to improve.
C for household waste to be collected by the local council.

Summary completion

WARNING

If you use more than three words you will lose the mark. One mark can make a big difference to your final band score.

4 1.11 You are now going to hear the rest of the conversation. Read and answer questions **5–10**. Complete the notes using **NO MORE THAN THREE WORDS** for each answer.

The one message that is not getting enough attention is that the **5** .... also has a responsibility. The reasons why their waste levels are rising is due to changes in **6** .... and an increase in wealth. There has also been an increase in the sale of **7** .... and pre-packed goods which is a result of people wanting their lives to **8** .... However, unless we can change our current **9** ...., recycling will remain challenging. This ultimately comes down to the role of **10** .... and them being more willing to buy recycled goods.

5 Find synonyms or parallel expressions for the following words / phrases. Use a dictionary to help you.

1 a growing trend
2 commercial waste
3 pre-packed goods
4 world-wide recession

Pronunciation

Final consonants

Pronunciation mistakes can make you lose unnecessary marks in your Speaking test. If the examiner cannot understand what you are saying, it is difficult to give you a good mark. A common mistake is to swallow sounds that should be pronounced at the ends of words or sentences. In particular, sounds like /s/, /z/, /d/, /k/, /n/ and /l/.

1 1.12 Look at the words below. They are all words from this unit about the environment.

Put them in the correct category according to their final consonant sound. Listen to check your answers.

1 importance
2 futile
3 solution
4 targets
5 public
6 household
7 conventional
8 convenience
9 policies
10 appliance
11 fundamental
12 sustain
13 domestic
14 sustainable
15 recycles
16 propose

/s/	/z/	/d/	/k/	/n/	/l/

TIP

Just as you can train the muscles in your body, you can train the muscles in your mouth and face to help you pronounce sounds correctly. To do this effectively, you need to know what the following parts are doing as they are extremely important for pronunciation:

1 your tongue
2 your teeth
3 your lips
4 your mouth

2 1.13 Work with a partner and practise the following sentences. Listen to each other and make sure that the final consonants are pronounced where necessary.

1 The UK has less recycled household waste and rather more industrial and commercial waste.
2 The government needs to start and sustain changes in refuse collection.
3 The general public needs to think more about recycling and develop a fundamental change in the way they get rid of their domestic waste.
4 He made the suggestion that a sustainable solution required an expansion in the market.

Now listen and check your pronunciation.

Speaking

TIP

You will be given limited prompts in the IELTS speaking test. In Parts 1 and 2 the examiner can repeat the question. In Part 3 the examiner can rephrase the question.

1 Work in pairs. Discuss the following questions with a partner.

1 How does speaking in an exam situation differ from everyday conversation?
2 What style of language would you use in the IELTS speaking test?

Speaking practice: Part 3
Introducing and organizing your opinions

2 Use the three 'stepping stones' below to help you organize what you're saying.

Sentence starter
'Basically I feel that ... '

Your main idea
'it is not only the government's responsibility to sort out the waste problem.'

Extra information to make your idea clearer
'... The main reason for thinking this is that if we don't all try and do something to sort out the waste problem, it probably won't go away.'

3 Study the words and phrases in the Useful language box below. Use them when you speak and make them part of your speaking vocabulary. Keep adding new expressions that you see and hear to your vocabulary book.

WARNING

If you don't use a variety of words, you will lose marks.

Useful language: prepositions of place and location

Sentence starters: Introducing your opinions
Basically, I feel that ...
I guess you could say the main issue is getting people to ...
In my view ...
Personally speaking ...
It would seem to me that ...
I really believe that ...

Extra information to make your idea clearer: Giving examples
One example that springs to mind is ...
Probably the best example I can think of is ...
(In my country) for example/ for instance ...

4 Find appropriate phrases from the Useful language box to complete the following main ideas. Use your own ideas to make your ideas clearer where necessary.

0 Renewable energy will become even more popular in the future.

1 Governments really don't have a choice anymore. They have to pump more money into renewable energy sources.

2 We need to think of ways to encourage people to recycle more.

3 Using nuclear power to create energy has more negative effects than positive ones.

4 We are living in a 'throw-away' culture.

I really believe that renewable energy will become even more popular in the future. Actually many countries are already doing this. One example that springs to mind is Greece which uses solar power to heat water.

5 In pairs discuss questions **1–3** below. Think about how you will organize your answers before you speak. Use the Useful language box phrases and the 'stepping stones' on page 49 to help you.

1 What changes could happen to the design of the car in the future? Which changes will be positive and which will be negative?
2 Compare the way the average house looks now in your country to how it will look in 10 years' time. Which one would you prefer to live in and why?
3 Do you think governments should spend more money researching alternative forms of energy? What might be their reasons for choosing not to do this?

Speaking strategy

In the IELTS speaking test make each answer you give the examiner about 30 seconds long to ensure fluency.

Writing

Task 1

1 In today's high-tech world people use more energy than ever before. Answer these questions.

1 What different types of energy do you use?
2 How many different types of fuel can you name?
3 Which energy sources are fossil fuels and which are renewables?

2 Read this Task 1 question and look at the diagram below.

The bar chart shows the average consumption by car drivers, of two types of fuel for a range of different age groups in 2005.

Summarize the information by selecting and reporting the main features, and make comparisons where relevant.

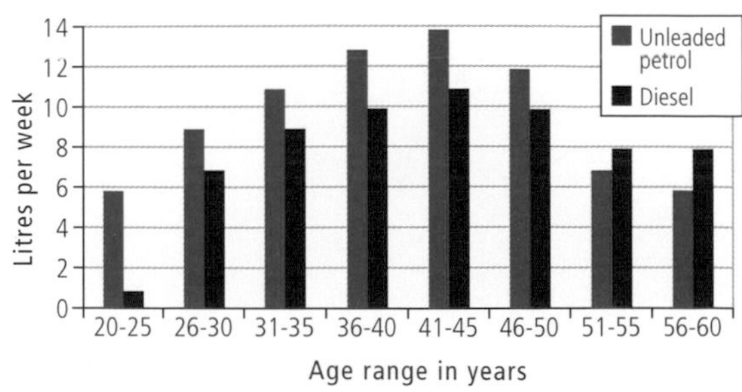

Task 1: Selecting significant information

3 Put these steps in the correct order.

1 Look at the columns and identify the main patterns and significant differences. These are often the largest/smallest amounts, or places where something happens that is different from the general pattern.
2 Look at each axis in turn to understand exactly what is being shown.
3 Read the question carefully.
4 Look at the columns and try to find the overall pattern.

TIP

There is usually more than one way to organize the answer. Choose the easiest way for you.

4 Study the diagram to answer the following questions.

1 What are the main features?
2 Which type of fuel has the highest consumption overall?
3 Which age group shows the largest difference between diesel and unleaded?
4 Are there any places in the diagram where there is an exception to the main pattern?
5 In what different ways could your answer be organized?

Exam strategy

Your answer should not try to describe every detail of the diagram. Task 1 needs a summary of the main features of the diagram with comparisons made where relevant.

5 Read these opening paragraphs from three model answers. Which do you think is better? Why?

Text A

First observations on studying the bar chart reveal a significant difference across the age ranges. You can see that fuel consumption increased dramatically up to 41–45, then fell to 56–60. This could be because older people don't enjoy driving so much.

Text B

The bar chart illustrates the average amount of unleaded petrol and diesel consumed in a week for age groups ranging from 20-60 years of age. Generally, unleaded petrol was consumed at a higher rate than diesel the highest being 14 litres of unleaded per week for the 41-45 year age group. This is a difference of more than 3 litres in comparison with diesel.

Text C

The bar chart shows the average consumption by car drivers of two types of fuel for a range of different age groups. The largest amount of fuel was consumed by the 41 to 45 age group (14 and 11 litres respectively for unleaded and diesel). This is a considerably greater use than the 20 to 25 age group (approximately 6 and 1 litres respectively for unleaded and diesel).

Task 1: Fixed time diagrams

Some diagrams do not show changes over time but show information in one fixed time. These diagrams need language to make comparisons.

6 Read the complete model answer below and summarize the main points that the writer makes under the headings in the strategy box.

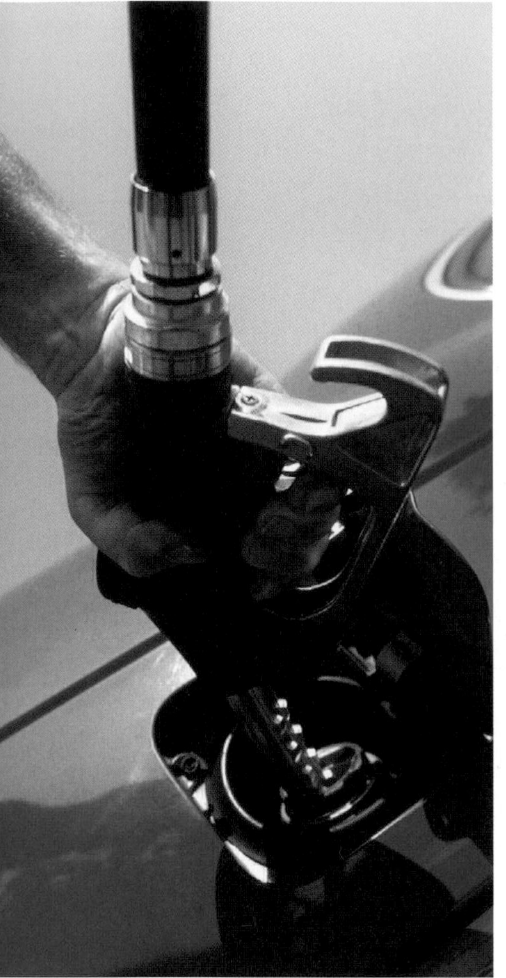

Strategy

Paragraph 1 0 Says what the diagram shows 1	The bar chart illustrates the average amount of unleaded petrol and diesel consumed in a week for age groups ranging from 20 to 60 years of age. Generally, unleaded petrol was consumed at a higher rate than diesel, the **highest** (0) being 14 litres of unleaded per week for the 41 to 45 year age group. This is a difference of more than 3 litres **in comparison with** (1) diesel.
Paragraph 2 2 3 4	The 20 to 25 year range shows **the largest** (2) variation in fuel use with leaded petrol consumption being over five times **as large as** (3) diesel. **In contrast,** (4) for the two oldest age groups the pattern is reversed with the amount of diesel consumed being about 1 litre higher. In addition, the consumption of diesel was the same for the 51 to 55 age group as it was for the 56 to 60 age group (7 litres per week).
Summarizing sentence 5	Overall, it can be seen that there is **a significant difference** (5) in consumption across the age ranges with the middle age groups using by far **the most** (6) fuel. 172 words

Task 1: Making comparisons

In Task 1 of the Writing module you will often need to compare and contrast information in a graph, bar chart, pie chart, table or illustration.

Useful language: Making comparisons

A and *B* represent elements in a diagram such as leaded and unleaded petrol, China and Australia, or nuclear and wind power.

x and *y* represent amounts such as $120 million, 67%, or 200 units.

Introducing differences

Generally, there is	**a significant difference**	**between** *A* **and** *B*.
	a wide disparity	**in** + (noun).

Comparative structures

In contrast (to *B*), **In comparison (with** *B*),	*A* is	larger / smaller	**by a narrow margin.** **by** *x*.
A is **just/well**	**under/** **over**	*x*	(larger / smaller**)** **than** *B*.
A is **approximately**			
A is	**(over)**	**twice** **two/three/four** **times**	**as** large / great / high **as** *B*.
	(under)		
A uses / produces	**more/** **less**	+ (noun U)	**than** *B*.
	more/ **fewer**	+ (noun C)	
A	**is**	**considerably** **marginally**	greater / higher / smaller **than** *B*.
A is	**almost**	**as** (large / high) **as that in**	*B*.

Superlative structures

A	is	**the** (second / third) largest / smallest	+ (noun C).
	has	**the** greatest / widest / most significant	+ (noun U & C).
A	uses produces consumes	**the** largest / highest / smallest / lowest	**proportion of** + (noun U). **number of** + (noun C). **amount of** + (noun U) . **quantity of** + (noun U & C).

7 Study the sentences below and say whether they are comparative or superlative structures. Then complete the gaps by studying the bar chart below.

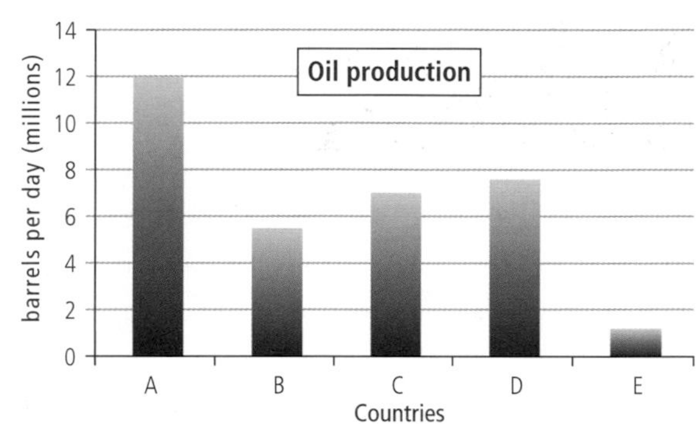

0 D is the second largest producer of oil.
1 Production in ____ is marginally higher than in ____.
2 Oil production in ____ is approximately 2 million barrels larger than in ____.
3 Production of oil in ____ is under half the size of production in ____.
4 ____ is the largest producer of oil of all the five countries.
5 In comparison with ____, oil production in ____ is larger by a narrow margin.
6 ____ produces the least amount of oil.
7 Production of oil in ____ is almost as large as in ____.
8 ____ produces less oil than all the other four countries.

8 Look at the following diagrams. Write two sentences for each that use different ways to describe the data. Use the Useful language section to help you.

Journeys made by road or rail

Rail 22%

Road 78%

0 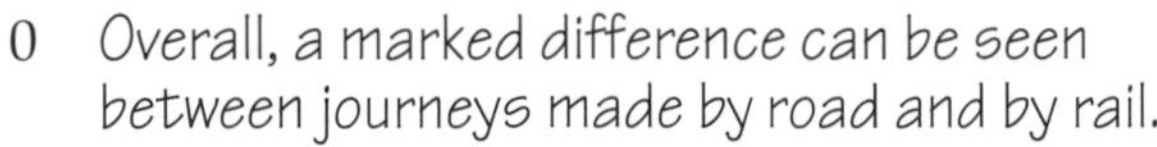
Overall, a marked difference can be seen between journeys made by road and by rail.

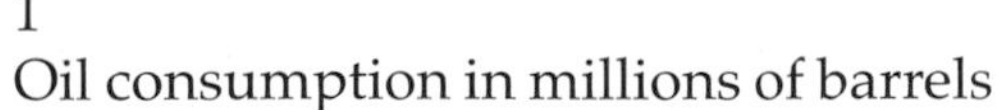
Journeys by road are over three times as common as by rail.

1

Oil consumption in millions of barrels

Russia	Germany
949	985

3

Electricity production in Europe

Britain	Sweden	Belgium
26%	10%	5.5%

2

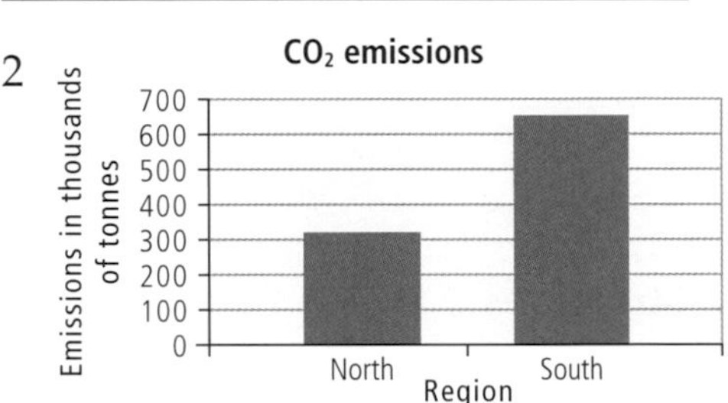

4

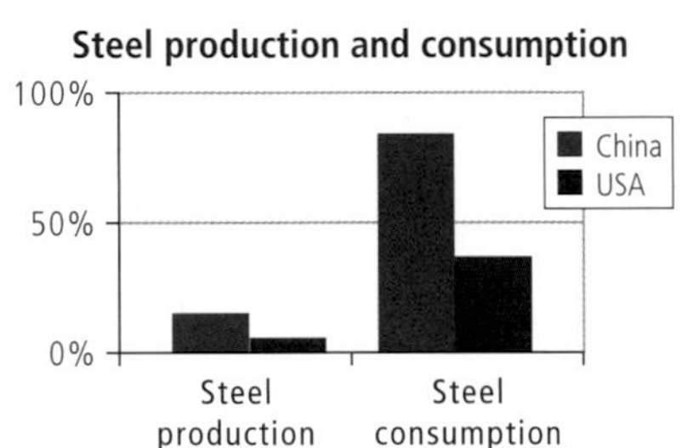

9 Look at the model answer on page 52. Use language from the Making comparisons section of the Useful language table to replace the words/ phrases in bold (marked 1–6), with a suitable alternative.

1
2
3
4
5
6

Task 1: further practice

10 Study the Task 1 question and answer the questions below.

1 What do the numbers refer to?
2 What are the significant differences in the table?
3 How would you organize your answer?

The table below shows the percentage use of four different fuel types to generate electricity in five European countries in 2001.

Summarize the information by selecting and reporting the main features, and make comparisons where relevant. Write at least 150 words.

Fuel type used to generate electricity (%)

	Nuclear	Coal & lignite	Petroleum products	Hydro & wind	Other
Germany	29	50	1	6	13
Britain	23	34	2	2	39
Italy	0	11	27	20	42
Sweden	45	1	2	49	44
Belgium	58	12	2	2	26

Study skills

Recording vocabulary for Writing Task 1

1 In the box below is some useful vocabulary for Task 1. Add the words in the box to the table below.

> ***TIP***
> Don't forget that 'changes over time' diagrams require different words and phrases from fixed time diagrams. Look at the diagrams in Units 1 and 3. What type is each one?

A fluctuated considerably from … to …
The given data illustrates …
A and B experienced an identical increase.
The USA consumes the greatest proportion of energy.
In general, the most significant change occurred in …
This table/graph/chart clearly shows …
A was over twice as large as B.
The exception to this trend is/was …

Introductory phrases to Writing Task 1	Describing overall trends or features	Describing changes over time Don't forget to learn DIFFERENT PATTERNS: adjective + noun (eg a substantial increase) verb + adverb (eg increased significantly)	Making comparisons

Dictionary focus

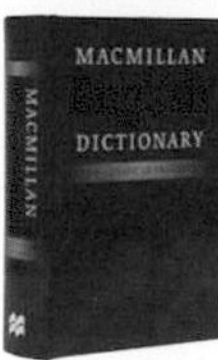

1 Find these words in the unit.

synthetic p.41	inflation p.41	recycled p.47
capacity p.41	commercial p.47	consume p.53

1 Decide what kind of words they are. (*Example: Is it a noun? Verb?*)
2 Read the sentence the word is in and try to guess its meaning from the context.
3 Now check their meaning in your dictionary and record them.

2 Use your dictionary to check the meanings of the words as they are used in the text from Reading 1.

4 Healthy body, healthy mind

Speaking

1 What do you think 'a balanced diet' is? In your country, what are the main foods people eat in these groups: carbohydrate, fat, protein, fruit and vegetable?

2 Vice or virtue? Make two lists, one your 'good' or healthy habits and the other for things you do which are 'bad' or unhealthy.

Reading 1

Using headings to identify purpose and organization

1 Skim read these headings for a passage about chocolate quickly and answer question 1.

List of headings

0 Chocolate could boost concentration
1 Chocolate makes us feel better
2 Chocolate is good for stress
3 Chocolate does not give you spots
4 Chocolate makes you live longer
5 Chocolate is nutritious
6 Chocolate boosts the appetite
7 Chocolate helps us digest milk
8 Chocolate can make you more alert

TIP

Table completion and short answer questions often require you to scan read the passage for factual information.

1 The purpose of the article is to

A present a problem and a solution
B present one side of an argument
C describe cause and effect
D describe both sides of an argument

2 Read the passage quickly and match the headings (**1–8**) with the paragraphs in the passage (**A–I**).

Why eating chocolate is good for you

It's many people's favourite vice, but if the latest evidence is to be believed, the last thing you should feel when you secretly tuck into a hunk of chocolate is guilty. Scientists have revealed that eating chocolate, in reasonable amounts, makes you feel emotionally better and so improves the smooth running of your body's endorphins. It even protects against heart disease.

A Researchers at Harvard University in the U.S. studied 8,000 men and found that those who ate modest amounts of chocolate up to three times a month lived almost a year longer than those who didn't eat any. They concluded that this is likely to be due to the fact that cocoa contains anti-oxidants called polyphenols, also found in red wine, which prevent the oxidation of harmful cholesterol. Anti-oxidants are also known to protect against cancer.

B This is thought to be because it contains valeric acid, which is a relaxant and tranquilliser. Also, the sugar in chocolate may reduce stress – sugar has been shown to have a calming and pain-relieving effect on babies and animals because sweet tastes activate the opiate-like substances in our brain.

C There are a number of scientific reasons for this. The smell of chocolate has been found to slow down brain waves, making us feel calm. Most of the time our brains are dominated by beta waves, the normal waking frequency. When our brain activity slows to alpha waves, we experience a pleasant feeling of calm but alert relaxation. Also, because most of us find eating chocolate so pleasurable, we release endorphins in the brain. These have similar pharmacological actions to morphine, acting as pain-relievers and giving us a sense of well-being.

D Although many teenagers blame chocolate for their acne, there's no scientific data to confirm this link. Scientists at Missouri University even gave spot-prone subjects chocolate to eat and observed their skin for the next week, with no effect.

Chocolate could boost concentration

E This can occur, for example, if you eat it mid-afternoon, when blood sugar levels get a bit low. Chocolate has a reasonably low glycaemic index (GI), which means it gives long-lasting energy because it doesn't raise blood sugar too quickly. For example, a typical bar of chocolate has a GI of 70, compared with 73 for a bowl of cornflakes. This means a chocolate bar will keep you going for longer. Also, chocolate is a good source of chromium, which helps control blood sugar because it is involved in making glucose available in the body.

F This means it is good for those who are lactose-intolerant. Researchers at Rhode Island University have shown that cocoa stimulates activity of the enzyme lactase in the intestine. We need this to digest lactose, the sugar found in milk. Lactose-intolerant patients showed a reduction in bloating, cramping and diarrhoea when one-and-a-half teaspoons of cocoa were added to a cup of milk.

G This could be because it contains cannabinoid-like substances that are known to affect the hypothalamus, the part of the brain that controls hunger. This isn't ideal if you're on a diet but, for those who need to put on weight or who are convalescing, chocolate could be just what you need to help you get your appetite back.

H It contains a stimulant called theobromine, a caffeine-like substance that is thought to make us more alert. But theobromine doesn't have the side-effect of making us nervous, like caffeine, and chocolate contains only minute amounts of caffeine – a mug of coffee has about 85mg compared with just 1mg in three squares of chocolate.

I A 50g bar of plain chocolate contains 1.2mg of iron, and 45mg of magnesium. Milk chocolate is a reasonable source of calcium – a 50g bar contains 110mg. However, we'd need to eat about seven bars to get the recommended daily allowances of these minerals.

Question strategy

Completing tables

1 Look at the table and the examples given and check what information is needed.

2 Check if you should use words from the passage or a list in your answer.

3 Scan-read the passage for technical terms, eg polyphenols and parallel expressions.

Completing tables, diagrams, notes

3 Answer questions **1–6**. Complete the table. Choose no more than **TWO WORDS** from the passage for your answer.

SUBSTANCE FOUND IN CHOCOLATE	EFFECT ON HEALTH
Polyphenols	Prevent oxygen mixing with **1** _____
Valeric acid	Causes a lowering of **2** _____
3 _____	Eases pain
Chromium	Regulates **4** _____
5 _____	Aids digestion of lactose
6 _____	Increases levels of anxiety

Short answer questions

Exam information

These questions ask for factual information.

Question strategy

1 Decide what sort of information you are looking for, eg a number, a substance.

2 Use words from the passage for your answer.

4 Read the text again and answer these questions. Write no more than **THREE WORDS AND/OR A NUMBER** for each answer.

Questions **7–11**

7 Which antioxidants are found in both chocolate and red wine?
8 What is the glycaemic index of a bar of chocolate?
9 Which three symptoms of indigestion are mentioned in the passage?
10 Which part of the brain affects appetite?
11 What three minerals can be found in chocolate?

Language focus

TIP

In academic writing:

Which is the most commonly used relative pronoun.

Subject relative pronouns are much more common than object relative pronouns.

Defining and non-defining relative clauses

See Grammar reference, page 172–173.

1 Study the sentences about chocolate. Underline the relative clause(s) in sentences **1–4** and circle the relative pronoun.

0 Chocolate is something (which) many people feel guilty about eating.
1 Chocolate is good for people who are lactose-intolerant.
2 Teenagers whose skin is affected by acne can safely eat chocolate.
3 Chocolate contains valeric acid, which is a relaxant and tranquillizer.
4 Chocolate has a reasonably low GI, which means it gives a long-lasting energy.

2 Read the grammar summary on page 172–173. Answer the questions about the relative clauses in sentences **0–4** in exercise 1.

1 Which relative pronoun tells you about
a people?
b things?
c something a person owns or possesses?

2 In which sentences could you
a replace the relative pronoun with *that*?
b omit the relative pronoun?

3 Why are there commas in sentences 3 and 4?

3 Sentences **0–2** contain defining relative clauses. The information in the relative clause is part of the main idea of the sentence. The relative clauses in sentences **3** and **4** are non-defining: the information they contain is not part of the main idea of the sentence.

Underline the correct alternative in these rules for forming defining and non-defining relative clauses.

a The relative pronoun can be left out in some *defining/non-defining* relative clauses.
b *That* can replace *which* in *defining/non-defining* relative clauses.
c Commas separate the main clause from a *defining/non-defining* relative clause.

4 Add more information from the box to each of the sentences by adding a relative pronoun and punctuation as necessary.

- promotes sweating and hastens healing
- the body temperature is lower
- the immune system is the only cure for
- panic or get distressed
- people respond to illness
- infects them
- is more dominant
- is 75 years
- is so tiny that 50,000 of them could fit on the head of a pin
- causes coughing, sneezing and a runny nose to wash out the virus

10 things you never knew about colds

a The 'common cold' is caused by a virus **0** ____.
0 which is so tiny that 50,000 of them could fit on the head of a pin.
b During an average lifetime **1** ____ a person will suffer about 210 colds.
c The symptoms of a cold are caused by our immune system **2** ____.
d It is possible to catch a cold from a horse as the virus **3** ____ is similar to the human version.
e Cold viruses like to live in the nose **4** ____.
f When we have a cold, the nostril **5** ____ stays open while the other nostril will be blocked.
g Ginger **6** ____ is a natural remedy for the symptoms of cold.
h The way **7** ____ is a factor in how quickly they recover.
i People **8** ____ have more severe symptoms because their brain prepares for the worst.
j The 'common cold is an illness **9** ____.

Participle clauses: -ing and -ed

1 Read sentences 1a and b. Are the verbs in the relative clauses active or passive?

1 a Chocolate has a reasonably low GI, which *means* it gives a long-lasting energy.
1 b Chocolate contains polyphenols, which *are* also *found* in red wine.

2 In Sentences 2 a and b the relative pronouns and any auxiliary verbs have been left out. Study sentences 2a and b and underline the correct alternative in the rules.

2 a Chocolate has a reasonably low GI, *meaning* it gives a long-lasting energy.
2 b Chocolate contains polyphenols, also *found* in red wine.

1 In place of a relative clause with an active verb we can use a *present/ past* participle.
2 In place of a relative clause with a passive verb we can use a *present/ past* participle.

3 Re-write these sentences using a past or present participle. If the verb is active, change it to a present participle. If the verb is passive, change it to a past participle.

0 The cold virus has the genetic ability to change the cells *which line the nose* so that they produce new viruses.
The cold virus has the genetic ability to change the cells lining the nose so that they produce new viruses.
1 The hypothalamus is the part of the brain *which controls hunger.*
2 Chocolate contains substances *which are thought to make us more alert.*
3 We need lactose to digest the sugar *which is found in milk.*

4 We may have more colds in the winter because we huddle together more for warmth, *which makes cross-infection more likely.*
5 Coughing is a reaction to the irritation in the throat *which is caused by colds.*
6 A cough is a rush of air through the voice box *which produces a sound unique to each individual.*
7 Chocolate slows downs brain waves, *which makes us feel calm.*

Speaking

1 Work in pairs and answer the following questions.

1 What kinds of food do you like to cook?
2 Do people in your country like cooking meals for friends in their homes, or do they prefer going out to eat in restaurants?
3 Are people healthier in your country now than they were in the past?
4 Do you think fast food will still be popular in the future?

2 Make up three more questions around the topics of Food and Health. Ask your partner your questions.

3 Read the following Part 2 topic. Take 1 minute to make notes and then speak to your partner about it for about 1 or 2 minutes.

Describe a popular dish from your country that you enjoy making.

You should say:
What this dish is
Why you enjoy making it
When you usually make it

You should also say why it is a popular dish in your country.

4 Work with a new partner and discuss the following Part 3 questions.

1 Do you think large fast food companies should be allowed to target children in their advertising campaigns? Give reasons for your answer.
2 How important is food as a representative of a country's culture?
3 Compare the importance of local and imported goods for the economy of a country.

Reading 2

Following an argument in a passage

1 Read the passage quickly and match the paragraph numbers in 1–3 with the best summary of that section of the passage (a–c).

1 Paragraphs 1–4	a Writer's views and conclusions
2 Paragraphs 5–7	b Anecdote about the writer's own experience
3 Paragraphs 8 and 9	c Reasons why responsibility for healthcare is shifting

Your own medicine *How too much self-help can be bad for your health*

1 'One of the first duties of the physician is to educate the masses not to take medicine,' observed William Osler, one of the giants of 19th-century medicine. It is a lesson that I, as a pill-popping member of the public, have learned the hard way. Several years ago, I was given a prescription for an acne medication which worked wonders for my complexion – so much so that when the prescription ran out, I kept refilling it, thanks to a friendly neighbourhood pharmacist.

2 I pride myself on being a fully empowered health-care consumer, being well-informed (keeping up with medical developments is, after all, my job), with a doctorate in immunology, and with enough money and determination to take treatment of minor complaints into my own hands. In this case, I was also extremely foolish.

3 After a few months on the medication, I started to experience dizzy spells. I dismissed them as overwork, and continued to take the pills. About a year later, those spells became a curse. I awoke one morning to find the world spinning around me. For a week, I lay in a darkened room with my eyes tightly shut. Every time I opened them, I would start to vomit. Doctors have a word for this living hell – auditory nerve damage. Thankfully, I recovered, but not without losing my balance for several weeks and becoming permanently deaf in one ear. There is no proof that my illness was caused by do-it-yourself doctoring. But once I stopped taking the pills the dizziness and other side effects ceased.

4 An experience like that would give anyone a healthy appreciation of the limits to self-help. But these days, people are being encouraged – indeed, expected – to take personal control of their own bodies. This is sound advice when it comes to staying healthy: sticking to a sensible diet, taking regular exercise, and refraining from smoking. But I wonder about the wisdom of such an approach when it comes to making people better as opposed to merely keeping them well. On the road to recovery, who should be in the driver's seat – doctor or patient?

5 Certainly there are powerful forces – social, political and legal as well as economic – that are jostling doctors out of taking full charge of their patient's health. For one thing, professional paternalism is no longer fashionable in western society. Today, your banker, lawyer and, above all, your physician is supposed to be an advisor, not an unquestioned authority who single-mindedly determines the course of action necessary. Malpractice litigation, especially in America, has pushed the medical profession into shifting much of the responsibility for taking decisions on to the patients themselves. For another thing, easy access to medical information on the Internet and elsewhere is giving patients an illusion of expert knowledge with which to challenge – and, increasingly, dictate – their doctor's decisions.

6 Pharmaceutical companies have been quick to take advantage of this trend. When a blitz of television commercials encourages viewers to 'ask your doctor' about the latest wonder drug, chances are your doctor will prescribe it for you. As one American expert on medical ethics has noted, in many branches of medicine, the doctor has become simply a waiter, and the patient a customer ordering from a menu of treatments.

7 Meanwhile, as governments and employers struggle to pay for expensive new medicines, they are trying to move more of the cost of treatment, and therefore more of the responsibility, on to patients. Drugmakers have also caught on to this economic trend, switching many of their products from being available only on prescription – where doctors and insurance firms control access – to becoming available as over-the-counter remedies that consumers choose and pay for themselves.

8 The drive to turn patients into self-reliant health-care consumers needs to be watched carefully – for the simple reason that shopping for medical treatment will never be the same as shopping for a flat-screen TV. There is a fundamental inequality in the doctor–patient relationship that no amount of education and empowerment can resolve. You wouldn't try to buy a new car with a complicated lease agreement when feeling like death. Likewise, a sick patient visiting a healthy care-giver, will inevitably be entering into a one-sided relationship.

9 This is not to say that public education in health matters should be discouraged. Nor does it mean that people should be dissuaded from doing all that they can to look after themselves. As the history of AIDS has shown, informed patients can be a powerful force for change when it comes to improving medical practices. But this needs to be part of a partnership between doctors and patients, not a substitute for it.

> **TIP**
> Remember: (a) the correct answer to the question is the one given in the text, and not your opinion; (b) words from an incorrect option may appear in the text.

Multiple-choice questions: multiple answers

2 Answer questions **1** and **2**.

1 According to Shereen El Feki, which of the following benefit when patients become more responsible for their healthcare?

Choose three answers from **A–F**.

A doctors
B drug companies
C lawyers
D governments
E insurance companies
F television companies

2 According to the writer, responsibility for healthcare is being transferred to patients because of …

Choose three answers from **A–F**.

A changes in public attitude.
B the availability of information.
C advances in healthcare.
D legal action against patients.
E the availability of non-prescription medicines.
F the high cost of healthcare.

Yes, No, Not given

Exam information

True/False/Not Given questions **(See Unit 2, pages 30–31)** ask you to identify whether a statement agrees with or contradicts **information** in the passage. **Yes/No/Not Given** questions ask you to say whether a statement agrees with or contradicts **the writer's views.**

> **TIP**
> Read the question carefully to see whether it asks you to identify information or the writer's views.

3 Read paragraphs **1–4** in the passage. Then study the example, questions **3–5** and the answers.

3 The writer suffered from a skin complaint. **YES**
She was given a prescription for an acne medication. (Paragraph 1)

4 The writer is certain that the medication was responsible for her illness. The passage says *There is no proof that…* (Paragraph 3) **NO**

5 The writer eats sensibly and takes regular exercise. **NG**
The passage says she thinks this is sensible advice, but not whether she follows it. (Paragraph 4)

4 Answer questions **6–12**.

Do the following questions agree with the views of the writer? Write:

YES if the statement agrees with the views of the writer
NO if the statement contradicts the views of the writer
NOT GIVEN if it is impossible to say what the writer thinks about this

6 People should be encouraged to take responsibility for maintaining their health.
7 Patients expect their doctor to take responsibility for making them well.
8 Doctors are making more use of the Internet than in the past.
9 Patients have more influence over their doctors' decisions than in the past.
10 A relationship between a doctor and a patient is always unbalanced.
11 Patients should do more to improve medical practices.

12 Which of the following best **summarizes** the writer's view of the doctor–patient relationship?

A Doctors will always have more power than patients.
B Patients can be as well-informed as doctors.
C Doctors are like waiters and patients are like their customers.
D Doctor and patient should be like parent and child.

Vocabulary

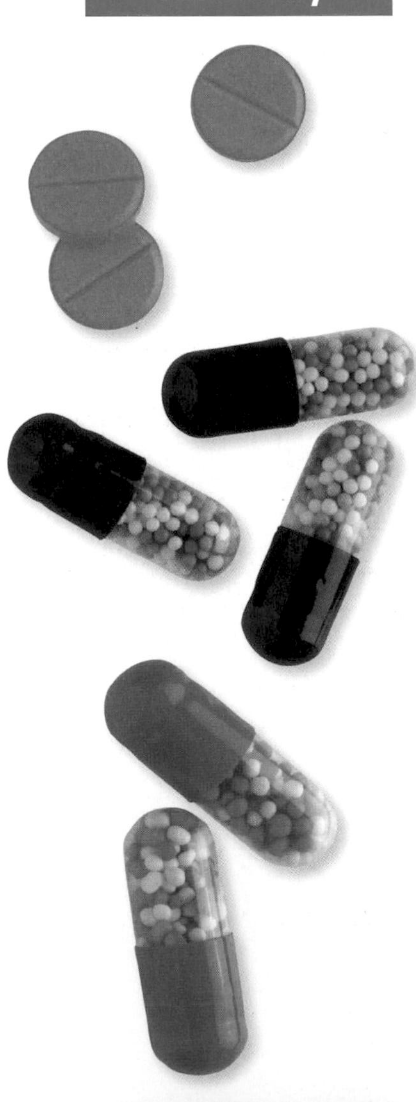

Medical terms

1 If you had these common conditions or illnesses, what symptoms would you have? Write your answers in column A.

ILLNESS	A SYMPTOMS	B TREATMENT
0 indigestion	c	4
1 a cold		
2 influenza / the flu		
3 chickenpox		
4 a hangover		
5 hay fever		

a sneezing, runny nose, red eyes
b nausea, dizziness, tiredness
c bloating, cramps, diarrhoea
d weakness, tiredness, nausea, painful joints
e a skin rash or spots, a temperature, itchiness
f coughing, sneezing, a temperature, a sore throat

2 How would you treat the illnesses in exercise 1? Write your answers in Column B.

1 rest in bed
2 take medication
3 take a painkiller
4 suck a lozenge
5 apply salve or ointment
6 see a doctor
7 other

3 Work in pairs. Discuss these questions. When was the last time you were unwell? What was the illness and how long were you ill? What were your symptoms? How did you treat the illness?

Writing 1

Task 2: Essay sections

1 Read the following extracts taken from several different essays.

1 Decide whether each sentence comes from the Introduction, Body or Conclusion of an essay.

1 A further point is that Western doctors usually only have time to treat the symptoms of disease not the fundamental causes.

2 To conclude, while it is true to say that there are benefits to having a free health service, the risk of inefficiency and spiralling costs are significant, and support the view that any health care system should include both private and public systems.

3 For instance, given the health scares over intensively farmed meat, vegetarianism offers a potentially healthier diet.

4 The focus of this essay will be to examine the various arguments surrounding the use of genetically modified products in food.

2 Which words or phrases in the sentences above help to organize the essay by linking ideas together?

Exam information

The body of the essay

The body is the main section of the essay where you explain and support your ideas/ opinions/arguments. It should consist of two or three paragraphs.

Paragraph plan for the body of the essay

1 Main idea
2 Development
3 Opposing idea (where relevant)
4 Paragraph conclusion

Paragraph structure: The body of the essay

2 The paragraph plan below may be used for any Task 2 question and can be used to help structure paragraphs in the body of the essay.

1 Match the explanations below to the sections of the plan in the margin. In this part of the body paragraph you should:

A refute the opposing argument and bring the essay back to your view.
B state your idea, argument or point.
C state the opposing argument or what other people might think.
D support the main idea with explanations, examples and reasons.

3 Read the sentences below.

1 Order the sentences to make one complete body paragraph from an essay on the topic of obesity.
2 Label each sentence according to the four types in the body paragraph plan.

1 These foods are often high in sugar and fat, both of which can lead to weight gain.
2 However, some forms of obesity are a result of genetic disorders and not diet.
3 Furthermore, many nutrients are lost from processed food during preparation making it less healthy to eat.
4 The first point to consider is the link between the consumption of processed food and obesity.
5 Nevertheless, what many people are concerned about is the recent increase in obesity rates, particularly in children, which I believe is partly a result of an increase in processed food consumption.

TIP

Read the question carefully to see whether it asks you to identify information or the writer's views.

4 Look at the following question and the 'Main Idea' sentence below taken from the body of a model answer.

The increasing use of modern drug technology encourages the treatment of symptoms instead of treating the causes.

To what extent do you agree or disagree with this?

Main idea
It is my view that drugs are often prescribed for recurring ailments such as headaches with no attempt to discover the reasons why they may keep happening.

1 Complete the paragraph by using the paragraph plan on page 65.
2 Ask the following questions to check:

1 Is the main idea clearly stated?
2 Is there enough evidence to support the main idea even in short paragraphs?
3 Do any of the ideas need to be explained further?
4 Have opposing arguments been included?
5 Does the paragraph conclude properly?
6 Are there enough linking words and phrases?

Listening

Section 4

1 Put the following strategies in an appropriate order.

Exam strategies

1 Predict possible answers and grammar
2 Highlight key words
3 Read the questions before you listen
4 Be aware that answers may come before or after a keyword
5 Check your answers for spelling
6 Pay attention to the instructions
7 Listen for synonyms or parallel expressions of key words

TIP
A difference of one mark may be significant in your overall Listening band score, so keep focused in Section 4 and guess the answer if you're not sure. Don't leave any answer spaces blank.

2 1.14 Look at questions **1–6** then listen to the first part of the lecture. Complete the notes below. Write **NO MORE THAN THREE WORDS** for each answer.

TIP
Be prepared to hear a range of different accents in the Listening module.

Tiredness is increasing

Evidence
- High number of complaints to doctors
- Popularity of **1** ____________ drinks
- Increased use of **2** ____________ stimulants

Dr Liebhold

Believes tiredness due to:
- Financial pressure
- **3** ____________
- Coming to work when ill

Other reasons
- Low levels of **4** ____________ at work
- Poor diet

Dr Mansfield

Solutions to sleep loss:
- Regular waking and sleeping hours
- Limit **5** ____________ intake

Sleep loss research

Without sleep humans:
- Get confused
- Become **6** ____________
- Have hallucinations

Multiple choice

3 1.15 Look at questions **7–8** and listen to the second part of the lecture. Circle the correct answer.

7 Professor Lloyd believes that chronic fatigue syndrome is a result of
- **A** brain site problems.
- **B** structural abnormality.
- **C** abnormal brain function.

8 According to Leonie McMahon, to avoid fatigue we should
- **A** eat a larger breakfast.
- **B** eat more protein at breakfast.
- **C** eat less protein.

Question strategy

Summary completion

Sentence, note and summary completion question types are all similar. In a summary completion quesion the gaps are in a complete paragraph which summarizes a section of the listening. Use the strategies given for note completion (page 24) to help.

Summary completion

4 1.16 Read questions **9–12** and listen to the final part of the lecture. Complete the summary using **NO MORE THAN TWO WORDS.**

Trent Watson is **9** ____________ by Leonie McMahon's ideas because the body does not like to burn protein, hence it doesn't add to **10** ____________ . Carbohydrate is a more common fuel. As a consequence, diets based on low-carbohydrate consumption can result in **11** ____________ . Red meat, leafy vegetables and **12** ____________ are good for strengthening red blood cells.

Writing 2

Task 2: Planning: Finding ideas 1

It is important before you start writing to make a plan. The first step is to spend a couple of minutes thinking of two or three main ideas for the body of the essay so that when you write you can concentrate on:

1 Remembering your grammar and writing as accurately as possible.
2 Linking your ideas logically and clearly.

1 Study the ways of finding ideas given below and think of another of your own.

PERSPECTIVE	Personal	Local	International
TIME	Past	Present	Future
AGE	Teenagers	Middle-aged people	Old-aged people
YOUR IDEA	?	?	?

Exam strategy

This method can be used for:

1 The main ideas of the body of the essay. (For example: Using the 'time' perspective, a paragraph on the popularity of vegetarianism could compare the past, present and future.)

2 Support for a main idea. (For example: A paragraph on stress could be supported by contrasting three age groups.)

2 Put the following sentences into the correct category – *personal, local/ national or global/international.*

1 The increase in the sale of GM foods is fast-becoming a world-wide phenomenon.
2 In my own experience, the attraction of fast-food is that it is much more convenient.
3 An increasing number of people in the UK are now using alternative medicine, such as acupuncture.
4 Governments need to be putting more money into researching cures for fatal diseases like AIDS and cancer.
5 Countries, like China, appear to have far fewer cases of obesity amongst children.
6 My viewpoint is that choosing to eat organic food is by far the safest option.

TIP

Local/national and global/international arguments and ideas are more important because they are more academic in style. The personal ideas should form a smaller part of your overall arguments.

3 Read the essay question below and think of two or three main ideas using one of the ways suggested in exercise 1.

An increasing number of people are turning to vegetarianism. Some people believe that people are following a vegetarian diet for reasons other than animal rights issues.

Do you agree with this?

Give reasons why some people are choosing to become vegetarian.

Argument/opinion questions 2: The opinion essay

See the balanced argument approach in Unit 2, page 35. A second approach to an argument / opinion essay is to take a position in the introduction and continue supporting it throughout the essay. This is called an opinion essay – your essay leads from your opinion.

Question strategy

Be flexible. Don't learn only one essay approach. The key to a good Writing mark is to read the question carefully then choose the most suitable essay approach.

5 Look at the Task 2 question below. Which essay approach would be most suitable for you, a balanced argument or an opinion essay?

Supermarkets should only sell food produced from within their own country rather than imports from overseas.

What are your opinions on this?

6 Read the model answer on page 69 noting the opinion essay structure.
1 Does the writer take a clear position and is it supported throughout the essay?
2 Underline the language used to describe opinions.

Structure	Writing Task 2 – Opinion essay
INTRODUCTION Topic introduced and writer's opinion given.	Nowadays, supermarkets are stocked with food products from around the world. Some would argue that it would be better if food produce was not imported. I firmly believe that this view is correct, and will discuss the reasons why in this essay.
BODY 1 First idea plus examples for support. Describes what others may argue but refutes it by restating the writer's view.	It is certainly the case that importing food can have a negative effect on local culture. This can be seen in countries such as Japan where imported food has become more popular than traditional, local produce, eroding people's understanding of their own food traditions. Although some would claim that this is a natural part of economic development in an increasingly global world, I feel strongly that any loss of regional culture would be detrimental.
BODY 2 Second idea described and explained. Opposing idea given then refuted by giving the writer's view.	A second major reason to reduce imports is the environmental cost. Currently, many food imports, such as fruit, are transported thousands of miles by road, sea and air, making the product more expensive to buy and increasing pollution from exhaust fumes. Despite the fact that the trade in food exports has existed for many years, I am convinced that a reduction would bring significant financial and environmental gains.
BODY 3 Short paragraph starts with an opposing view then refutes it.	However, many jobs depend on food exports and some less developed countries may even depend on this trade for economic survival. In spite of this, the importance of developing local trade should not be undervalued.
CONCLUSION Writer's view restated and future implication briefly described.	In conclusion, I am certain that reducing food imports would have cultural and environmental benefits. What is more, the local economy should, in time, prosper commercially as the demand for local and regional products remains high resisting the competition from overseas. 259 words

7 It is important in an essay to use a range of expressions to describe yours and other's opinions. Add the opinion phrases 1–6 to the appropriate category in the language box.

1 It is widely believed that …
2 I partially support …
3 It is certainly true that …
4 My personal view is that …
5 I totally disagree with …
6 Many consider that …

Useful language: Expressing opinions

Describing your own opinion	Describing other people's opinions
Agreeing with an idea (+ reasons) I am certain that … For me it is obvious that … I am convinced that … It has long been my belief that ...	It is often said that … It is often claimed that … It seems apparent that … Scientists are convinced that … Many researchers have found that ... Some people believe that … X argues / asserts / believes / claims / concludes / confirms / insists / maintains / states / points out / that + sb + v
Disagreeing with an idea (+ reasons) There is no justification for … I am completely against … I believe there is no evidence to support … I do not agree with the idea that …	
Giving an opinion In my view … I would agree that … I feel strongly that … It seems to me that … I would argue that …	
No strong opinion There could be a case for saying that … It would appear that …	

Writing: Further practice

8 Use the language and ideas presented in this unit to write an opinion essay to the following question.

There are serious concerns about the sale and production of genetically modified food. Yet this is necessary if we are to meet the demands of an increasing world population.

Give your opinions on this.

Study skills

Planning: Finding ideas 2

Another method of finding ideas for a Task 2 question is to form adjectives that end in the suffix –al. *For example: politic**al***

1 Complete the mind map below using adjectives that end in -al. An example has been done for you. Check your answers with a partner.

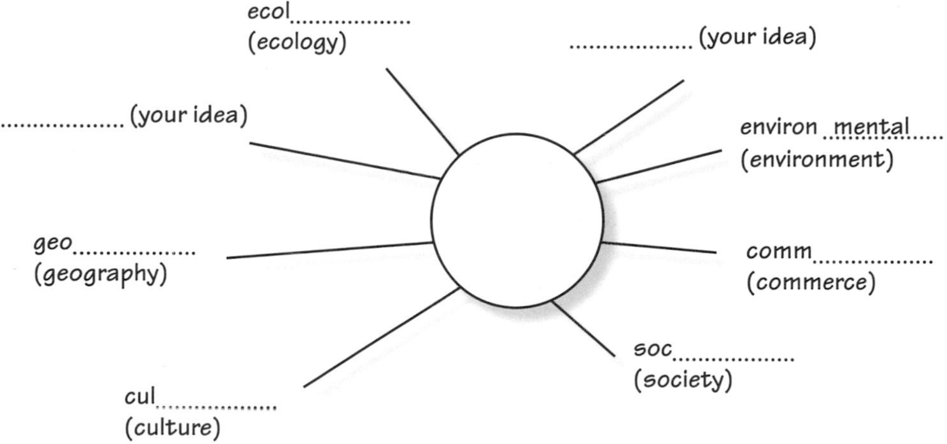

2 Complete the following sentences using appropriate words from the mind map in question 1.

1 It would appear as if food is, in many ways, a .... issue. Therefore, people's food choices are inextricably linked to their beliefs and traditions.
2 It is largely due to .... reasons that food companies continue to promote fast food in their advertising campaigns.
3 Research has shown that producing GM crops has not only health, but also .... implications such as the effects on crops of cross-pollination, which are currently unknown.
4 Peer pressure has a major .... influence on young people's attitudes to what constitutes a healthy diet.

3 Now look at the model answer from Writing 1, Exercise 5 on modern drug technology on page 190 and identify which planning method was used.

Dictionary focus

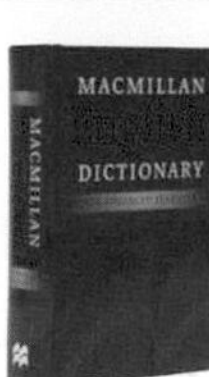

1 Find the following words in the unit.

1 Guess each word's part of speech and meaning from its context.
2 Look up the word in your dictionary and record them in your Writing Task 2 vocabulary bank.

appetite p.57	activate p.57	fundamental p.62
dominate p.57	remedy p.60	fatigue p.67

5 The world we live in

1 Look at these pictures. What do they show? What natural disaster could have caused the damage in the pictures?

2 Work in pairs. Discuss these questions. Do you know of any countries that have experienced these or other natural disasters? Who should be responsible for dealing with the effects of natural disasters, local or international communities?

Reading

1 Skim read the passage in 2–3 minutes and answer question **1**.

1 The writer's purpose is to

A present a problem and a solution.
B present an argument.
C describe cause and effect.
D describe a phenomenon.

Hurricanes

A A hurricane is a tropical cyclone, an area of intense low pressure in the tropics surrounded by a violent rotating storm. It is called a hurricane in the North Atlantic, the Northeast Pacific east of the dateline, and the South Pacific Ocean east of 160E; west of the dateline it is called a typhoon, and in the Indian Ocean, a cyclone. It becomes a hurricane officially if its wind speeds reach 75mph, or force 12 on the Beaufort scale; below that it is a tropical storm. Every year there are about 100 tropical storms and about 50 of them reach hurricane strength. The name comes from "Hurican", the Carib god of evil.

B Hurricanes need precise meteorological conditions to form: the sea surface temperature needs to be above 26.5°C. They are formed over the tropical ocean when strong clusters of thunderstorms drift over warm water. Warm air from the storm and the ocean surface combine and begin to rise, creating an area of low pressure on the ocean surface. Rising warm air causes pressure to decrease at higher altitudes. Air rises faster and faster to fill the low pressure, in turn drawing more warm air up off the sea and sucking cold air downwards. The cluster of thunderstorms merge to become a huge storm, which moves west with the trade winds. While it remains over warm water the tropical wave begins to grow. Wind speeds increase as air is sucked into the low pressure centre. If the depression strengthens and its wind speed climbs above 40mph it becomes a tropical storm and is named by the US National Hurricane Centre. Once the sustained winds exceed 74mph, the storm becomes a hurricane. It can take as long as several days or only a few hours for a depression to develop into a full-blown hurricane. The fully developed hurricane is made up of an eye of calm winds surrounded by a spinning vortex of high winds and heavy rainstorms.

C Hurricanes produce the highest wind speeds, up to 200mph in the most extreme cases, which only the strongest structures can withstand. They produce enormous amounts of rain which can lead to catastrophic flash floods. Sometimes most seriously, they produce a phenomenon known as a storm surge. This is a huge raising of the sea level, caused jointly by the huge winds and the very low atmospheric pressure. In the most extreme cases it can be as much as 25ft above normal. The hurricane pushes this heightened sea along in front of its path and when it hits the coastline, especially the low-lying coasts, there can be disastrous inundations, especially when the surge combines with torrential rain. Once a hurricane reaches land, it tends to die out fairly quickly as there is no more warm water to supply heat, but out in the open ocean it can last for a fortnight or more.

D Hurricanes are now measured between strengths 1 and 5 on the Saffir-Simpson scale, formulated in 1969 by Herbert Saffir, a consulting engineer, and Dr Bob Simpson, the director of the US National Hurricane Center. The scale was devised in the aftermath of Hurricane Camille in 1969, one of the most violent storms ever to hit the continental United States. Its categories run like this:

Category one (minimal): winds 75 to 95mph, minor flooding, slight structural damage, storm surge up to 1.5m.

Category two (moderate): winds between 96 and 110mph, roof and tree damage, storm surge 1.8 to 2.4m.

Category three (extensive): winds between 111 and 130mph, houses damaged, severe flooding, storm surge 2.7 to 3.7m.

Category four (extreme): winds of between 131 and 155mph, major structural damage to houses and some roofs destroyed, storm surge of between 4 and 5.5m.

Category five (catastrophic): winds above 155mph, many buildings destroyed, smaller ones blown away completely, severe inland flooding, storm surge of more than 5.5m.

E Although global warming is confidently expected to produce more violent storms, scientists cannot yet prove a link between current hurricane rates and climate change. There does seem to have been an increase in the number of category five hurricanes worldwide. 2004 was more active than 2003 and 2002 but less active than the four years before that.

F All tropical storms are named, to provide ease of communication between forecasters and the general public about forecasts, watches and warnings. Since the storms can often be long-lasting and more than one can be occurring in the same region at the same time, names can reduce the confusion about which storm is being described. Before the 20th century, especially in the Caribbean, hurricanes were sometimes named after the saint's day on which they struck land. During the Second World War, US Navy meteorologists gave them the female names of wives and loved ones, but by 1950 a formal naming strategy was in place for North Atlantic cyclones, based on the phonetic alphabet of the time (Able, Baker, Charlie and so on.) In 1953 the US Weather Bureau decided to switch to female first names, and with the agreement of the World Meteorological Association, included male first names in the list in 1979. Each meteorological region of the world now has an agreed list of names. The letters Q, U, X, Y and Z are not used because few names begin with these letters. Quite a few hurricane names, including Andrew, Betsy, Bob, Camille, Hugo and Hilda, have been officially retired because the storms concerned caused damage on a scale unlikely to be repeated. About 50 names have been retired; a country can request retirement.

Question strategy

1. Put a line through the letter beside the example passage and heading before you start the exercise.
2. Read each section for a general idea of its meaning and purpose. Remember: the main idea of a paragraph is usually given in the first, or topic, sentence.
3. Look in the passage for repetitions of words in the headings and for synonyms or parallel expressions.
4. If there are two possible headings for a section or paragraph, choose both. When you have answered all the questions go back and decide which heading best summarises the section or paragraph.
5. Choose the heading which best describes the overall meaning of the section. A heading which picks up on a detail or an example is usually not the correct answer.

2 Skim read Paragraph A and underline key words. Notice the use of: *is called; becomes; the name comes from*. These phrases suggest that hurricanes are being defined in the paragraph. In fact, the best heading for Paragraph A is *iii Defining characteristics*. Heading x, the Carib god of evil is mentioned in Paragraph A, but this is only a detail.

Read the passage and answer questions **1–5**. Use key words in the paragraphs to help you to find the correct heading.

The reading passage has six sections, **A–F**. Choose the correct heading for sections **B–F** from the list of headings below.

List of headings

i Process of formation
ii Effect of a storm surge
iii Defining characteristics
iv Systems for identifying
v Damaging effects
vi History of hurricanes
vii System for classification
viii Speculation about cause
ix Effect of low pressure
x The Carib god of evil

0 Section A iii
1 Section B ____
2 Section C ____
3 Section D ____
4 Section E ____
5 Section F ____

Summary completion

TIP

A summary completion question can require you to summarize the entire passage or just a section of it.

Exam information

Summary completion (from the passage)

See Unit 2, page 30 for more information on summary completion using words from a list. For this type of summary question you must use words taken from the passage for your answers.

Remember: the correct answer must complete the summary grammatically and agree with what is said in the text.

3 Read the summary. Does it summarize all or part of the passage?

Complete the summary. Write **NO MORE THAN THREE WORDS** from the passage for each answer. Write the words in the space provided.

> Hurricanes, also known as cyclones and typhoons, commonly occur in the **6**____________. The lowest **7**____________ hurricane may cause only minor damage, while the most severe will see **8**____________ or even blown away completely. No proof yet exists of a connection between an increased number of severe hurricanes and **9**____________. Various systems have been used for identifying hurricanes, but only since 1979 have they been described using **10**____________. Hurricane names are allocated to a **11**____________ and in special circumstances can be **12**____________.

Labelling a diagram

Exam information

You may be asked to choose words or phrases from a box or list, or words from the passage. If you are asked to choose words or phrases from a box or list there will be more words than you need.

Question strategy

Study the diagram and question carefully. Use the labels you are given in the question to help you understand the diagram.

Label the diagrams. Use **NO MORE THAN TWO WORDS** from the passage.

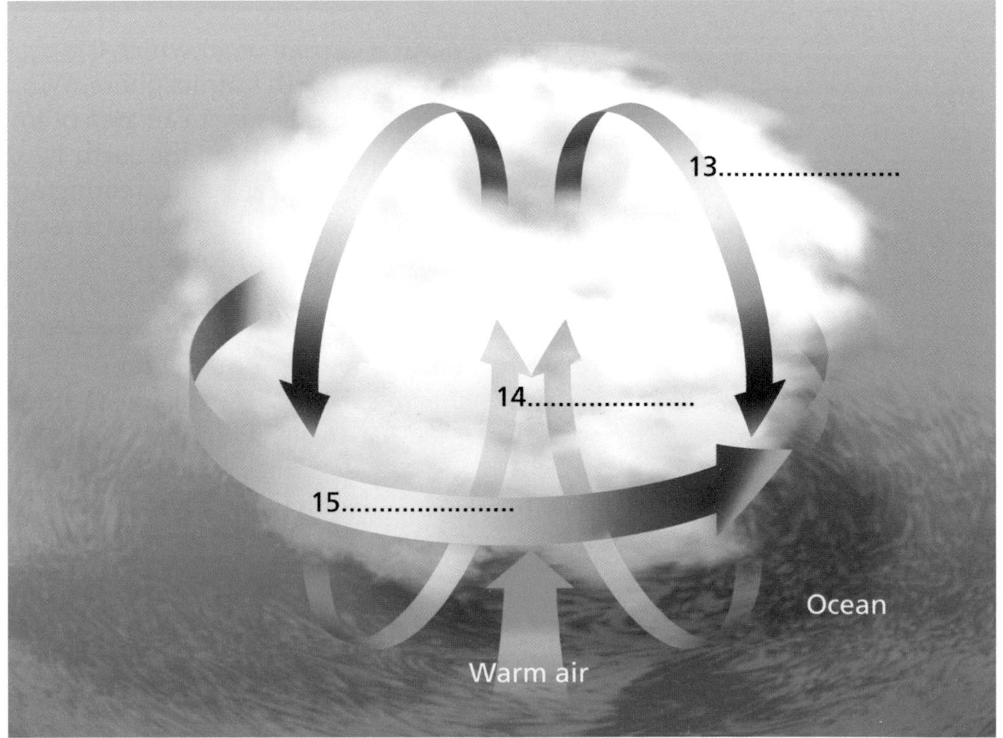

Language focus

The passive

See Grammar reference, page 173.

We use the passive when the action is more important than who did the action. When we want to say who or what did the action, we use ***by*** + agent.

a Active: Herbert Saffir and Bob Simpson *devised* the Saffir–Simpson scale. (It is more important who devised the scale.)

b Passive: The Saffir–Simpson scale *was devised* **by** Herbert Saffir and Bob Simpson. (The Saffir–Simpson scale is more important.)

1 Match sentence halves in **A** and **B** to form true sentences about hurricanes.

A	B
1 All tropical hurricanes	a *can be requested* by a country.
2 Names can reduce confusion	b *have been retired.*
3 Some hurricane names	c *are named.*
4 Retirement of a hurricane name	d about which storm *is being described.*

2 Look at sentences in exercise 1 and answer the following questions.

1 Are the verbs in italics active or passive?
2 How do we form the passive?
3 What tense is each verb in italics?
4 Which sentence contains an agent? Why?

3 Complete the text with passive verbs from the box in the appropriate tense.

cause devise give heat (x2) measure rate (x2)

Wind is a natural current of air which **0** is caused by differences in air pressure within the earth's atmosphere. Wind occurs when air flows from an area of high pressure to an area of lower pressure. Wind can be global or local. Certain parts of the earth **1** ________ more than others by the sun, causing air to rise and creating an area of low pressure. Air flowing from higher pressure areas to these areas of lower pressure creates wind. Wind occurs near water because the air above the land **2** ________ more than the air above the water. Winds that always happen at the same time or in the same way **3** ________ names, for example, the mistral in southern France and the sirocco in North Africa. Wind speed **4** ________ using a rating system called the Beaufort scale. The scale, which **5** ________ by Sir Francis Beaufort, a British admiral, describes wind behaviour at various speeds: a calm day **6** ________ as zero while a hurricane **7** ________ as 12 on the scale.

Vocabulary 1

TIP

1 To retain a word you need to test yourself progressively and often.

2 To help remember a word, make personal associations with the word – think of connections or contexts for the word.

Adjectives and nouns

1 The adjective forms of these nouns are used in the passage on hurricanes.

a Change the nouns to adjectives and write the adjective form of each noun under the correct adjective ending.
b Write the adjective form for the word which does not fit in the table.
c Which ending is most common?

act disaster globe meteorology catastrophe
structure torrent tropics violence

-al	-ent	-ive	-ous
0 tropical			

2 The adjective forms of the following nouns are common in more formal writing. Write the adjective forms in the table in exercise 1.

attraction creation effect expense centre dependence
difference efficiency fame frequency nation norm
politics religion variety

3 Write an appropriate adjective from exercises **1** and **2** in each sentence. In each sentence a noun which collocates with the adjective is written in italics.

0 The economic *consequences* of large-scale military action can be disastrous for a country.
1 We chose the premises because their ____________ *location* meant easy access by public transport.
2 The earthquake caused major ____________ *damage* to buildings in the area.
3 Statistics show a fall in incidences of ____________ *crime* involving harm to a person or property.
4 A vaccine can be an ____________ *means* of controlling the spread of a disease.
5 There is not just one but ____________ *ways* of solving the problem.
6 In some parts of the world people are still persecuted for their ____________ *beliefs*.
7 The accounts are inspected regularly and at ____________ *intervals*.
8 It is ____________ *practice* in some countries for women to give birth at home rather than at hospital.

Listening 1

Section 2

1 Answer the following questions then discuss in pairs.

1 Can you name any wild animals that tourists pay to see in their natural surroundings?
2 Are there any costs or benefits to wildlife tourism?
3 What different environmental problems might these animals face?

Flow chart

Question strategy

Flow charts

Put the following steps into the correct order:

1 Make sure your answers are grammatical.
2 Predict the grammar needed for each gap and any possible answers.
3 Check the instructions and the maximum word limit.
4 Use the stages of the flow chart to help you keep up with the listening.
5 Check you haven't exceeded the maximum word limit.
6 Quickly look at the chart to understand what it shows.

2 1.17 Listen to the first part of a radio programme and fill in the answers using **NO MORE THAN TWO WORDS AND/OR A NUMBER.**

Polar Bear Migratory Cycle

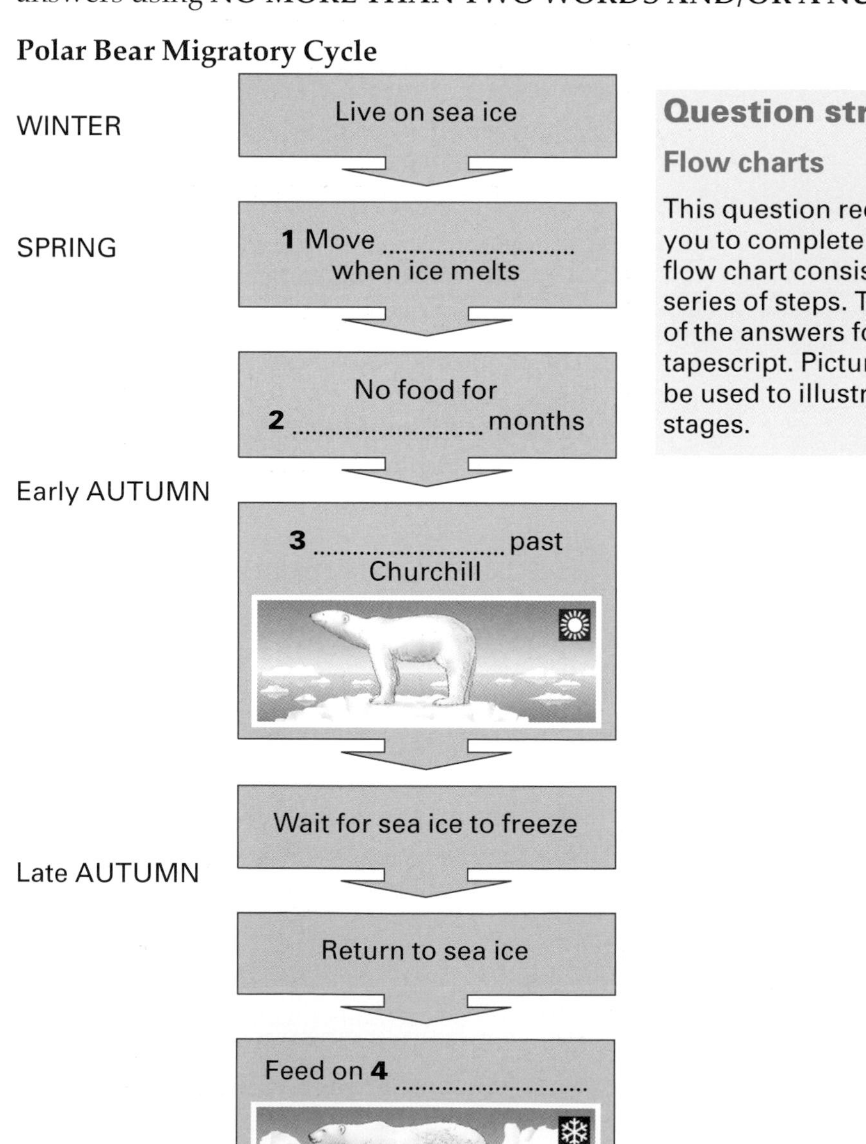

Question strategy

Flow charts

This question requires you to complete gaps in a flow chart consisting of a series of steps. The order of the answers follows the tapescript. Pictures may be used to illustrate the stages.

3 1.18 Listen to the second part of the radio programme. Write **NO MORE THAN THREE WORDS** for each answer.

The Bear Alert Programme

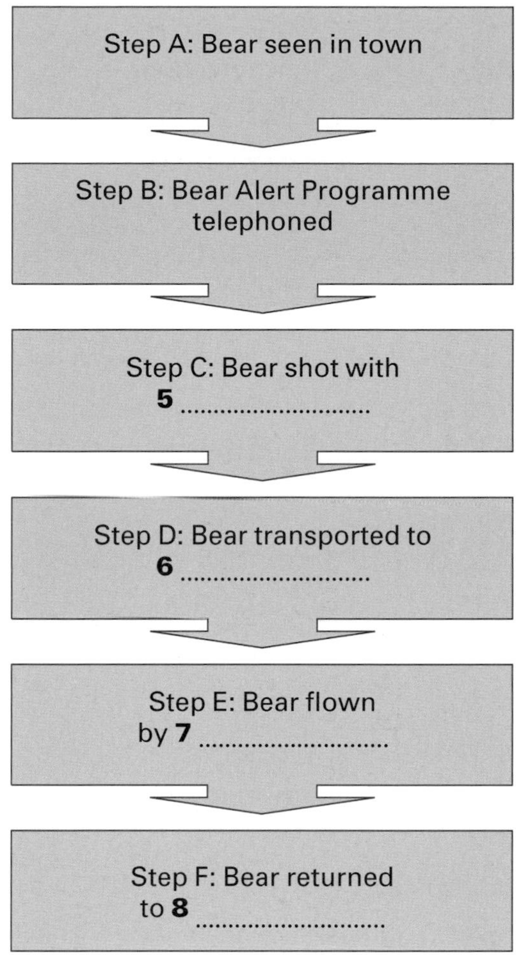

Step A: Bear seen in town
Step B: Bear Alert Programme telephoned
Step C: Bear shot with **5** ....
Step D: Bear transported to **6** ....
Step E: Bear flown by **7** ....
Step F: Bear returned to **8** ....

Short answers

Question strategy

Note the word limit then read the questions to decide what kind of information you are listening for *eg a date, number, place, activity, name, etc.* Underline key words in the questions to help you pick out the answer.

Exam information

This question type may consist of a series of questions or sentences with gaps. In either form, the number of words in your answer must match that given in the task instructions.

4 1.19 Listen and answer the questions using **NO MORE THAN THREE WORDS AND/OR A NUMBER.**

9 How much does Manitoba Province earn in one year from Bear Tourism?
10 What might cause the bears to disappear according to Darren Ottaway?
11 What do tourists come to do?
12 What is the estimated number of Hudson Bay Bears?
13 What do Japanese tourists want to see?
14 Which movie, filmed in Churchill, is yet to be released?

Pronunciation

TIP

The schwa sound /ə/ is the most common vowel sound in English. Many unstressed syllables have the schwa sound. Many short, one-syllable words, eg articles, prepositions, auxiliary verbs, have a schwa sound when they are said quickly in a sentence.

The schwa sound /ə/

1 Mark the stressed syllable and the schwa sound(s) /ə/ in these words from the reading and listening passages.

1 area
2 category
3 community
4 economy
5 enormous
6 estimate (n)
7 minor
8 phenomenon
9 potential
10 region
11 resident
12 strategy

2 1.20 Listen and check your answers. Then take turn reading the words to your partner.

3 Mark the stressed syllables and the schwa sounds /ə/ in these sentences.

1 The Hudson Bay polar bears are an unusual group.
2 Sometimes the officers capture four bears in a day.
3 The town of Churchill has good reason to look after the bears.
4 Polar bears are not currently an endangered species.
5 The bears have been in our community for years.

4 1.21 Listen and check. Then take turns reading the sentences to your partner.

Speaking

Exam strategy

Never give a one word answer to a question. For every answer, give:

1 A reason

2 An example

For example: *Examiner: Do you think people will still visit zoos in the future?*
Candidate: Yes I think they will because zoos are an easy way for people to look at wild animals, especially people who live in big cities for example.

1 Work in pairs. Take it in turns to be the examiner and the candidate. Ask each other the following Part 1 questions.

Topic: Zoos

1 Do you like zoos? (Why / Why not?)
2 Are zoos popular in your country?
3 Do you think there will still be zoos in the future?

Topic: Pets

1 Do you have a pet? (Why / Why not?)
2 Are pets important in your country?
3 Do you think people spend too much money on their pets?

2 Look at the following Part 2 topics. Take 1 minute to make notes about one of these. Then speak to your partner about it for 1–2 minutes.

Describe your favourite animal.

You should say:
a What this animal is
b What it looks like
c Where you first saw it
d Why you like it

e And you should also say if it is an important animal in your culture.

Describe a mountain, sea or lake that you have visited.

You should say:
Where it was
What it looked like
Why you chose to go there

And you should also say who you think is responsible for looking after this place.

3 1.22 Now listen to a student answering one of these questions. Do they answer each part of the question?

Exam strategy

Give longer answers to the questions in Part 3.

1 Explain what you mean and be as specific as you can. Think of answers to wh- questions on the topic. For example: Who? Where? Why? When?

2 Give as much information about the topic as you can. A good Part 3 answer is about 30 seconds long.

4 Read the following Part 3 questions. Expand your answer by completing the appropriate wh- questions in the table. Discuss your answers with your partner.

0 *Example: Who should solve the problems caused by pollution?*
1 Who is responsible for protecting wild animals?
2 Is it necessary for cities to have public areas like parks?
3 Compare the climate in your country now to what it was when you were a child.

Who?	What?	Where?	Why?

5 1.23 Listen to an answer to question 1 in exercise 4 and compare it with your own answer.

6 1.23 Listen to the answer again and read the text on page 200 at the same time. Underline any phrases used for explaining ideas.

Listing 2

Section 4

1 Look up the meaning of the word 'cloning' in a dictionary.

2 Look at the pictures and discuss the following questions.

1 Which of these has / have already been cloned?
2 Give possible reasons for cloning.
3 What do you think is the future of cloning?

3 1.24 Before you listen, read questions **1–3**.

Short answer type questions

Write **NO MORE THAN THREE WORDS** for each answer.

1 Who does Idaho Gem look like?

....

2 Where was the first cloned kitten made?

....

3 What could cloned pigs be used for?

....

Matching

TIP

In matching listening questions focus on the questions first. Then refer to the options.

Exam information

In matching listening questions you will be given a list of options to choose from. There will usually be more options than you need to answer the questions. The options are sometimes listed alphabetically and **not in the order** you will hear them. The questions will be listed in the order that you will hear them.

Question strategy

1 Before you listen:
- Read the questions first.
- Then read the options.
- Underline the keywords.

2 Listen out for the keywords in the question and match them to the keywords in the options.

Remember

You may hear more than one of the options you have been given and you may hear them very close together. As with the reading, an option must answer the question. (See Question strategy on page 74.)

4 1.25 Before you listen, read questions **4–10**.

Questions **4–6**

How are these types of cloning defined? Choose your answers from the box and write them next to the statements in questions **4–6**. There are more definitions than are needed.

A Nuclear transfer
B Cell replacement
C Plant reproduction
D Human transplants
E Embryo splitting

4 A natural process where identical copies form around the parent ...
5 It is used to produce new farm animals …
6 An embryo is made in a laboratory and placed in a donor mother …

> **TIP**
> For matching questions, you must keep up with the tape. If you hear a keyword in the next question, then answer that question next. You are given time at the end of the test. Use this time to go back and answer questions you have missed.

Questions **7–10**

Circle the correct letter **A**, **B** or **C**.

7 What does Neil Blackwood think about cloning?
A He strongly disagrees
B He strongly agrees
C He is not sure

What is Sheila Halliday's opinion about the following?

A She strongly disagrees
B She strongly agrees
C She is not sure

Write the letters **A**, **B** or **C** next to questions **8–10**.

8 Cloning pigs could save human lives in the future
9 Pigs would pass infections to humans
10 Further medical research is needed

5 Are there any situations where cloning is justifiable? Discuss these situations with a partner. Give reasons for your answer.

Writing

Task 1: Process diagrams 1

Exam information

A process diagram shows a series of steps in a system, cycle or process. To describe a process diagram, a different approach is needed to the approach you use for graphs, tables and charts.

> **Question strategy**
> 1 Identify which type of process – system, cycle or process – the diagram shows and which type of language is required.
> 2 Choose a suitable starting point *eg If it is a cycle, where would be a logical place to start?*
> 3 Describe each step in a logical sequence and the purpose or result of that step if appropriate.

1 Study the process diagrams below.

1 Describe what each one shows to a partner.
2 How is the type of process in diagram A different from that in diagram B?

Diagram A

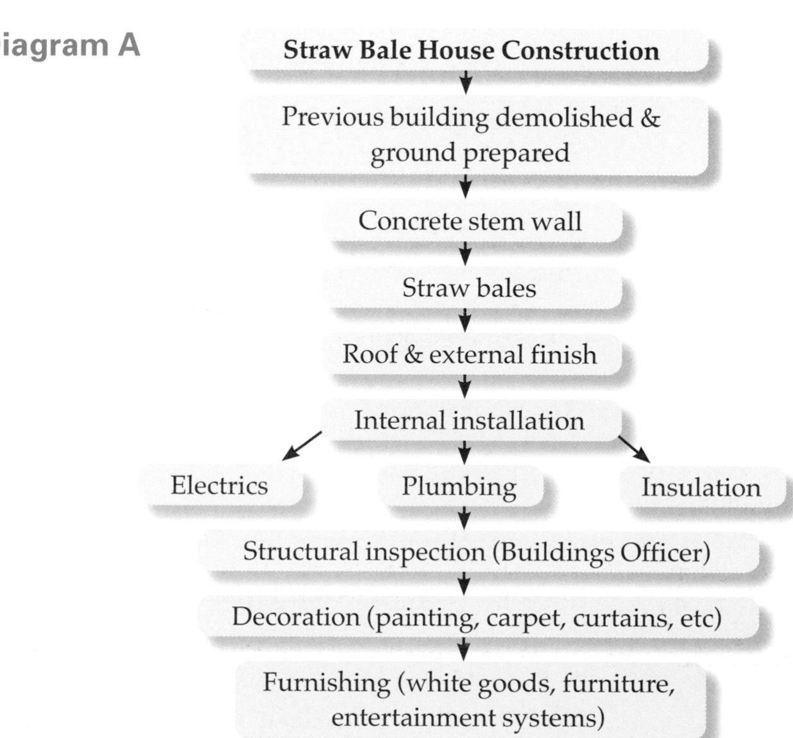

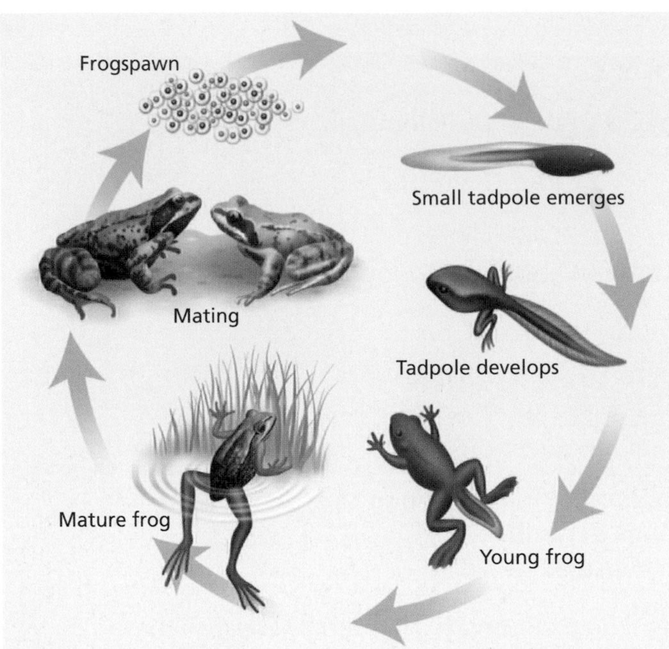

3 The words and phrases below are used to describe different types of processes. Check their meaning in your dictionary then match the words to the appropriate diagram, A or B.

pictorial	linear process	natural
cyclical process	man-made	non-pictorial

2 Match the extracts below to the appropriate diagram.

i The body enlarges and the tail becomes longer. At this stage, the lungs and legs appear in order to prepare the tadpole for its future life on land.

ii The next stage of the process is when the structure is inspected by the buildings officer to ensure safety requirements are met. Before the property can be furnished it must be decorated.

1 Look at the verbs in extracts i and ii. What tenses are used? Why?

2 What is the difference between the verbs in the two extracts?

3 The sentences below explain how to approach a process question. Use the words in the box to try and complete the sentences.

passive	changed	present	active	order	different	purpose

1 Process questions require **1** .... language to graphs, charts and tables.
2 All process questions require language to show the **2** .... and **3** .... of different stages.
3 Words in the diagram often need to have their grammar **4** .... in the answer.
4 Man-made processes require mostly **5** .... verb forms.
5 Natural processes require mostly **6** .... verb forms.
6 Processes usually require **7** .... tenses.

TIP

It is not always easy to find the first step of a process. A linear process has a single starting point but a cyclical process may have several equally logical starting points *eg Look back to the frog life cycle – the frogs mating and the eggs are both possible first stages.* Think logically, look for a stage where something is just beginning.

4 Can you think of another example of (a) a man-made linear process, (b) a man-made cyclical process, (c) a natural linear process, (d) a natural cyclical process?

5 Complete the model answer to diagram B using the words from the box below.

~~Initially~~, Gradually, in order to As a result of
Having completed all these steps The step after this
The final stage of the cycle is when At this point in the cycle, Over time,

Diagram B: Life Cycle of a Frog

The diagram shows the life cycle of a frog from egg to mature frog. **0** Initially, the eggs, which are called frogspawn, float on the surface of the pond. **1** .... is the emergence of the small tadpole, which has a small body and a long tail. **2** .... the tadpole develops and its body enlarges while the tail becomes longer. **3** .... the legs appear

4 .... prepare the tadpole for its future life on land. Eventually, the tadpole starts to change into a young frog with a wider mouth, a reduced tail and bigger legs. At this point the young frog continues to live in the pond. 5 .... the frog matures and moves onto the land.
6 .... being on land, it breathes air and it loses its tail.
7 .... the frog finds a mate so as to produce eggs.
8 .... the lifecycle begins again.

6 Study the Useful language box.

1 Add the words from exercise 5 into the appropriate place in the box below.
2 Find an alternative word or phrase for gaps 0–4 in exercise 5.

Useful language: Ordering, purpose and result

<table>
<tr><td>

Ordering
First stage
The first stage is when + noun + verb
To begin with,
The process commences with

Middle stages
Eventually,
This step involves + ing
After this stage is complete,
The next step is when +noun + verb
By this stage,
The step after this + verb
At the same time,
While / As
Once A has finished, B is able to start.

Last stage
Once the final stage has been completed,

</td><td>

Expressing purpose
A is done (so as) to produce B.
A is done in order that B can be produced.
so that,

Expressing cause and result
As a result,
This results in + noun
A results from B
in B
A happens, which results in B
which leads to B
which causes B
with the result that B happens.

</td></tr>
</table>

7 Look at the sentences describing how bees pollinate flowers. Add suitable ordering phrases from the box above plus relative clauses where necessary, to produce one paragraph.

1 The bee searches for suitable flowers.
2 The bee finds a flower and extracts nectar. Bees make honey from nectar.
3 Pollen from the flower sticks to the bee's legs.
4 The bee finds another flower and repeats the process. This helps pollinate the flower.

8 Rewrite the sentences below using the phrases in italics. You may need to change vocabulary as well. Make sure you keep the same meaning.

0 Buildings require insulation. Non-insulated buildings waste energy. ***so as to***
Buildings require insulation so as to avoid wasting energy.
1 Apples are carefully packed in boxes. Apples bruise easily. ***in order to***
2 Yeast is mixed into the bread dough. Yeast helps the bread rise. ***so that***
3 A drop in the ocean floor produces a tsunami wave. ***as a result of***
4 The temperature drops below zero degrees. Snowflakes form. ***which results in***

TIP

If you consistently copy words from the diagram your vocabulary mark will go down. Learn to recognize which words have different forms and can be changed *eg prepare (v) – preparation (n)* and those which cannot change *eg straw (n only)*

9 Read the model answer to diagram A in exercise 1 on page 00.

1 Underline any words in the answer that have been taken from the diagram and grammatically changed. How have they been changed?

0 *demolition (n) – demolished (v)*

2 Underline all the verbs and identify the tenses stating if they are passive or active.

Further practice

10 Using the paragraph plan underneath, write a complete answer to the following question.

You should spend about 20 minutes on this task.

The diagram below shows part of the carbon cycle.

Summarize the information by selecting and reporting the main features, and make comparisons where relevant.

Write at least 150 words.

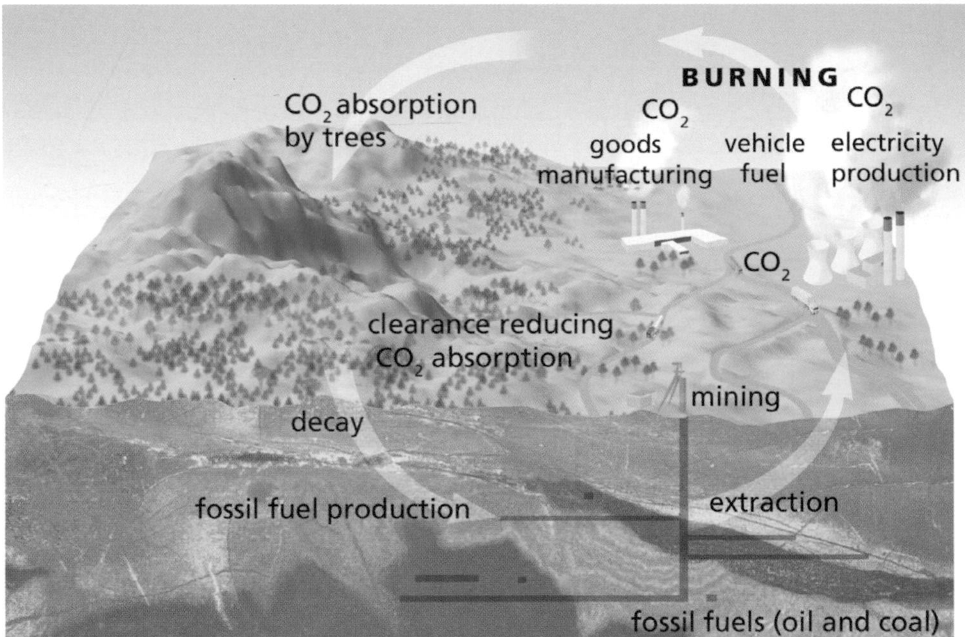

Process Question Paragraph Plan
Paragraph 1: Say what the diagram shows in your own words. Choose a logical starting point and describe the first half of the process including the purpose or result of the main stages where necessary.
Paragraph 2: Describe the second half of the process.
Summarizing sentence: End by stating what the process has produced and whether the process has finished, or whether it starts again.

Study skills

TIP

To achieve a good band score in IELTS it is important to use a formal, academic style of language.

Academic vocabulary

1 Match the informal language with a more formal, academic alternative.

Informal language	Academic language
1 I will write about …	A People are concerned about the issue of …
2 I think …	B These days, many people depend on technology for various aspects of their work and social life.
3 Everyone is worried about …	C This process has many advantages, such as …
4 … but this is wrong.	D This essay will discuss …
5 This is a good way to do things.	E The solution is not immediately obvious.
6 Everyone knows that …	F … however, this may be incorrect.
7 I don't know the answer to this.	G It is my belief that …
8 Today, we all use machines all the time for many things.	H It is clear that …

The Academic Word List (AWL) was developed by Averil Coxhead and consists of some of the most common words used in the academic tests. See www.vuw.ac.nz/lals/research/awl/

2 Read the text below on climate change. The underlined words are all taken from the AWL.

Climate Change

Analysis of environmental data indicates that the world is getting warmer. Evidence for such climate change comes from many sources and has led to governments being asked to consider creating new policies which require both individuals and businesses to adopt procedures which will reduce CO_2 – a major greenhouse gas. Researchers have identified significant benefits to such legislation stating that it will lead to improved long term financial and economic stability.

1 Check the meaning of any words you don't understand and add them to your vocabulary book.

Dictionary focus

1 Find the following words in this unit.

area p.73	strategy p.73	consequences p.77
structural p.73	combine p.73	involve p.200
formulated p.73	occur p.75	
categories p.73	location p.77	

1 Check their meaning in your dictionary.
2 Do these words look like they come from the Academic Word List?
3 Add the words to the table above.

6 Going places

Discuss the following questions with a partner.

1 What types of holiday are popular in your country? Why?
2 Is tourism an important industry in your country? Why?/Why not?
3 Describe the forms of transport that are most frequently used in your country.

Listening 1

Section 1

1 1.26 You are going to listen to a student, Ingrid, booking a holiday. Before you listen, read questions **1–6**.

Questions **1–2**

Write **NO MORE THAN TWO WORDS AND/OR A NUMBER** for each answer.

1 Where does she want to begin her journey?

....

2 How much is she prepared to pay?

....

Questions **3–6**
What forms of transport does the travel agent suggest?

Write
A If she **RECOMMENDS** it.
B If she **DOES NOT RECOMMEND** it.

Example: Travelling on foot
Tapescript: Well, because of the time limit, I don't think walking is a viable option. *Answer* **B**

3 Travelling by train
4 Travelling by bus
5 Travelling by car
6 Travelling by taxi

2 1.27 Now read questions **7–9** before listening to the rest of the recording.

Circle the correct letter **A**, **B** or **C**.

7 How will Ingrid travel to France?

A

B

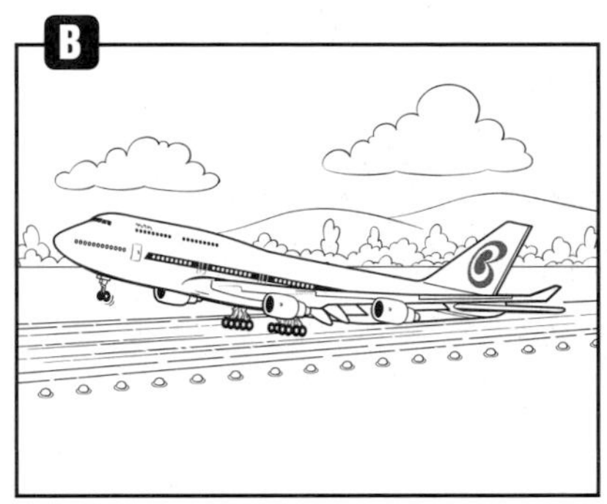

C

8 How will Ingrid pay for her trip?

A

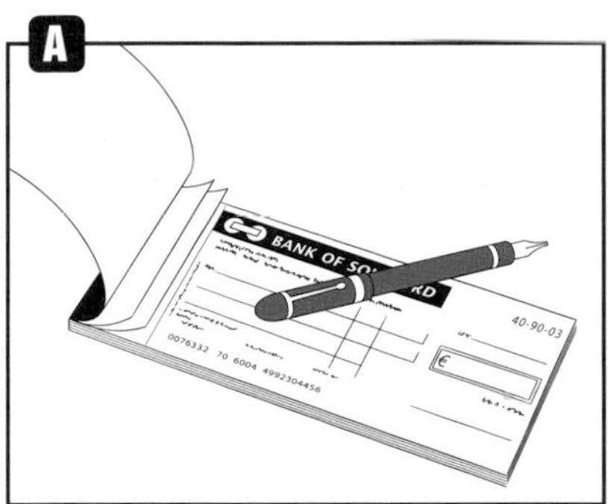

B

C

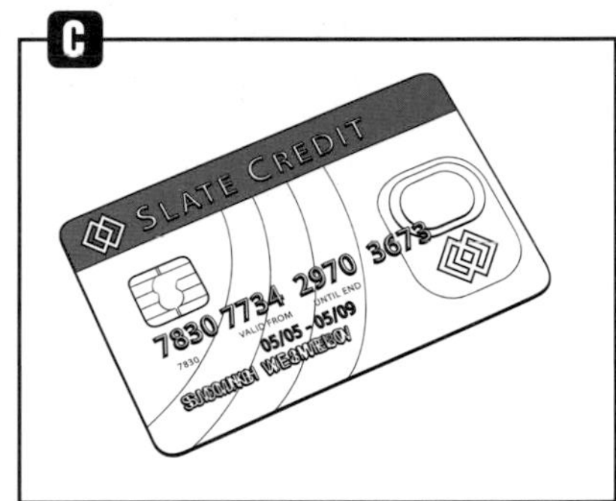

9 What flight does Ingrid choose?

A

B

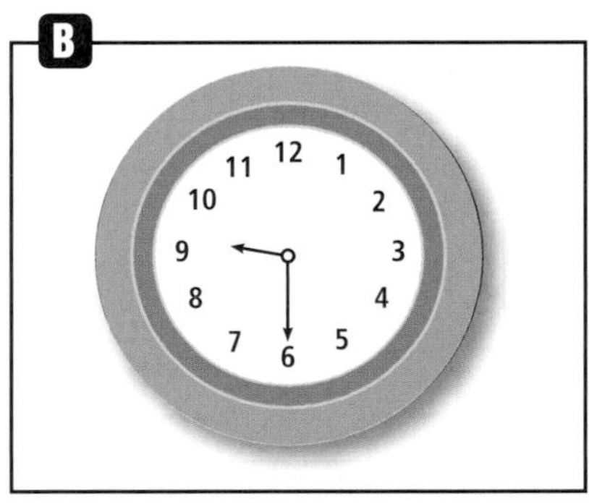

C

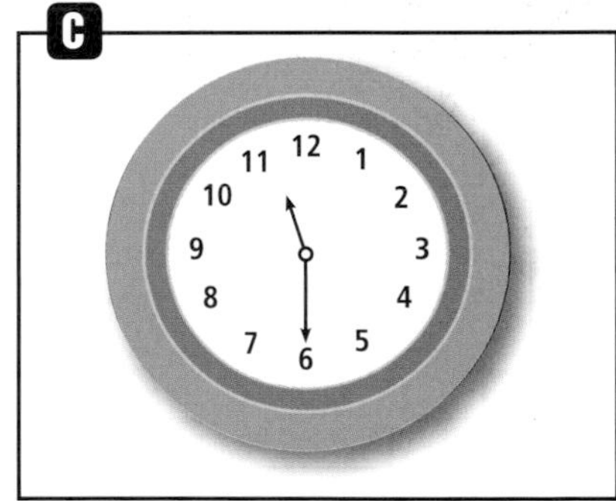

3 Do you think it is a good idea for university students to travel after they have finished studying instead of starting their careers? Why? / Why not?

Listening 2

Section 4

1 1.28 You are going to listen to a lecture about transport in different countries. Before you listen, read questions **1–6**.

> **TIP**
> Refer to Unit 4 for suggested approach to table completion questions.

Questions **1–6**

Complete the table of notes below.
Write **NO MORE THAN TWO WORDS AND/OR A NUMBER** for each answer.

Colombia	**Venezuela**	**Belgium**	**United Kingdom**
Made aviation history by establishing the first **1**	Iron ore mines can be found in **3**	Extensive inland waterways and canals.	About **4** .... of inland waterways, but only **5** .... used for business purposes.
Over **2** .... airports.	Main seaports are Puerto Cabello and Guanta.	Main seaport is Antwerpen, the third largest port internationally.	Proportion of road travellers is around **6** ....

2 1.29 Now listen to the rest of the recording.

Questions **7–12**

Complete the summary using **NO MORE THAN THREE WORDS OR A NUMBER** for each answer.

Transport development in China has been affected by its **7** .... Due to the wide use of roads and railways, bridges have been built such as the Yangtse which has **8** ...., one for cars and people and one for **9** .... Japan has a highly developed railway network with trains that can travel up to **10** .... per hour. Ships are also used for both **11** .... and **12** .... transport.

Reading

Recognizing opinions in a passage

The purpose of some passages will be to present the writer's view or opinion. Opposing arguments may be introduced but these will be refuted. In other passages, the writer will present the opinions of others, but not necessarily his or her own. You will come across both types of IELTS reading passages.

1 Read the passage in **2–3** minutes. Answer questions **1** and **2**.

1 Does the writer give his/her opinion about the proposal described in the passage?

2 The purpose of the passage is to

A present a problem and a solution
B describe advantages and disadvantages
C present an argument
D describe cause and effect

The town that tired of life in the shadows

Overshadowed by the Alps, the Austrian town of Rattenberg receives no direct sunlight. Now villagers hope giant mirrors will end their eternal gloom.

It is midday in the west Austrian village of Rattenberg and bright blue skies tower overhead, but the inhabitants of the town are squinting in an unworldly twilight. The cause is the Stadtberg, a 2,650 ft limestone mountain covered in dense pine forest that stands to the immediate south of the village and completely blocks the low winter sun as *it* tracks from east to west along the length of the village.

From mid-November to mid-February the village sits permanently in shadow. The result is an all-pervading seasonal gloom that Rattenberg's leaders argue strikes down *its* citizens with winter depression and threatens their economic future by driving inhabitants and tourists away.

Even at the end of March the effects of the Stadtberg's shadow can still be felt, casting parts of the village into half-light. But just as the obstacle that blights Rattenberg is a force of nature, *so too* is the solution which, after nine centuries, the village has chosen: to harness the power of the sun to create *one* of its very own. For 370 years, Rattenberg has built its reputation and wealth on the production of crystal glass. Now it is hoped that another type of glass will banish the winter twilight and revive Rattenberg's pride and fortune – mirrors.

Thirty computer-controlled 8ft-square reflectors, or 'heliostats', will be placed half a mile to the north of the village in the town of Kramsach. The hi-tech mirrors, precision-engineered to ensure *they* are completely flat and thus reflect the light accurately, will bounce the sun rays back to another array of reflectors. The second set of mirrors will be fixed to the remains of a 17th-century fort overlooking Rattenberg from the slopes of the Stadtberg. These mirrors will direct the sunshine into the village at a dozen strategic points, bathing the village in winter sunshine for the first time since the 1100s.

Helmar Zangerl, the joint managing director of the Bartenbach Light Laboratory, a private academy specialising in illumination allied to the University of Innsbruck, can barely contain his fervour. He said: 'The principle is very simple – to take the sunshine from where it is plentiful into a place where it is not using a material we have had for millennia. Of course the practice is more difficult, but this project will have massive psychological benefit by giving people sunshine when they have learnt not to expect *it*.

At the moment, people are moving away from Rattenberg because they can no longer stand the winter shadow. They complain of depressive illness and the tourists do not want to come in winter. This project has the potential to change all of that, I can see bus loads of Japanese tourists queuing to see the sun in the city where there is no sun.'

The scheme was drawn up after Rattenberg's leaders conducted a survey in 2003 asking what improvements could be made to village life. The predominant issue, placed top by nearly 60 per cent of the population, was the lack of winter sun. One in five of Rattenberg's inhabitants suffer from seasonal affective disorder (SAD), the syndrome created by a shortage of sunlight *which* provokes anything from a bad mood to full-blown depression. Opinion on Rattenberg's impressive main street confirms the pervading sense of solar deprivation. Manfred Kohler, 47, who has two children and works in one of the crystal glass studios said: 'I think it is a brilliant idea. It is ironic that we rely on this magic of light and glass for our living but we spend a large part of the year longing to see sunlight.'

Franz Wurzenrainer, Rattenberg's mayor said that the need to overcome the sunshine problem and reinvigorate the economic life of the village is increasingly urgent. While up to 3,000 tourists a day flow through Rattenberg in high season, the number falls to almost zero during the winter, creating a knock-on effect for the shops reliant on the tourists for the sale of their crystal. The permanent population has fallen by 10 per cent in recent years with people moving to neighbouring communes in search of the sun. With an ageing population and a birth rate of just five babies a year, the authorities are desperate to attract young families.

While most are overwhelmingly in favour of the idea, the citizens of Rattenberg are learning that there are problems associated with the project. The 2 million euro cost of the mirrors could push the village into bankruptcy unless *they* obtain European Union funding. Concerns have been raised that the glare from the mirrors will blind motorists travelling along the motorway between the reflectors and Rattenberg. The designers at Bartenbach reject *these* concerns, insisting the effect of looking at the mirrors will be no more than looking at the winter sun and naturally averting the eyes.

There is also controversy about the effect of placing the mirrors on the sides of the fort, a historic monument. But the greatest difficulties are technical. Scientists have stressed that the mirrors will by no means bathe the entire village in light. To *do so* would require mirrors covering a space four times the size of Rattenberg.

Dr Peter Erhard, the town's doctor said that while *he* deals with patients suffering from SAD, he believes the rate is not higher than in Austria's major cities. He said: 'Of course it would be nice to have a little more light in our city – it has a lot of dark corners. People complain of the lack of sun but I cannot see the justification for the project on medical grounds.' The doctor added that other issues, such as a plan to shut down a regional court house, which provides 50 jobs, were likely to have a more detrimental effect on Rattenberg's sense of well being. 'There is nothing wrong with this dream of mirrors. But there are other problems here we need to deal with. It feels like a continuation of an old joke that if we want to get more sunshine, all we have to do is move the mountain.'

Franz Wurzenrainer, the town's mayor and leader of the planning scheme, said of the project: 'It has captured our imagination and *that* of a lot of people elsewhere. I've had calls from Australia and Canada. After all, how many places on earth can claim to have their own second sun?'

Multiple-choice questions

See Unit 3, page 42 for advice on how to approach this type of question.

2 Answer questions **1** and **2**.
Circle the best alternative **A–D**.

1 Which of the following in Rattenberg may **NOT** be affected by the presence of the mountain?

A economic activity
B health of the inhabitants
C tourist numbers
D population growth

2 The townspeople are **NOT** worried about

A the cost of the project.
B the effect on driving conditions.
C a sudden influx of people into the town.
D the possibility of damage to a historic building.

Completing a map

3 Questions **3–5**
Complete the labels on the map. Write **ONE WORD** from the passage for each answer.

Question strategy

1. Study the map carefully. Look at any labels which are given on the map.
2. Scan read to the appropriate part of the passage. Use proper nouns eg names of people and places, to help you locate the part of the passage containing the answer.
3. Study that part of the passage carefully to find the answer.
4. If you are asked to choose words from the passage, do not use any more words than you are allowed.

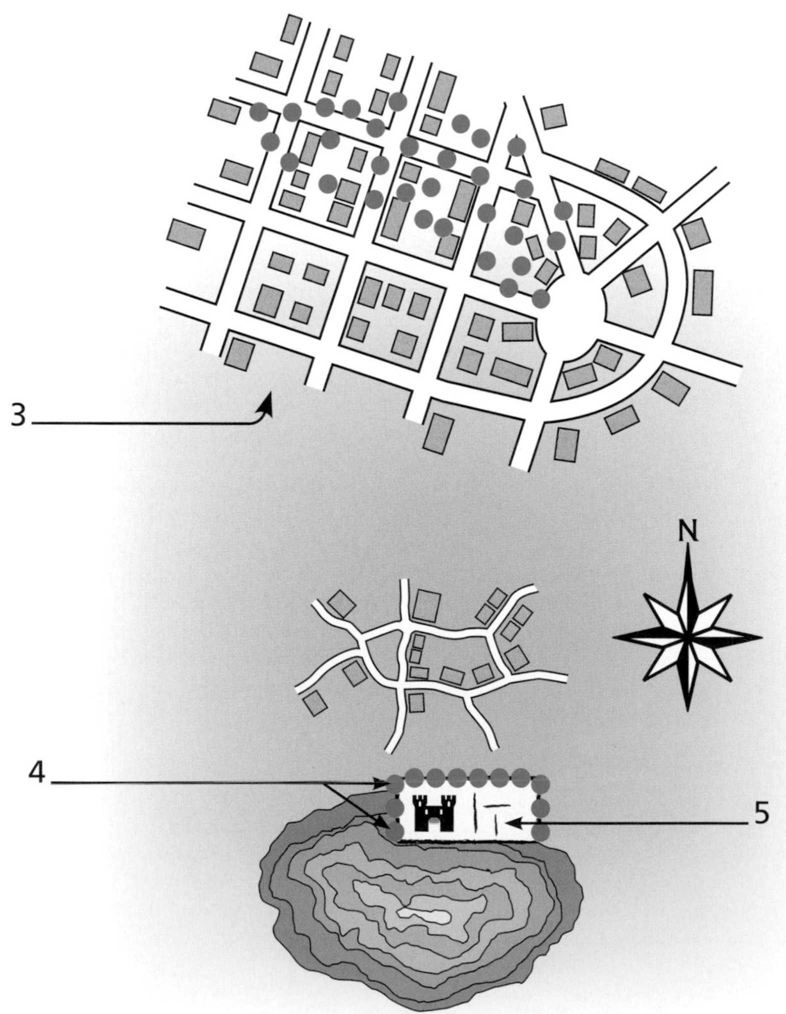

Sentence completion (no list)

TIP

Some of the words in the questions will be the same as those in the passage. Some will be parallel expressions.

Exam information

See Unit 1, page 12 for information on completing sentences using words from a box or list. Follow the same strategy, but for this type of question complete the sentences using words from the passage.

4 Find parallel expressions in the passage for the words and phrases in italics in questions **6–12**.

5 Answer questions **6–12**.
Choose **NO MORE THAN THREE WORDS** from the reading passage for each answer.

6 The absence of sun in the winter is *causing* both ____________ *to avoid the village.*
7 *Traditionally, the main industry* in Rattenberg has been ________.
8 The heliostats must be ____________ to *reflect the sun rays precisely.*
9 *Twenty per cent* of Rattenberg's inhabitants are affected by a *condition* called ____________.
10 The ten per cent *decline* in the ____________ has alarmed the town leaders.
11 One objection to the mirrors is that reflected light could *affect the vision* of ____________.
12 Rattenberg's doctor is concerned about the effect of a *decision to close* a ____________.

Matching: People and opinions

Exam information

The names of the people in the list will follow the order in which the names appear in the passage. You may not need to use all of the names in your answers. Some names you may need to use more than once.

Question strategy

1 Scan read to find the names of the people (**A–D**).
2 Read each opinion and then read the relevant section of the passage to see if it matches any of the people.
3 You can write your answers in any order if more than one is correct.

6 Answer questions **13–18**
Match the opinions to the people that express them.

13 The scheme has brought the town worldwide attention. ___
14, 15 The scheme will bring more tourists to Rattenberg. ___, ___
16 The presence of the mountain does not affect the health of the inhabitants. ___
17, 18 The town should use its resources to solve the problem. ___, ___

A Helmar Zangerl
B Manfred Kohler
C Franz Wurzenrainer
D Peter Erhard

TIP

We use reference words, like pronouns, to avoid repeating a word or expression. Understanding how these reference words are used will improve your reading and listening and make your writing more cohesive.

Understanding reference and substitution

1 What do the pronouns in italics refer back to in the passage on page 91.

1	*it* l.10?	5	*which* l.83?
2	*its* l.16?	6	*they* l.117?
3	*they* l.39?	7	*these* l.122?
4	*it* l.63?	8	*he* l.137?

2 What words or phrases do the following replace in the reading passage?

1 *so (too)* l.24?
2 *one* l.27?
3 *do so* l.133?
4 *that* l.160?

3 Read about Walt Disney executives' attempts to set up theme parks in Paris and Hong Kong. Use the reference or substitution links in the box to replace the underlined section.

did so do so it (x2) its one so that those

When building the new entrance to Hong Kong Disneyland, Walt Disney executives decided to shift the angle of the front gate by 12 degrees. They (1) shifted the angle of the front gate after consulting a feng shui specialist, who said the change would ensure prosperity for the park. Hong Kong Disneyworld is the first of the parks that Disney wants to build in China, including (2) a park in Shanghai, and company executives are being careful not to repeat the mistakes of the past.

When Disney opened Disneyland Paris in 1992, (3) Disney was criticised for being culturally insensitive to its guests. The company failed to understand that, unlike Americans, who often book their holidays directly with Disney, Europeans tend to (4) book their holidays more through travel agents. Another big marketing mistake was (5) the mistake of not offering wine when the park opened. But today, just as company executives are respecting local traditions in Hong Kong, (6) respecting local traditions too are Euro Disney executives in Paris.

Euro Disney are still recovering from the blunders of their planning executives and (7) the blunders of their marketing executives. Though (8) Euro Disney's finances have been re-structured, Euro Disney is still about $2 billion in debt. Back in Hong Kong, while using feng shui may seem strange to some Western sensibilities, Disney executives now claim that as a practice (9) using feng shui is just common sense.

Vocabulary

TIP

Certain words in a text help the reader to follow the organization of ideas in the text, eg to describe a problem and solution or a cause and its effect. These words also help to avoid repetition.

Lexical cohesion

Look at the use of text-organizing vocabulary in these extracts from the passage on page 91.

(Problem / cause) It is midday in the west Austrian village of Rattenberg and bright blue skies tower overhead, but the inhabitants of the town are squinting in an unworldly twilight. The **cause** is the Stadtberg, …
(Problem / result) From mid-November to mid-February the village sits permanently in shadow. The **result** is an all-pervading seasonal gloom …
(Problem / solution)But just as the **obstacle** that blights Rattenberg is a force of nature, *so too* is the **solution** ...

1 Write the text-organizing words in the box next to the appropriate category.

alternative amount answer consequence controversy debate discussion dispute event extent number outcome project result scheme scope suggestion viewpoint

0 problem / cause: issue, concern, reason, obstacle
1 solution / effect:
2 action / activity:
3 size / quantity:
4 argument / opinion:

2 Complete each sentence using any one of the words from exercise 1. You may need to use plural forms. In some questions more than one answer is possible.

The **problem** of environmentally friendly tourism is a major **issue/concern** for many countries. In few parts of the world is the **0** _problem_ so acute as in Hawaii, where tourism accounts for one third of the economy. Many inhabitants of states like Hawaii, which attract large **1** ________ of tourists, do not want to ban tourism, but would rather encourage ecotourism. For example, one **2** ________ to the problem of large numbers of tourists destroying wildlife in certain areas is to allow only a certain number of tourists per month to visit those areas where wildlife is being affected by human **3** ________. It is hoped that **4** ________ such as this will make tourists more aware of the **5** ____ of the activities they engage in. However, there is an **6** ________ that ecotourism brings problems of its own. For example, the **7** ________ of ecotourism for many of those employed in more traditional tourist activities, like luxury hotels, has been a loss of revenue. The **8** ________ of the problem for environmentally fragile areas, like Hawaii, cannot be under-estimated. Nor can the importance of finding workable **9** ________ .

Language focus

Conditional sentences

See Grammar reference, page 174.

Real conditionals

1 First conditional sentences can describe the results of possible actions, events or situations. We can use them in academic writing to develop arguments or describe problems and solutions.

If the people of Rattenberg ***obtain*** European Union funding for the cost of mirrors, they ***will/may/might/could be saved*** from bankruptcy.

1 What is the problem and what is the solution?

2 Re-write the sentence with these words and say if the meaning changes.
   a Provided (that) …
   b Unless …
   c Supposing (that) …
   d As / so long as …

2 Use first conditional sentences to suggest possible solutions to these problems. Use *will, may/might,* or *could* to show how certain you are about the result of the action.

0 global warming
   If we improve public transport, carbon emissions from private cars will be reduced and global warming may be slowed.
1 environmental and / or economic damage caused by tourism
2 threats to endangered species of plants and wildlife
3 road accidents
4 traffic congestion

Unreal conditionals

1 We can use second conditional forms to hypothesize about the present or future and third conditional forms to hypothesize about the past. Mixed conditionals combine speculation about the present and the past.

a **If** Hawaii ***banned*** tourism, the economy ***would/may/might/could be*** badly affected.
b **If** fewer tourists ***had been allowed*** to visit ecologically vulnerable areas, there ***would/may/might/could have been*** less damage to those areas.
c **If** Walt Disney executives ***had paid*** more attention to local custom in France, Euro Disney ***would/might*** not ***be*** in debt.

1 Which sentence, a, b, or c, speculates about:
   1 the past?
   2 the present or future?
   3 the effects of a past action on a present situation?

2 Develop these arguments about the use of public transport using conditional forms.

0 Private cars should be banned from city centres.
If private cars were banned from city centres more people would be forced to use public transport.
1 There should be congestion charges for all privately owned vehicles entering city centres.
2 Penalties on the use of private cars are unfair to people who live in areas which are poorly served by public transport service.
3 Laws to discourage the use of private transport should have been introduced before cities became so polluted.
4 Taxes on petrol should have been increased and the money invested in public transport.
5 Politicians should worry less about winning votes and more about addressing the problem of pollution in our cities.

Writing 1

Exam information

A clear introduction will help you to write a well-organized essay and help the examiner to follow your arguments. An introduction needs to show the examiner two things. Re-write the jumbled sentences:

1 the-understand-you-question-show.

2 question-say-the-how-answer-you-to-going-are.

Task 2: Understanding introductions

1 Look at the Task 2 question below.

1 What is the topic you need to write about?
2 What is the task?

Write about the following topic:

Private car ownership has grown dramatically in recent years. This has led to a rise in traffic congestion.

What could governments and individuals do to reduce congestion?

Give reasons for your answer and include any relevant examples from your own knowledge or experience.

Write at least 250 words.

2 Read the example introduction.

1 Complete the paragraph plan for sentences 2 and 3 of the introduction.

Paragraph Plan	Introduction
1 Introduces the topic (paraphrases the question, and describes the situation now). **2** **3**	**1** In recent times, as standards of living continue to rise, more people have been able to afford their own cars. Growing car ownership has resulted in an increase in traffic congestion. **2** It is my belief that the solutions to reducing congestion are the responsibility of both individuals and governments. **3** This essay will outline possible solutions to the problem of traffic congestion and evaluate their potential effectiveness.

2 Would this be a suitable plan for all Task 2 introductions?

TIP

Your introduction needs to paraphrase the question: you must not copy the question.

Paraphrasing the question

3 An important skill in writing introductions is to paraphrase the question. **Paraphrasing involves expressing an idea in a different way by:**

1 finding synonyms *eg price* ⟶ *cost*
2 using different grammar *eg Travel by train avoids traffic jams.* ⟶ *Avoiding traffic jams is one advantage of travel by train. (verb to +ing noun).*

Look at the underlined words in the question. Find examples of paraphrases in the model introduction.

Example: in recent years ⟶ in recent times

Private car ownership has grown dramatically in recent years. This has led to a rise in traffic congestion.
What could governments and individuals do to reduce congestion?

4 The following words are common in Task 2 questions. Match each word to a suitable synonym.

Word	Synonym
1 solution 2 issue 3 opinion 4 concern 5 important 6 justify 7 develop 8 attitude 9 influence	belief affect significant answer explain improve problem view worry

TIP

Gerund subjects are common in academic language. Use them in your essay to improve the level of your grammar mark. *eg*

(subject) ***Developing fuel-efficient forms of transport*** *(verb)* *is* *a priority for governments.*

5 Look at the sentences below and paraphrase each one. Change the underlined word into an +ing noun (gerund) and the words in italics to a synonym. Change the grammar where necessary.

0 If people used their own *cars* less, it would reduce pollution.
Using private vehicles less would reduce pollution.
1 It is *not easy* to solve the problem of noise near airports.
2 It is important for *politicians* to encourage environmentally friendly forms of transport.
3 It is better for the environment to transport freight *by train*.
4 People are *worried* about how oil prices have risen.
5 A government's *main priority* should be to reduce energy *loss*.

Writing introductions

6 Look at the Useful language box on introductory phrases.

1 Add a phrase to each section from the introductory paragraph about congestion.
2 Underline examples of these phrases in the introductions of the essays in Units 2, 4, 8 and 10. (pages 189, 190, 194 and 196)

Useful language: Introductory phrases

Introducing the topic	Explaining the focus of your essay
Some people think that + noun + verb Research has shown that + noun + verb It is often reported that + noun + verb Recent advances in A have led to B. ... is an ever-increasing problem. The issue of ... is one which needs to be looked at carefully. It has become apparent in recent years, that ... is an issue that many people feel strongly about. Recently, …	In this essay the arguments / issues surrounding ... will be examined. The arguments both for and against ... will be evaluated in this essay. This essay will discuss the topic of … in more detail. This essay will consider the problem of ... and outline possible solutions.
Expressing opinions See Unit 4, page 70.	

7 Write introductory paragraphs to the two questions below using the paragraph plan and language presented in this section.

Question 1

In some countries privately owned transport systems have a poor safety record. Yet it is the government who have ultimate responsibility for public safety.

How can governments ensure that private transport companies do not neglect safety regulations?

Question 2

Today's low-cost airlines are able to offer fast and cheap travel. However, some people believe this is at a cost to the planet.

Suggest ways that governments and individuals could tackle the environmental impact of low-cost flights.

Speaking

1 Put these words into the correct category.

commuter bicycle train bus fare car
tram tollbooth motorway taxi motorcycle

A Public transport	B Private transport

2 Fill in the table with the advantages and disadvantages of public and private transport. Discuss your answers in pairs.

Public transport		Private transport	
Advantages	Disadvantages	Advantages	Disadvantages
0 cheap 1 2	*0 overcrowded* 1 2	*0 more convenient* 1 2	*0 increasing petrol prices* 1 2

Exam information

In Part 2 you are given suggestions to help you structure what you say. The first two questions usually require shorter answers. The last two questions require more information.

See Unit 2, pages 25 and 26 for information on this question type.

3 Work in pairs. Student A look at the Part 2 speaking topic on page 186. Student B look at the topic on page 188. Student A make notes about the topic and speak to your partner about it for 1 minute. Student B listen and write down the four questions your partner is discussing.

Example: Student A: I first went to Hong Kong when I was 16 years old. I guess that was about 5 years ago, but I remember it was in summer, during my school holidays.
Student B: Where is it and when did you go there?

4 Take it in turns to be the candidate and the examiner. Ask each other the following Part 3 questions. There is another topic on page 186.

TOPIC: TRANSPORT

1 What do you think is the most dangerous form of transport? Give reasons for your answer.
2 Do you think the bicycle will still be popular in the future?
3 What forms of transport are most suitable for cities?
4 Compare forms of transport today to what they were in your grandparents' day.
5 Give the advantages and disadvantages of travelling by plane.
6 Who is responsible for making sure roads are safe to drive on?

Writing 2

Task 2: Problem and solution questions

Exam information

Some Task 2 questions describe a problem and ask you to suggest or evaluate possible solutions. These questions require a different approach from argument and opinion questions.

1 Look back at the different Task 2 questions in Unit 2 (page 35), Unit 4 (page 65) and in this unit (page 97). What is different about the three tasks?

2 Look at the paragraph below, suggesting a solution to the problem of over-crowding on public transport during rush hour.

1 Which words are used to avoid repeating 'problem' and 'solution'?
2 Look at the underlined language and explain why it is needed.

One possible answer to the issue of over-crowding on buses and trains would be to introduce a range of ticket prices, with the highest being for peak hour travel. If this was done, it might encourage people whose journeys were not essential to travel at other times. A drawback of such a policy would be that people who had to travel during peak hours for work would suffer the most. It is very probable that this would lead to significant opposition to such a proposal.

TIP

In order to think of possible solutions, it sometimes helps to consider what would happen if no action was taken. For example:

No investment in public transport may lead to more people using their own cars and hence create more congestion.

3 Work with a partner taking turns. Student A should suggest a solution to the problems below. Student B should form an opposing argument.

Problem 0: Over-crowding on public transport during peak hours
Student A: *One suggestion of how to improve this negative situation is to offer cheap fares at off-peak times to discourage non-essential travel in rush hour.*
Student B: *The drawback of this idea is that it forces working people to pay the highest fares.*

Problem 1: Road accidents
Problem 2: Insufficient car parking in city centres
Problem 3: Erosion of historical buildings as a result of tourism
Problem 4: Car drivers breaking the speed limit
Problem 5 : Your own idea

TIP

In academic writing, opinions or predictions are not usually expressed as absolute statements. Words like *all, every* and *always* are often avoided.

4 Look at the Useful language box, then rewrite the sentences underneath replacing the words in italics with language from the box.

Useful language: Avoiding absolute statements

Expressing probability			
This solution	would	certainly probably	have a positive effect.
Such a policy	may could might	possibly	make the situation worse.
It seems	highly	possible (un)likely	that the problem will get worse.

Avoiding 'all' or 'every'	**Avoiding 'always'**
certain + noun the majority of a minority of a large number of	sometimes often occasionally at certain times
many + countable noun a few	
much + uncountable noun a little	

Exam information

Problem and solution questions need:

1 Words and phrases to offer solutions and hypothesize.

2 Words and phrases to show you are suggesting ideas rather than expressing absolute certainty (see Useful language: Avoiding absolute statements).

0 It is *not true* that poor road conditions are the only explanation for road accidents.
It seems unlikely that poor road conditions are the only explanation for road accidents.
1 *All* road accidents cause fatal injuries.
2 *Everyone* believes that drivers *always* drive too fast.
3 Higher fines for speeding *will* reduce the number of accidents.
4 Having speed cameras on *all* streets *is* the best solution to the problem of speeding.
5 It is *a fact* that *every* accident involves drivers who have consumed alcohol.

TIP

Develop your solution (and evaluation of it) by describing the results it might have. For example: *One way of reducing traffic accidents would be to cut speed limits.* (solution) *If drivers were forced to drive more slowly, it is likely that there would be fewer accidents.* (result)

5 Choose three of the problems from exercise 4 and write a paragraph for each suggesting a solution and evaluating the advantages or disadvantages of the solution. Use the words and phrases and grammatical structures presented in this unit where appropriate.

Further practice

6 Use the paragraph plan to write a complete answer to the question below.

In some countries privately owned transport systems have a poor safety record. Yet it is the government who have ultimate responsibility for public safety.

How can governments ensure that private transport companies do not neglect safety regulations?

Problem and solution essay paragraph plan
INTRODUCTION: Introduce the background to the topic. Identify and fully describe the problem, and its implications. You may also choose to give your own view. Explain the focus of your essay.
BODY 1: Describe your first solution. Discuss the advantages and / or disadvantages of it.
BODY 2: Describe your second solution and discuss the advantages and / or disadvantages of it.
(BODY 3): Describe your third solution if necessary.
CONCLUSION: Summarize the solutions and make a recommendation about which solution you feel is the best.

Use this mind map to help you.

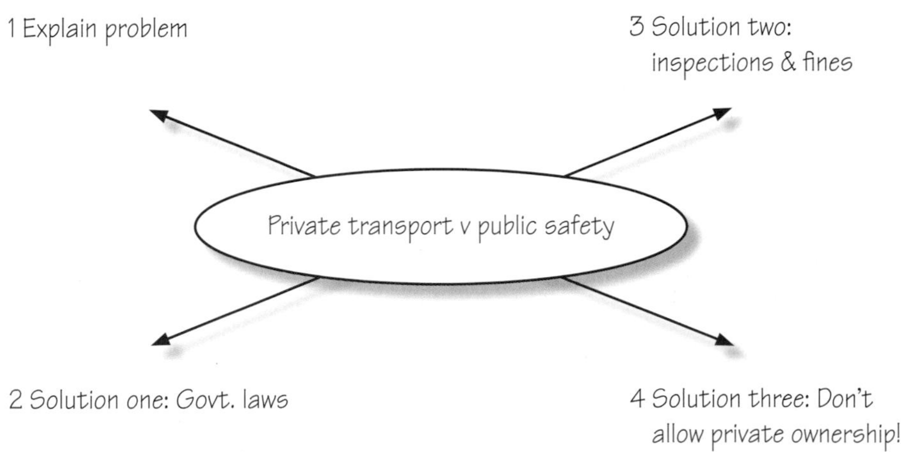

7 Compare your answer with the model on page 192.

Study skills

Editing 1: Editing your writing

1 In Writing Task 2, you have about 40 minutes to write 250 words. Leave at least 2 minutes at the end to check your work.

1 Match the grammar mistake to the example.
2 Correct each mistake.

Grammar mistake	Example
1 Subject–verb agreement	A Playing computer games a common pastime for young people is fast becoming a major cause of poor social skills.
2 Punctuation	B Tourism is a much needed source of income in developing country.
3 Plurals	C It is undeniable that the young children are easily attracted by advertising campaigns.
4 Articles	D This suggests to have a fast and efficient train system will encourage the general public to using private transport less.
5 Repetition	E Older people are more reluctant to travel long-distances because older people are less prepared to take risks.
6 Use of 'that' clause	F Relaxing visa regulations would be fairer for overseas students, particularly as their tuition fees is normally much higher than those for home students.
7 Word order	G On the another hand, other groups argue that it is the responsible of governments to maintain roads.
8 Word form	H These two charts are clear examples that different climate conditions in European countries.
9 Verb pattern	I In other words, their daily lives elements of traditional culture also include such as language, food and fashion.

2 Discuss with a partner what your main grammar mistakes are.

Dictionary focus

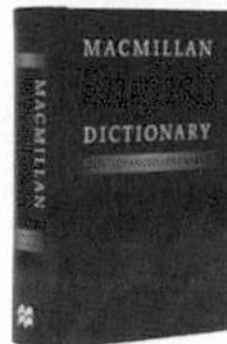

Find these words in the unit. Check their meaning in your dictionary and record them. Make sure you record what part of speech each word is.

For example: issue – noun

detrimental p.91
obtain p.91
syndrome p.91
reinvigorate p.91
predominant p.91
re-structured p.94
controversy p.95
environmentally friendly p.95
maintain p.103

7 The world of work

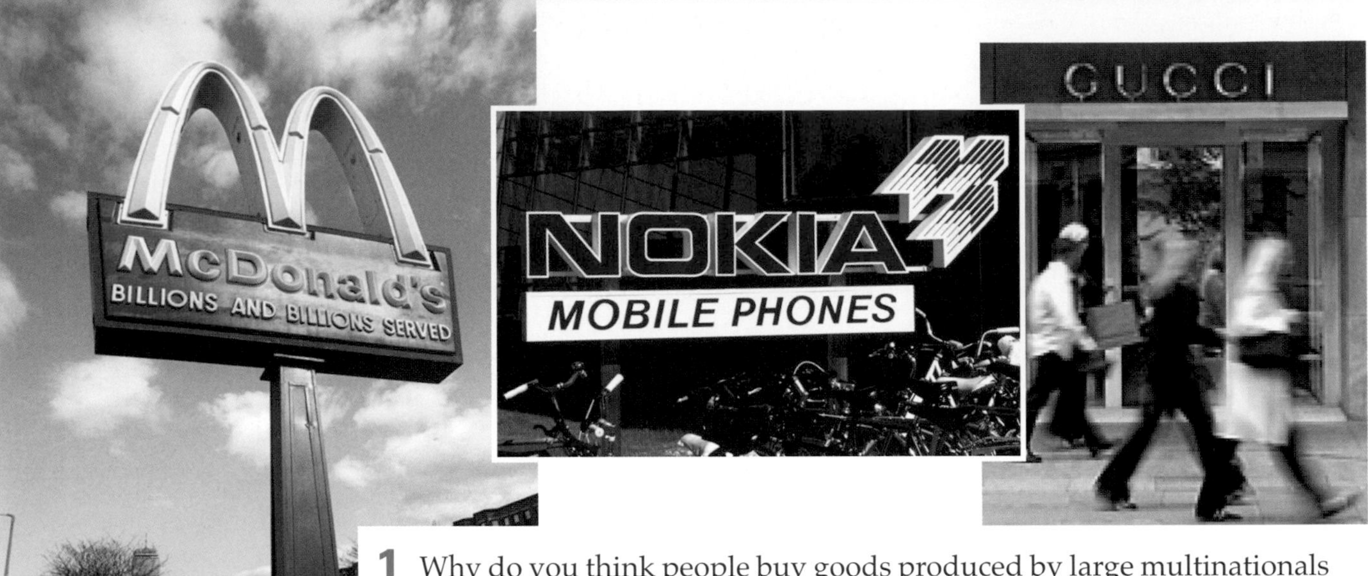

1 Why do you think people buy goods produced by large multinationals instead of products produced locally in their own countries?

2 What effects can large corporations have on local cultures and economies?

Reading 1

Prediction

Reading strategy

Use the following to help you predict what a text is about:

1 the title and subtitle and any illustrations

2 your knowledge of the world and the topic.

1 Work in pairs. Discuss these questions.

1 What do you know about McDonald's?
2 Do you think it is large enough to influence what and how much food is produced in the United States?

2 Look at the title and sub-title of the article. Before you read the passage, predict the answers to questions **1** and **2**.

1 The writer's purpose is to
 A present a problem and a solution.
 B describe a cause and an effect.
 C present one side of an argument.
 D present both sides of an argument.
2 The passage describes McDonald's recent impact on
 A advertising.
 B beef farming.
 C apple growing.
 D restaurant menus.

3 Skim read the passage and check your answers.

You Want Any Fruit With That Big Mac?

McDonald's buys so much food that its product decisions affect United States farmers.

Approximate annual purchases by McDonald's	BEEF **1 billion pounds**	POTATOES **1 billion pounds**	LETTUCE **110 million pounds**	TOMATOES **50 million pounds**	FRESH APPLES **54 million pounds** ('05 expected)	*GRAPES* ***11 million pounds*** *('05 expected)*
'04 U.S. production	24.5 billion pounds	45.6 billion pounds	220 billion pounds	72 billion pounds	10 billion pounds	*12 billion pounds*
McDonald's share	4.1%	2.2%	0.05%	0.07%	0.5%	*0.09%*

(A planned fruit-and-walnut salad will contain apples and grapes.)

Each day, 50,000 shiny red, Gala apples work their way through a sprawling factory in Swedesboro, New Jersey, where 26 machines wash them, core them, peel them, seed them, slice them and chill them. At the end of the line, they are dunked in a solution of calcium ascorbate and then deposited into green bags featuring a jogging Ronald McDonald. The bags make their way in refrigerated trucks to cavernous distribution centers and then to thousands of McDonald's restaurants in the eastern United States. No more than 14 days after leaving the plant, the fruit will take the place of French fries in some child's Happy Meal.

The apple slices, called Apple Dippers, are a symbol of how McDonald's is trying to offer healthier foods to its customers. McDonald's has also introduced 'premium salads' that will soon be joined by a salad of grapes, walnuts – and, of course, apples. No one knows whether these new offerings will assuage the concerns of public health officials and other critics of McDonald's highly processed fat-and-calorie-laden sandwiches, drinks and fries. So far they have not entirely done so. But this much is already clear: just as its hamburgers and French fries have made McDonald's the largest buyer of beef and potatoes in America, its new focus on fresh fruits and vegetables is making it a major player in the $80 billion American produce industry.

Some believe that McDonald's could influence not only the volume, variety and prices of fruit and produce in the United States, but also *how* they are grown.

The company now buys more fresh apples than any other restaurant or food service operation, by far. This year, it expects to buy 24,500,000 kilograms of fresh apples – 54 million pounds, or about 135 million individual pieces of fruit. That is up from zero apples just two years ago. (This does not include fruit used to make juice and pies, which use a different quality of apple.) McDonald's is also among the top five food-service buyers of grape tomatoes and spring mix lettuce. Of course, other fast-food chains have similar salads and fruit choices, but they have not had a comparable influence on the market because of their smaller size. Burger King, for example, has 7,600 restaurants in the United States, while Wendy's has 5,900. McDonald's has 13,700.

Missa Bay, the company that runs the Swedesboro plant, one of six McDonald's apple slicing facilities around the United States, could not be happier about that. In a few months, Missa Bay will also be supplying roughly one-quarter of the 13,700 restaurants with sliced green apples for the new fruit salad. These two items will increase Missa Bay's revenue by at least 10 percent this year.

Just as the enormous size of McDonald's once helped the company turn the nation's beef, chicken and potato industries into highly mechanized, consistent and low-cost businesses, McDonald's is using its purchasing power to build a reliable supply of fresh fruits and vegetables that meet its exacting specifications. At the U.S. Apple Association's annual marketing conference in Chicago, the McDonald's director of quality systems in the United States told a crowd of growers that if they wanted to work with McDonald's, they should grow Cameo and Pink Lady apples. Already, Cameo production in Washington State is up 58 percent in the current crop year from a year earlier, according to the Yakima Valley Growers-Shippers Association.

Eventually, a bigger supply of certain varieties will drive prices down, which will be good for McDonald's. But at present, the company's huge presence in the market is keeping prices high. However, if the new power that McDonald's exerts over the produce industry ends up reducing prices and squeezing profit margins, said James R. Cranney Jr., vice-president of the apple association, it would be a trade-off that many growers and producers seem willing to accept.

'Apple consumption has been flat over the past 10 to 15 years,' he said. 'This is exactly what the apple industry needs because we think it's going to increase consumption.'

True, False, Not Given

Pay special attention to words in the questions and passage which show:

1 number or amount, eg all, every, half, a few, few
2 time or frequency, eg always, already
3 negativity, eg not, none
4 comparison, eg more / less than, most
5 probability, eg will, may

These words can have a significant effect on meaning.

> ### Remember
> **True/False/Not Given** questions ask you to identify whether a statement agrees with or contradicts **information** in the passage.
>
> **Yes/No/Not Given** questions ask you to say whether a statement agrees with or contradicts **the writer's views**.

4 Answer questions **1–6.** Use the words in *italics* to help you find the answers.

Do the following statements agree with the information given in the passage?

Write: **TRUE** if the statement agrees with the information
FALSE if the statement contradicts the information
NOT GIVEN if there is no information on this

1 McDonald's has *already* introduced salads with fruit.
2 The introduction of fruit and produce into McDonald's menus *may* reassure health officials.
3 Criticism of the calorie and fat content of McDonald's food has affected sales.
4 Other fast-food chains have *not* affected food production.
5 Missa Bay's income is predicted to rise by *less than 10%*.
6 McDonald's has influenced the efficiency of parts of the American food producing industry.

Flow chart completion

> ### TIP
> To find answers to complete a flow chart, skim read to locate a section of the passage which describes a series of steps or stages.

5 Answer questions **7–9**.

Complete the flow chart. Use no more than **TWO WORDS AND/OR A NUMBER** from the passage for each answer.

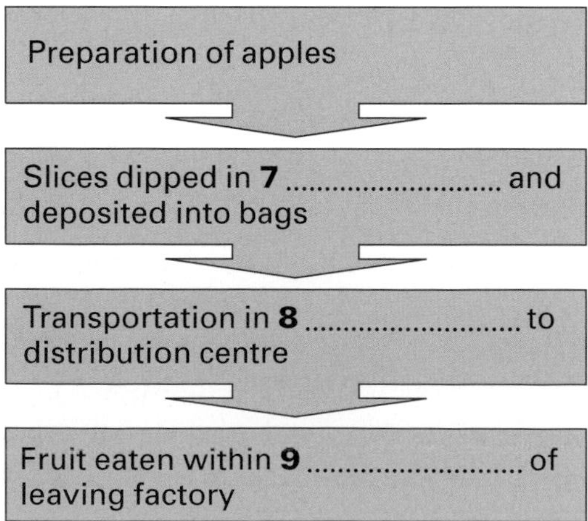

Preparation of apples
Slices dipped in **7** .... and deposited into bags
Transportation in **8** .... to distribution centre
Fruit eaten within **9** .... of leaving factory

Remember

These questions ask for factual information.

TIP

Answers to reading questions may also be found in tables, graphs or other illustrations.

Short answer questions

Question strategy

See Unit 4, page 58 for a suggested approach to answering these questions.

Answer the questions. Write **NO MORE THAN THREE WORDS AND/OR A NUMBER** for each answer.

10 Which two fruits will go into the fruit and walnut salad?
11 What percent of the total number of potatoes sold in the United States are bought by McDonald's?
12 What proportion of McDonald's restaurants will Missa Bay be supplying apples to?
13 Which two types of apples is McDonald's encouraging growers to produce?

Language focus

that-clauses

See Grammar reference, page 175.

1 These sentences all contain clauses beginning with *that*.

A Missa Bay is the company that (~~Missa Bay~~) **will be supplying one-quarter of McDonald's restaurants with sliced apples**.
B Missa Bay is the company that **McDonald's has chosen (~~Missa Bay~~) for its apple slicing facilities**.
C Missa Bay reported that **sales revenue should increase by 10% in 2005**.

Which sentence contains:

1 a defining relative clause where the pronoun replaces the object?
2 a defining relative clause where the pronoun replaces the subject?
3 a *that*-clause which could function independently as a sentence?

TIP

Clauses beginning with ***that*** may be used to report speech, information or opinions.

eg Some believe that McDonald's could influence not only the volume, variety and prices of fruit, but also how they are grown. (Opinion)

2 Decide whether these expressions would introduce a fact or an attitude/opinion. Which is **NOT** a main clause containing a subject and a verb?

0 Experts have found that <u>fact</u>

1 It has been proven that …
2 Tests indicate that …
3 Scientists can confirm that …
4 It is certain that …
5 Results show that …
6 It is interesting that …
7 In spite of/Despite the fact that …
8 It is doubtful that …
9 Many would argue that …
10 Some believe that …

3 Notice that the base structure of sentence 1 is the same as that of sentence 2.

Sentence 1: Alex advised John that if he wanted the job, he should apply for it.

Sentence 2: At the U.S. Apple Association's annual marketing conference in Chicago, the McDonald's director of quality systems in the United States told a crowd of growers that if they wanted to work with McDonald's, they should grow Cameo and Pink Lady apples.

> **TIP**
> It is easier to make mistakes in longer, more complex sentences. Understanding how sentences break down into their parts will help you to avoid errors.

Subject: Noun phrase	Reporting verb	(Object: Noun phrase)	That	Complement
Alex	advised	John	that	if he wanted the job, he should apply for it.
At the U.S. Apple Association's annual marketing conference in Chicago, *the McDonald's director of quality systems in the United States*	told	a crowd of growers	that	if they wanted to work with McDonald's, they should grow Cameo and Pink Lady apples.

> **TIP**
> Academic writing often uses very long noun phrases and short verb phrases.

4 Put the sentence phrases in the correct order.

0 managers / on people at work / are the single greatest influence / it has long been recognized / that

It has long been recognized that managers are the single greatest influence on people at work.

1 managers exhibit one of two management styles / and 'democratic' / authorities on management styles / argue / which are described as 'authoritarian' / that

2 believe / and will avoid work and responsibility / are basically lazy / managers exhibiting an authoritarian style of management / people / that

3 work is natural to people / believe / and can be enjoyed / managers employing a democratic style of management / that

4 argue / as their abilities and their employers will allow / employees will assume / democratic managers / as much responsibility / that

5 their ability to lead / recognize / effective managers / is a direct extension / of their personal credibility / that

5 Decide if each sentence is right (R) or wrong (W). If the sentence is wrong, then correct it.

0 The company assured that the faulty item would be replaced. W

The company assured me/us/them that the faulty item would be replaced.

1 Peter Chan, the new sales representative, is the man that I was telling you about him.

2 It could be argued that globalization has been responsible for the decline of local industry in developing countries worldwide.

3 The diagram shows that unemployment throughout the 1980's in Southern European countries.

4 In my opinion that the removal of trade barriers would enable developing countries to build strong economies and reduce their dependence on aid.

5 It is my opinion that we are on the verge of a breakthrough in information technology which it will have a profound impact on the global economy.

6 As can be seen, the charts show clearly that the number of boys and girls in all levels of education in developing and developed countries.
7 As we can see that there is only a slight difference between the two countries.
8 If we look at all three charts we can see that at all levels of education were able to achieve the final target.
9 In conclusion, it could be stated that the number of employees in all sectors of the economy fell.

Vocabulary

Synonyms for people

Exam information

To achieve a higher band score you need to avoid repetition and show precision of meaning.

For example:

Some people feel that globalization gives multinational companies too much power. However, consumers can influence manufacturers by changing their purchasing habits.

1 Place the words into an appropriate part of the table.

the general public ~~the unemployed~~ employees ~~everyone~~
national/religious leaders students consumers ~~politicians~~
~~the old/young~~ the middle-aged managers parents voters celebrities
manufacturers representatives home owners teenagers
entrepreneurs workers individuals employers human beings

Useful language: Synonyms for people

People – in general	People and work	People and power	People – specific groups
everyone	the unemployed	politicians	the old / young

2 Use words from the table to replace the underlined language.

0 <u>People with children</u> are a common target for marketing campaigns.
Parents are a common target for marketing campaigns.
1 Many people think governments only listen to the views of <u>people</u> during election campaigns.
2 <u>People with original business ideas</u> should be given investment by governments as they are a potential source of jobs.
3 Product design is influenced by the views of <u>people who buy things</u>.
4 It is up to <u>people on their own</u> to decide if they believe a company's business is unethical.
5 <u>People out of work</u> need to be given training to help them find productive work.

6 Changes in interest rates are of concern to people.
7 If people who make goods are unable to make a profit, they will cease trading.
8 Controlling inflation and balancing imports and exports is a key priority for people in government.
9 People in work will look for alternative employment if their salary is too low.
10 Some people think that high income groups such as famous people should pay higher taxes.

3 Check the meaning of any new words from the previous exercise and add them to your IELTS vocabulary bank.

Speaking

1 Look at the following Part 1 topics and related questions. Write your own question for each one.

Topic 1: Jobs

1 Do you have a job? If so, what do you do?
2 What job would you like to do in the future?
3 Is this a popular job in your country?
4 (Your idea) ....

Topic 2: Time

1 Are you always on time for meetings and appointments?
2 In what kind of situations is it important to be on time?
3 How do you organize your time (ie Do you keep a diary?)?
4 (Your idea) ....

2 Work in pairs. Take it in turns to be the candidate and the examiner. Ask each other the questions from exercise 1.

Exam information

In all parts of the speaking test you may need to make predictions about future events or situations.

Predicting the future

3 2.1 Read the following question and listen to a candidate answering the question. Fill in the gaps as you listen.

Do you think brand names will still be popular amongst young people in the future?

Well, I think **1** .... that young people, particularly in my country, will still be buying brand names like Nike and Adidas. Of course I **2** .... whether or not this will be the case in other countries. Having said that, it's **3** .... that brand names will still be popular amongst young people in Western countries because, if the present is anything to go by, then they will **4** .... still be trying to follow the latest fashions in the future.

4 Put the expressions from exercise 3 into the table below.

Certain	Fairly certain	Uncertain

5 Add the following expressions to the table.

1 There is a strong possibility that …
2 I'm not really sure if …
3 It might / could be the case that …
4 There is no question in my mind that …
5 I think it's debatable whether …
6 There is every chance that …
7 I can say without a doubt / most definitely that …
8 No one can predict whether …
9 I'm quite / totally / utterly convinced that …
10 It's impossible to say whether / if …

6 Work in pairs. Take it in turns to be the candidate and the examiner. Ask each other the following Part 3 questions. Use the expressions from the table to help you.

1 Is it likely that governments will increase their funding for local businesses?
2 Where will people shop more in the future, in big supermarkets or local markets?
3 What will be the most highly paid jobs in your country in 10 years' time?
4 Do you think large companies will continue to put money into making sure their employees work in a clean and safe environment?

Reading 2

1 Work in pairs. Discuss these questions.

1 How do you feel when you have too much work to do?
2 Does work ever affect your health or relationships? In what way(s)?

2 Read the passage and answer questions **1–6**.

Handling work overload

Advice for managers on how to cope with the pressures of work

A Non-managers are used to taking orders. Whether they are blue-collar workers on a production line or travelling sales people who spend most of their time away from the office they are on the receiving end of orders which they themselves must action. There is no additional stratum to which they can delegate the order. Sometimes their job allows virtually no discretion, as with the production line workers, and sometimes autonomy is encouraged and expected. In the final analysis, however, at this level in an organization you are on the receiving end of orders and, generally, do what is expected of you. Authority is, on the whole, accepted without question.

B Managers, on the other hand, are used to giving as well as receiving orders. Whether they are first line supervisors or middle ranking officers, they form a link in the chain of command translating corporate vision into reality on the 'shop floor'. The amount of discretion they are expected to exercise may vary, but managers are expected to be thinking beings, exercising their judgment in how they go about their tasks, and that judgment does not suddenly switch off when taking orders and switch on again when implementing them. They are more inclined, therefore, than their non-managerial colleagues to want to query or at least participate in receiving orders.

C There are, however, certain complications to add at this stage. First, some managers do not know what their subordinate managers do, not in detail anyway. To begin with they tend to only hear about the problems and not the ordinary, everyday, uneventful smooth running. Second, not only is the business environment exceptionally competitive, globally as well as locally, but the work ethic is enjoying a marked resurgence, which puts many managers under intense pressure to succeed. They are left with no apparent choice but to delegate more.

D Work overload farther down the chain is becoming a serious issue – 'serious' because of volume and because of another slight twist. Once you are in the management chain certain factors are triggered. You probably have a career, not just a job; you are expected to adhere to and uphold the corporate structure; you are assessed on achievement not on activity; you are probably salaried instead of paid hourly, and so are expected to work the hours necessary to achieve your objectives.

E Put all of these factors together and it is easy to see how the work can pile up. Rather than admit defeat, appear as if the job is too much for them, risk the reputation of someone who is anti-corporate culture, or risk the possibility of a poor annual appraisal with its repercussions for advancement, many managers soldier on, working longer hours, seeing less of the family and becoming more autocratic and stressed. They probably also wonder 'What's wrong with me?', and become suitable breeding ground for mid-life crisis.

F Managers who find themselves in this position need not just courage but diplomacy as well. Courage is internally generated not externally applied so managers have to look to their own self-image, life plan and rights. Most overloaded managers believe, first, that they are the ones at fault for not being able to handle the pressure. It is a real blow to their self-image to feel that the job 'is too much' for them. Second, they believe that to suggest that it is not they but the company which is out of step is corporate blasphemy and will result in personal excommunication or the corporate equivalent of immediate exile. In other words, people who feel this way are ignoring a fundamental right – to be their own judge.

G The courage that is required, therefore, is to make a decision. Do you want to live your life this way? If you do not, why should it be because there is something wrong with you? Why cannot it be because the way you want to be managed is something different from the way in which you are managed? Thinking this way, managers can at least approach the problem constructively.

H What is required next is action, but diplomatic action. Diplomatic action is easier if the situation can be viewed from the boss's perspective. He or she probably wants from you the same things that you want from your staff – results, honesty, trust, loyalty and so on. Therefore, the discussion should be approached from this angle. The way the argument is put over will have as much, if not more, effect than the argument itself. Part of the presentation to the boss will be the words used, while the other part will be verbal and non-verbal communication skills.

Note completion

Exam information

Note completion

These questions require you to read and understand a large section of a passage. The organization of information in the notes is usually the same as that in the text.

Question strategy

Use the note headings, eg *Non-managers* and *Managers* to help you to locate the sections of the text containing answers to the questions.

Questions **1–6**.

Complete these notes about the passage. Choose **NO MORE THAN THREE WORDS** from the passage for each answer.

A Non-managers

Accustomed to **0** taking orders
No scope for them to **1** ____________
2 ____________ may be possible

B Managers

Accustomed to giving and receiving orders
Expected to interpret and implement the **3** ____________ of those above them
Expected to use their **4** ____________
Pressure to succeed may force them to **5** ____________
May choose to accept too much work rather than **6** ____________
Overwork may lead to health or family problems

TIP

Read the question carefully to see whether it asks you to identify information or the writer's views.

Yes, No, Not Given

3 Answer questions **7–10**.

Do the following questions agree with the views of the writer? Write:

YES if the statement agrees with the views of the writer
NO if the statement contradicts the views of the writer
NOT GIVEN if it is impossible to say what the writer thinks about this

7 Only managers question the orders which they receive.
8 Competition and attitudes to work increase the expectations put on managers.
9 Managers worry about the effect their work has on family life.
10 Managers should give constructive feedback to their superiors.

Exam information

Matching details to paragraphs or sections

This question type requires you to find detailed information in the passage.

Matching details to paragraphs

Question strategy

Scan read the passage for vocabulary repetition or parallel expressions in the question and passage. Use these to help you to match details and paragraphs.

4 Answer questions **11–15**.

The passage has eight paragraphs, **A–H**. Which paragraph contains the following information? Write the correct letter **A–H** next to the question.

The words in *italics* appear in the passage or are a synonym for an expression in the passage. Use them to help you to answer the questions.

11 what managers *want from* the people who work for them ____
12 what managers may *believe* about themselves ____
13 effects on managers of not discussing an *excessive workload* with their manager ____
14 advice on how managers can change their *thinking* ____
15 how managers' performance is *evaluated* ____

Listening

Section 2

Exam strategy

Concentrating

Work with a partner and answer the following questions.

1 What do listening strategies help you to do?

2 You are given time to read the questions before you listen. What should you use this time for?

3 What keywords should you underline?

4 What words should you pay careful attention to?

Now turn to Unit 1, page 15 for the answers.

Prediction

1 Discuss the following questions with a partner.

1 Look at the sign above. What does it mean and where would you see it?
2 What kind of jobs are available in your country for disabled people?
3 Who is responsible for making sure companies provide suitable working conditions for disabled employees?

2 2.2 You are going to listen to a talk offering advice and support to students with special needs looking for temporary employment. Before you listen, read questions **1–7**.

Short answer questions

Questions **1–7**

Listen and answer these questions. Use **NO MORE THAN TWO WORDS** for each answer.

1 What kinds of jobs are the students interested in?

....

2 What should students make before applying for a job?

....

Sentence completion

Complete the sentences. Write **NO MORE THAN THREE WORDS** for each answer.

3 Students that are applying for jobs independently need to ....
4 .... in buildings must be barrier free for direct access.
5 The location of .... in the buildings is extremely important.
6 Students must ensure they get .... working hours.
7 Car owners need to check the availability of ....

Table completion

2.3 Now listen to the rest of the talk and answer questions **8–15**.

Fill in the table. Write **NO MORE THAN THREE WORDS OR A TIME** for each answer.

DAY/TIME	PLACE	JOB DESCRIPTION	START TIMES	REFRESHMENTS
Monday am	Hotel	**8** .... OR Conference organizer	**9**	Light lunch
10	**11**	Making handmade paper and cards	3.30 pm	**12** ....
Thursday am	Travel agency	Travel agent	8.00 am	**13** ....
Friday	**14**		**15**	

Pronunciation

Connected speech

When native speakers speak English, they join words together. Two things they do are:

1 Join final consonant sounds at word endings to initial vowel sounds at word beginnings, eg male‿and female.

Which words are joined together in these examples?

1 you will agree
2 one of the factors
3 to help answer

2 Add extra sounds when a vowel sound at a word ending is followed by a vowel sound at a word beginning. The two most common extra vowel sounds are /w/ and /j/.

What is the extra vowel sound in these phrases. Why is the sound used in each phrase?

1 you all have
2 we all have

After round lip vowels, eg /uː/ the intrusive sound in /w/. After spread lip vowels, eg /iː/ the intrusive sound is /j/.

3 How would you connect the words in these sentences.

1 Most of you I hope will be applying for jobs with companies the University has recommended.
2 Make sure you know before you even get to the interview stage that your needs will be met.
3 I know that some of you are applying for jobs independently, so for you it's best to plan ahead and be aware of what you might need.
4 Ask if all the lifts have this facility or if it's only certain ones.
5 When you arrive at the hotel, wait for someone to take you to your first session, which will be a talk.
6 The next place we'll be visiting will be on Tuesday afternoon.

4 2.4 Listen and check your answers.

Writing

Question Strategy

Task 1 questions may ask you to describe two or more graphs, charts or tables. If the fixed parts of each diagram are the same (eg When the vertical and horizontal axes in two graphs both measure the same thing), then your answer should focus on comparisons between the diagrams. However, if the fixed parts of each diagram differ, then your answer should describe each diagram separately with only the summarizing sentence making a comparison.

Task 1: Multiple diagrams 1

1 Look at the question strategy and multiple diagrams A and B below, then decide which approach each question requires.

A Average weekly income

Country	Wage
A	$180
B	$123
C	$159
D	$43

Average weekly expenditure (country A)

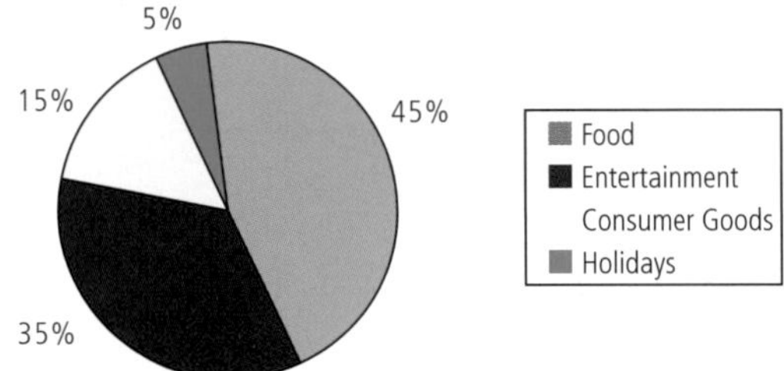

B Unemployment as a percentage in the 1990s

Year	Females
1990	12.30%
1995	13.40%
1999	14.70%

Year	Males
1990	7.50%
1995	7.30%
1999	5.80%

2 Look at the bar charts below and discuss questions 1–5 in pairs.

The charts below show the share of global manufacturing and exports for four countries between 1985 and 2005.

Summarize the information by selecting and reporting the main features, and make comparisons where relevant.

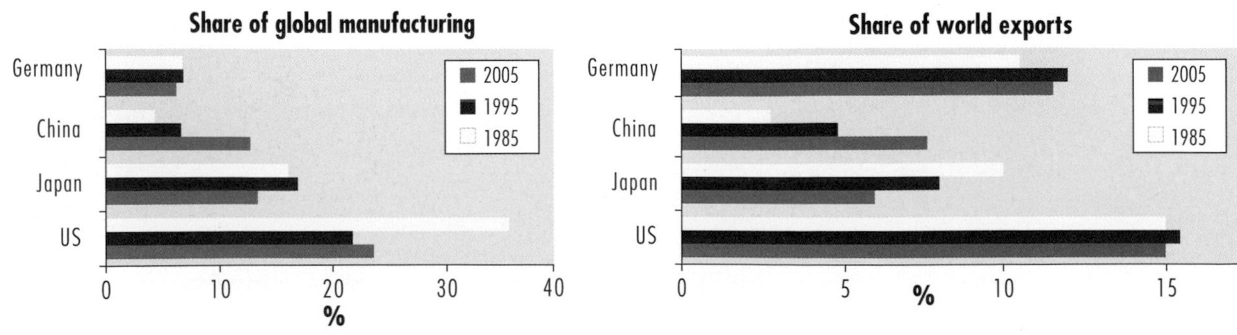

1 Look back to the bar chart on page 53 in Unit 3. What is different about the layout of the bar charts on page 116.
2 What do the two axes represent in each chart?
3 What do the coloured columns represent?
4 Should you make comparisons, describe changes or both?
5 Should you approach this question by comparing the charts or describing each separately?

3 Look at each chart in Exercise 2 and answer the questions.

1 Which countries have the largest percentage?
2 Which have the smallest percentage?
3 Which countries show the greatest change in the period?
4 Are there any opposite trends (ie the trend in one country moving in the opposite direction to another)?
5 Write a single overall trend sentence comparing both diagrams. Begin, *Overall, it can be seen that…*

TIP

A range of different diagrams may be used in Task 1. Practise 'reading' diagrams that lay out information in different ways by exploring the chart wizard on your computer. Use different ways of expressing figures to increase your vocabulary score. Similarly, repeating language will reduce the vocabulary score!

4 Write an answer to the question in Exercise 2 using the paragraph plan below. Compare it with the model answer in the back of the book on page 193.

Multiple diagram paragraph plan for diagrams with the same fixed parameters
Paragraph 1: Say what the diagrams show in your own words. Describe the most important features (biggest, smallest, greatest change, etc) and compare the diagrams.
Paragraph 2: Describe the other features and compare.
Summarizing sentence: End with an 'Overall, …' sentence summarizing the main feature of both diagrams.

Ways of describing data

5 Look back at the bar charts on page 116. Write four sentences comparing the data using language from the box below. For example, *US manufacturing in 1985 was approaching 40%.*

Useful language: Different ways of expressing figures or percentages

Approximating figures	Fractions
(well/just) over around about approximately approaching almost (well/just) under (slightly) more/less than	half a third two thirds a quarter three quarters a fifth a tenth

Catering

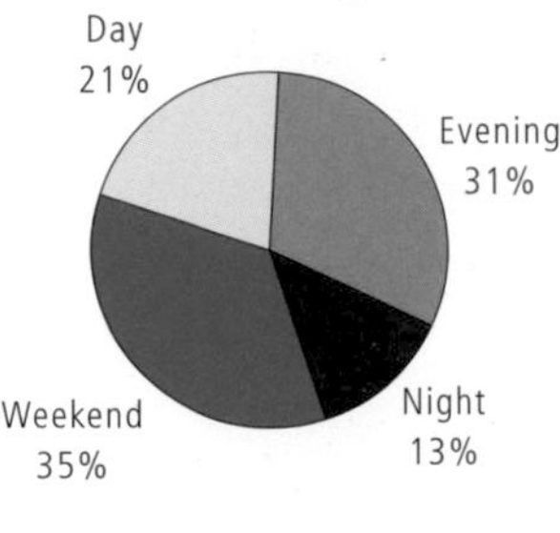

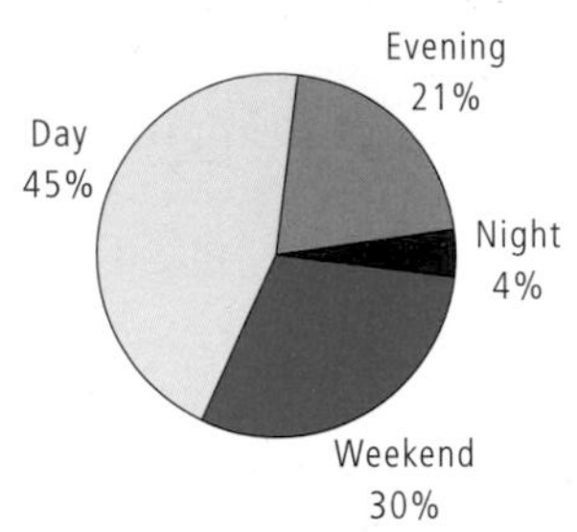

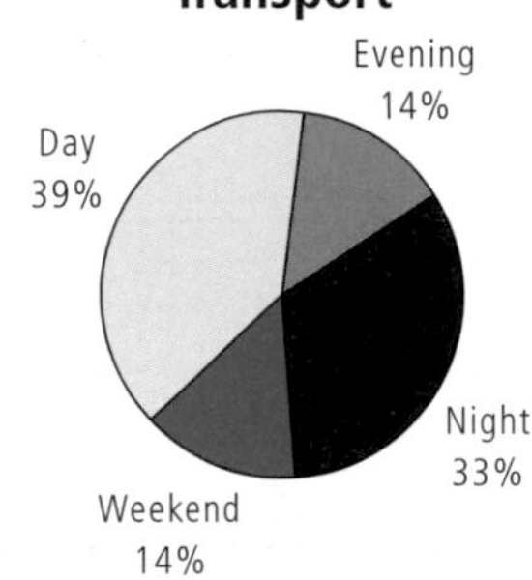

Finance

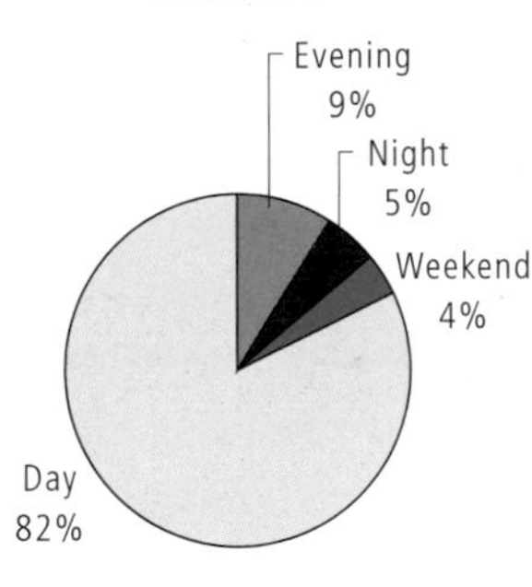

6 Look at the pie charts showing different work patterns. Use language from the box to describe the percentages in the Catering and Retail pie charts.

The charts show the work patterns for employees in four industries.

Summarize the information by selecting and reporting the main features, and make comparisons where relevant.

0 *Just under a third of workers in the catering industry work during the evening and slightly over two fifths work in the day.*

7 The following words are also useful for describing data in different ways.

Determiners
the (vast) majority of (very) few equal numbers of all none most a minority of many

1 Order the words from biggest to smallest.
2 Use some of these words to write sentences describing the percentages in the Transport and Finance charts.

0 *In the transport industry, equal numbers of workers are employed to work evening and weekend shifts.*

8 Suggest two ways of organizing an answer to this question. Which would make comparison easier?

9 Write the answer to the pie chart question from exercise 6 in 20 minutes following a plan with two paragraphs and a summarizing sentence.

Multiple diagrams 2

10 Study the question below and decide if the diagrams should be compared or described separately. Then write your answer in no more than 20 minutes using some of the language presented in this unit.

The diagrams below show the main reasons workers chose to work at home, and the hours males and females worked at home for the year 2005.

Summarize the information by selecting and reporting the main features, and make comparisons where relevant.

Main Reason for working at Home – 2005

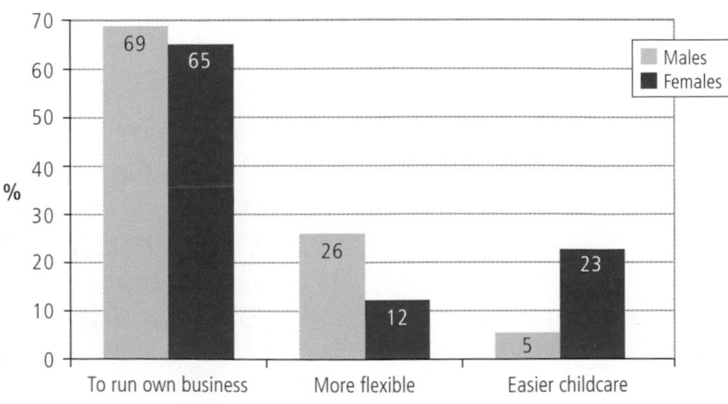

Hrs worked per week	Males (%)	Females (%)
Under 10	2	73
10–30	16	22
31+	82	5

Hours worked at home - 2005

Study skills

Editing your writing

1 Look at the two examples below. Look at criteria **5–8** in the table on page 187 and decide which one is an average writer and which one is a good writer? Discuss with a partner and give reasons for your choices.

Example 1

It is certainly true that governments should spend more money to develop local industry and trade, instead of only encouraging foreign investment. Some people say that poorer countries need this foreign aid to help build their economy, but this is over-simplification. In contrary, if more money is invested in local businesses, then less developed countries might not have to import as much, which often increases their international debt.

Example 2

Instead of import goods all the time a greater proportion of the government budget should be spent on develop local business. If the government develops local business, then the economy will growing more quickly. More people in that soceity will then have a beautiful life.

TIP

You will lose marks if the examiner cannot read your writing.

3 Now edit a piece of your writing and use the table on page 187 to decide what kind of writer you are.

The most common mistakes I am making as a writer are:	I am going to improve my writing by:

Dictionary focus

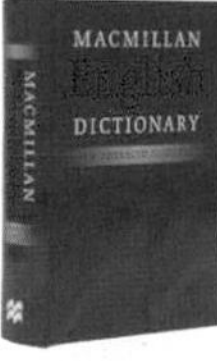

1 Find the following words in the unit. Look at the words that come before and / or after these words and note what kinds of words they are. The first one has been done for you as an example.

deposited: deposited into bags (deposited + preposition + noun)

deposited p.105	exerts p.105	world-wide p.193
focus p.105	marked p.112	variation p.194
comparable p.105	approximately p.117	

2 Complete these sentences with suitable endings using the words from the box below.

marked focus world-wide

1 Despite the rapid increase in sales in November, there was still a …
2 Although the negative effects of globalization can be seen in local trade, the effects on …
3 Having already successfully marketed their beauty products to older women, the company now has to …

3 Now look up the meaning of the words from exercise 1 in your dictionary and record them.

8 Art and the city

1 How has your town or city changed since you were a child?

2 What do / did you like and / or not like about living there?

3 What are the differences between city and country living?

Reading

classical curious eccentric elegant futuristic individualistic magnificent modern traditional

Distinguishing fact and opinion

1 Work in pairs. Discuss these questions.

1 In which cities or countries would you see these buildings?
2 For each building, which of these words would you use to describe the architectural style in which it is built?
Use a dictionary to check meanings of words you don't know.

2 Read paragraphs **A–D** of the passage on page 122. Which of the adjectives from the box on page 120 does the writer use to describe organic architecture? Do these adjectives suggest his opinion of organic architecture is mainly positive or negative?

3 Do the following sentences express facts or opinions about organic architecture?

1 Many of the buildings are made of natural materials.
2 The buildings look powerful and energetic.
3 Imre Makovecz established a school for architects in Hungary.
4 The buildings are both likeable and unusual.
5 It seems likely that organic architecture will continue to be popular.

4 Read paragraphs **A–D** of the passage again. Which of the facts and opinions listed in exercise 3 does the writer mention?

TIP

It is important to be able to distinguish fact from opinion when you are reading.

5 Skim read the entire passage and answer questions **1–2**.
Circle the appropriate letter **A–D**.

1 The main purpose of the passage is to discuss
A the background to two well-known buildings.
B the work of several different architects.
C one style of architecture.
D all of the above.

2 The passage is taken from
A an official report.
B a textbook.
C a newspaper article.
D a tourist guide book.

Organic Architecture

'The straight line belongs to man – the curve to God.' Antoni Gaudí

Organic vegetables, organic bread, organic toothpaste ... the word has been used as a kind of talisman to ward off the evils of consumer societies in which so many things, from what people eat to the homes they live in, have become mass-produced, unsettling and even unhealthy.

A Organic architecture is an equally loose term, yet it conveys an idea of buildings designed to grow naturally from the ground they stand on. It conjures too the idea of buildings that are made of natural materials, that seem somehow to belong in a way that Classical temples never do. It also conveys the idea of buildings that make a play on natural forms and employ geometries that have little to do with Euclid and mathematical perfection, as well as suggesting buildings that are designed to be wide open to the elements.

B In extreme cases, as with the work of Antoni Gaudí, buildings really do seem to be plants or animals growing naturally out of the ground rather than being projected unnaturally into the sky. Gaudí created a form of architecture made up of what appeared to be bones and sinews, or tendrils and shoots. Architects like Bruce Goff and Herb Greene shaped a shaggy architecture that might be home for animals and insects as well as human beings. Frank Lloyd Wright, one of the century's most influential architects, left a legacy of Organic buildings that fit into the depths of rural America as they do in the grid-iron Manhattan. Imre Makovecz, who founded an entire school of Organic architects and craftsmen in Hungary, described his designs as 'building beings', and indeed at their strange and haunting best they really do feel as if they are alive and breathing.

C What all the buildings of this type have in common is the sense of being close to nature, either in terms of location or materials used in their construction. Each of the buildings is highly individualistic and none is held back by precedent or convention. They are all in their own way highly emotional buildings, but unlike the architectural expression of Postmodernism, none is cynical, too clever or too knowing. Quite the reverse: most have an innocence about them, each an attempt to take architecture into unknown waters.

D Veering between the eccentric and the proudly magnificent, this loose fraternity of building includes some of the century's most likeable as well as curious. With increasing concern for ecological issues and the natural world, it seems likely that Organic architecture will blossom rather than wilt.

Casa Mila, Antoni Gaudí, 1910, Barcelona Spain

E This truly strange building is known locally as *la Pedrera*, or the quarry. Yet, far from being a heap of stones, it is a brilliantly resolved stone palazzo into which Gaudí has poured sinuous apartments that are like nothing else on earth. The seven-storey building is grouped around two courtyards so that each flat, large or small, is lit. Outside, the block appears to stand on the legs of stone elephants, while balconies and window mouldings jut out like strange lips beneath a roof garden which is like a Dali painting come to life.

F The architect, Antoni Gaudí I Cornet (1852–1926) was one of the most extraordinary architects ever. A devout Catholic, he lived the life of an ascetic monk and was taken for a tramp when admitted to hospital having been fatally knocked down by a tram while pondering on the construction of his unfinished masterpiece, the Cathedral of the Sagrada Familia (Sacred Family). Gaudí's was a highly individualistic attempt to reconcile Architecture to Nature. The truly remarkable thing about Gaudí's work is that it is always logical in its own wilful manner: he may have looked at the world in a way very different from the majority of twentieth-century architects, yet he is never gratuitous and never sinks into kitsch. So demanding is the alternative logic of Gaudí's sense of structure that it is obvious why he left no real followers, or no one competent to take the risks he did.

Sydney Opera House, Jørn Utzon, 1973, Sydney Australia

G It's fair to say that this highly memorable building put Sydney on the international map in a way that it had never been before. In truth, the Sydney Opera House is both brilliant and frustrating at one and the same time. No one can doubt the thrill of its roofline – whether you see there in those remarkable roofshells the beaks of seagulls, shark fins, waves or wimples – and the fascinating story there is to be had of its construction. The latter was left largely to Peter Rice, a very young structural engineer who was to be awarded the Royal Gold Medal for Architecture before he died in 1992. The interiors of the building, though, are rather pedestrian: the thrill of the exterior fails to survive the long haul through the lobbies to the auditorium itself. This is probably because Jørn Utzon (born 1918), the Danish architect, resigned – or was pushed off the project – in 1966 and the building was completed without his special genius. Rather like Gaudí, Utzon continued to work on the design of his buildings as he went along, so that we do not know quite how he would have finished his most ambitious work. His other buildings, mostly in his native Denmark, are all inventive and combine an intriguing marriage of experimentation with new materials and technologies and Organic forms.

Matching: People and descriptions

Remember

You may not need to use all of the options (**A–E**) to answer the questions. Some letters you may need to use more than once.

Scan read the passage to locate the names of the people in the question.

Question strategy

See Unit 6, page 93 for advice on how to approach this question type. If a question asks for **TWO** answers, you must give both answers to get one mark.

6 Answer questions **1–4**. Match each description to the correct architect(s) **A–E**. You may use any letter more than once.

1 These **TWO** architects did not complete a famous project ____ ____
2 These **TWO** architects strongly influenced many others. ____ ____
3 He designed buildings which resemble living things. ____
4 He designed buildings which are suitable for different environments. ____

A Antoni Gaudí
B Bruce Goff
C Frank Lloyd Wright
D Imre Makovecz
E Jørn Utzon

Summary completion (No list)

7 Answer questions **5–11**.

Complete the summary below. Choose **NO MORE THAN THREE WORDS** from the passage.

Buildings designed in the style of organic architecture use **5** ________ shapes and materials. Inside Antoni Gaudí's Casa Mila, which is constructed of **6** ________ , there are **7** ________ which ensure that each apartment receives sufficient light, while the roof of the building can be compared to **8** ________ . The Sydney Opera House also has an exciting **9** ________ with which many comparisons can be made. The Opera House's disappointing **10** ________ could be explained by the fact that Jørn Utzon was not given the opportunity to complete **11** ________ of the building.

Sentence completion (From a list)

8 Answer questions **12–15**.

Complete each sentence with the correct ending **A–F** from the list below.

12 The Casa Mila ____
13 The Sagrada Familia ____
14 The Sydney Opera House ____

A has a roof which is compared to moving water.
B was designed by a young structural engineer.
C was designed for people to live in.
D is built on stone elephants.
E was not completed before the death of its designer.
F was designed by a monk.

15 Which of the following best **summarizes** the writer's opinion of organic architecture?

A It is environmentally friendly.
B The buildings are unusual but attractive.
C It makes effective use of natural materials.
D The buildings seem to be alive and breathing.

Language focus

Linking expressions

See Grammar reference, page 176.

1 Match the sentence beginning (1–6) with an ending (a-f) to make true sentences about the reading passage.

1 The word 'organic' has been used to describe everything from vegetables to toothpaste. **In addition,** …
2 Casa Mila has two courtyards **in order to** …
3 Both Gaudí and Utzon left major projects unfinished. **However,** …
4 Utzon left the Sydney Opera House project before it was finished, **so** …
5 The interior of the Sydney Opera House is disappointing **because** …
6 Many of Gaudí's buildings resemble plants or animals. **For example,** …

a it was not designed by Utzon.
b allow light into each flat in the building.
c they did so for very different reasons: Gaudí was killed, while Utzon was dismissed.
d Casa Mila seems to stand on elephant legs.
e he did not complete its design.
f it describes a distinctive form of architecture.

2 Which of the expressions **in bold** in exercise 1 indicate:

1 a *reason* for an action, event or situation?
2 the *result* of an action, event or situation?
3 a *purpose*?
4 a *contrast* between two ideas?
5 support through an *example*?
6 an extra or *additional* argument or piece of information?

3 Match these linking expressions to the categories in exercise 2.

although as well as because of despite for instance
furthermore so that nevertheless in spite of
so as (not) to such as thus therefore whereas

4 Look at the expressions in exercises 2 and 3. Which of them usually connect:

1 two ideas in the same sentence?
2 ideas in different sentences or paragraphs?

5 Study the linking expressions in the sentences in exercise 1 and the expressions in exercise 3. Which expressions are usually followed by:
1 a clause?
2 a noun or -ing form?
3 a verb?

6 Rewrite the sentences so they that contain the word(s) in **CAPITAL** letters and the meaning stays the same.

1 Architects should express themselves freely. However, their work must also be practical. **ALTHOUGH**
Although ....
2 While living in a city can be stressful, there are still many advantages to doing so. **DESPITE**
3 Because people are concerned about the environment, organic architecture will probably remain popular. **BECAUSE OF**
4 The city invested in a new sports complex so that more people would be encouraged to exercise and get fit. **SO AS TO**

7 Complete the statement or argument appropriately.

1 I enjoyed / didn't enjoy growing up in …
  a because …
  b although …
  c so …
2 Cities offer more amenities than towns.
  a For example, …
  b However, …
  c Therefore, …

Vocabulary 1

1 Complete the following words and phrases for places where people live:

1 v _ l l _
2 s t _ d _ _ f _ _ t
3 a p _ r t _ e n _ b l _ _ k
4 b _ ng _ l _ w
5 b _ s _ m _ _ t f _ _ t
6 h _ g h r _ s _

2 Label the following features on the illustration.

balcony easy chair
air-conditioning unit
house plant
bookcase
satellite dish
rug blinds
music system
posters TV aerial
TV files

3 In pairs take it in turns to answer the Speaking Part 2 topic card below. Use the vocabulary from exercise 1 to help.

> Talk about your room in your house.
>
> You should say:
> What type of building the room is in
> What is in the room
> What you like / dislike about it
>
> and you should say how you would change the room if you could.

Listening

Section 3: Analysing multiple-choice options

1 Read the following multiple-choice question and the three possible answers. Discuss with your partner what you think the answer is.

Why is research important?

A For historical evidence to be protected.
B For ideas to be validated.
C For researchers as individuals.

2 2.5 Now listen to a postgraduate student talking about research and check your answer.

3 Read an extract from the listening text below. Why are options **A** and **C** incorrect?

> Well, I think research is important for us as individual researchers. We need to know that our ideas and suggestions are valid. But more importantly, it's for others. We cannot prove our ideas effectively, unless we look back at the past, to research that has been done before. We then check past evidence with present day evidence to see if it correlates. So without research being done, ideas will not be made valid.

Question strategy

For this type of multiple-choice question:

1 Don't mistake hearing words in an option for hearing the answer to a question. Always link the option to the question.
2 Keep listening even when you think you've found the answer.

4 2.6 You are going to hear two students, Miwako and Enrique, discussing their new research project. Before you listen, read questions **1–5** and underline the keywords.

Questions **1–3**
Choose **THREE** letters from **A–G**.
What do the students say makes a good research question?

A It should be based on lecture notes.
B It should show the purpose of the research.
C It should provide a definition of evaluation.
D It should only include past research.
E It should be focused on particular areas.
F It should assess problems.
G It should only include contemporary research.

1 ....
2 ....
3 ....

Short answer questions

Questions **4–5**
How long should the assignment be?

4 ....

What must the students do first?

5 ....

2.7 Before you listen, read questions **6–10**.

Note completion

Questions **6–10**
Complete the notes using **NO MORE THAN THREE WORDS**.

A successful city

- Offers **6** ....
- Attracts young people with talent and creativity.
- Encourages business development, which raises the **7** ....
- Offers a cleaner environment, with traffic control, less noise pollution and **8** .... (eg parks).
- Has both old and new buildings.
- Attracts people because it offers a **9** .... as well as a choice of day time activities.
- Has a **10** .... so that people feel safe to bring up their children.

Section 4

1 When you listen to lectures, you will hear the lecturer using discourse markers which act as 'signposts' helping to guide you through the talk. You are going to hear a lecture about contemporary art. Look at the following discourse markers from this lecture and discuss with a partner what kind of information you might expect to follow.

1 This morning I'd like to look at …
2 I think at this point, it's important for me to clarify that I am looking at art from two main perspectives. Firstly, …
3 … and secondly, …
4 Okay, so what is contemporary art? …

2 2.8 Now listen to the recording and check your answers.

3 2.9 Now listen to the complete lecture and answer questions **1–11.**

TIP

Follow the signposts and keep moving through the questions.

Questions **1–3**

Multiple choice

Choose the correct letter **A–C.**

1 One of the aims of this lecture is
A to describe how art supports society.
B to define contemporary art.
C to define artistic experiences.

2 It is important for the students to
A agree with the lecturer's ideas.
B utilize their past experiences.
C revisit galleries to look at contemporary art.

3 The students will ultimately have to
A write a critical analysis.
B write 2000 words.
C write an art-review.

Questions **4–8**

Sentence completion

Complete the sentences using **NO MORE THAN TWO WORDS AND/OR A NUMBER**.

4 The French revolution began in .... and marked the beginning of what is known as the modern era in art.
5 Contemporary art is best viewed as any works of art from the period beginning .... until today.
6 One of the disadvantages of official art is its .... nature.
7 Art is subsidized by governments or wealthy individuals like ....
8 .... art, also known as amateur art, is now becoming more widely acceptable.

Questions **9–11**

Short answer questions

Answer the following questions using **NO MORE THAN THREE WORDS** for each answer.

9 What do graffiti artists damage? ....
10 What can contemporary art teach us about? ....
11 What can contemporary art influence? ....

Vocabulary 2

1 Which of these would you associate with the visual arts (V) and which would you associate with the performing arts (P)? Which are places and which are art forms?

0 ceramics V - art form
1 the cinema
2 a concert
3 dance
4 a gallery
5 graphic design
6 a museum
7 music
8 a play
9 (a) painting
10 photography
11 (a) sculpture
12 the theatre

2 What other art forms do you know of?

3 Discuss. Which of the art forms in exercises 1 and 2 do you prefer and why? Talk about the last time you went to one of the places in exercise 1.

Speaking

Structuring what you say

Exam information

In all three parts of the speaking test you need to structure what you are saying. This makes it:

1 Easier for you to keep going and be more fluent

2 Easier for the examiner to follow what you are saying

1 Match the expressions below to one of the options **A–C**. Some options can be used in more than one category.

A Introducing what you say
B Explaining what you say
C Concluding what you say

1 I think what I'm trying to say is .... ☐
2 So basically I think that .... ☐
3 I'd like to talk about .... ☐
4 The final point I'd like to make is .... ☐
5 I think we can clearly see this in situations like .... ☐
6 For me this means that .... ☐
7 This topic makes me think about .... ☐
8 The best example I can think of is .... ☐
9 Ultimately I feel that .... ☐
10 I'd like to begin by talking about .... ☐

2 Look at the following Part 2 topics. Make notes about one of them for 1 minute and then speak to your partner about it for 1–2 minutes. Use the expressions from exercise 1 to help you structure your talk. Then ask each other the follow-up questions.

A

Buildings

Talk about an important building in your town/city

You should say:
Where it is
What it looks like
What it is used for
and you should also say whether or not it is important to protect historical buildings.

Follow-up questions:
1 When did you last see this building?
2 Is it a popular tourist attraction in your city/town?

B

Works of Art

Talk about a painting, sculpture or photograph that you really like

You should say:
Where it is
When you saw it
Why you like it
And you should also say whether or not art is important to you.

Follow-up questions:
1 Do your friends like art?
2 Have you ever made a work of art?

3 2.10 Now listen to a student answering topic B from exercise 2. Put a tick next to the expressions from exercise 1 that are used to structure their talk.

Example: Well, this topic makes me think about the very first time I visited an art gallery. I guess I must have been about 15 and it was organized by my school.

✔ *7 This topic makes me think about* ....

Writing

Task 2: Review: Balanced argument and opinion essays

1 Complete the definitions using words from the box.

accept conclusion supports reject refute introduction opposing

A In the introduction you **0** *accept* or **1** .... the idea, opinion or argument in the question. Each body paragraph **2** .... your view but should mention opposing arguments which you then refute.

B In the **3** .... you state that the essay will examine both sides of the issue. The body paragraphs look at issues both for and against in turn but also include mention of **4** .... arguments which you then **5** .... Your opinion results from the discussion of the two sides and is summed up in the **6** ....

Which paragraph describes the balanced argument essay and which describes the opinion essay?

2 In some questions the task makes it clear which approach to take. For example '*Discuss the advantages and disadvantages of this*' means that your answer must use the balanced argument approach. However, in other question tasks (eg '*To what extent do you agree or disagree?*') both essay approaches may be possible. In this case, it helps to consider how strong your own views are to help you decide which approach to take.

> **TIP**
>
> In a '*To what extent ...*' question, the key point is to explain in your essay how much you agree or disagree with the topic - *Do you strongly or partially agree or disagree?*

1 Match the statements.

1 If you have strong views ...
2 If you do not have strong views ...

A ... a balanced argument essay may be the best approach for you.
B ... an opinion essay may be the best approach for you.

2 Read the statement below and mark on the line how much you agree or disagree with it. This is a useful exercise to do before planning any argument / opinion essay.

There is no place for Art in a world where many people still live in poverty.

0% completely disagree	50% partially agree	100% completely agree

3 Compare your answers with a partner and justify your view.

Refuting opposing arguments

3 Some of the paragraphs in the body of your essay may include opposing ideas which you then say you believe to be false (refute). Look at the phrases below and divide them into those that are used to give opinions, and those that are used to refute ideas or make concessions and put them in the Useful language box below.

0 *Although ... , it does not necessarily follow that ...*
1 In spite of / Despite the fact that ... , ...
2 There is no doubt that ... ,
3 While it is true to say that ... , ...
4 ... Nevertheless, ...
5 The fact that ... does not necessarily mean that ...
6 The evidence for ... is undeniable,
7 It may be correct to say that ... but ...
8 It appears to be the case that ...
9 ... Having said that, ...
10 Despite + -ing ... ,

Useful language: Giving and refuting opinions

Giving opinions	Refuting opinions
	Although ...., it does not necessarily follow that ....

4 Combine the pairs of ideas so that the second idea refutes the first. Use language from exercise 3.

0 *While it is true to say that beautiful buildings are important in a city, it is the infrastructure that most affects quality of life.*

0 beautiful buildings are important in a city / it is the infrastructure that most affects quality of life
1 modern art is often criticized / all of it is bad
2 living in a city can be stressful / there are still many advantages
3 architects should express themselves freely / their work must also be practical
4 cities offer the opportunity to become wealthy / there remain many residents living in poverty
5 pop stars depend on computer technology / they are not good musicians

5 Study the statements below and then refute them.

0 New buildings should always blend in with their surroundings.

It is often accepted that the design of new buildings should match that of the surrounding architecture. Nevertheless, there are many examples where contrasting designs have been successful, such as Sydney Opera House.

1 An artist who cannot draw is not a true artist.
2 The increasing use of digital technology in music means that in the future there will be no real musicians.
3 Charity concerts do nothing to help world problems. They only promote the careers of the performers.
4 Historic cities should offer free parking in the city centre for visitors.
5 High rise buildings are the only solution to overcrowding in cities.

6 Read the question below and plan your answer. What essay type is required? Compare your ideas with a partner.

Some people believe that it is the duty of city authorities to provide cultural attractions such as museums and art galleries

Others believe that this is a waste of money, and that the focus should be on providing an effective infrastructure and efficient services.

Discuss both views and give your own opinion.

7 Read the extract below from a model answer and summarize the main points the writer makes in each paragraph.

Although putting a focus on infrastructure seems sensible, it does not necessarily mean that this would always be in the best interests of the city. In many cities, cultural facilities attract people, thus making them popular locations to work and visit. For instance, the popularity of London is partly due to the famous galleries and museums, despite the city having some serious infrastructure problems with an ageing underground and congested road system. Therefore, I believe that cultural attractions are a major factor in a city retaining a skilled workforce and remaining an attractive destination for tourists.

On the other hand, the fact that a city provides good cultural amenities does not necessarily mean that it will be economically strong. Investors, businesses and entrepreneurs, who are a vital part of a thriving city, require a dependable infrastructure before they choose their location. In addition, if investment in infrastructure falls, a city may cease to function properly resulting in growing economic instability and social tension. It is my view that poor transport, faulty communications or unreliable services will all lead to the decline of a city.

1 Compare the points to your own.
2 What part of the essay are these two paragraphs from?
3 Underline the refutation language and suggest alternative phrases.
4 Refer back to Unit 6, page 98–99 on writing introductions and write a suitable introduction.

Writing conclusions

8 Read the three conclusions to the question on public art and evaluate them by answering the questions below for each conclusion. Which is the most appropriate conclusion?

Writing conclusions: Self-check questions

1 Is it clear where the conclusion begins?
2 Does the conclusion summarize the main ideas from the body of the essay?
3 Is the view of the writer clear?
4 Has the writer expressed a final decision, recommendation or conclusion?
5 Have any new ideas been introduced? (There should not be any in the conclusion.)

Conclusion A

There are many competing demands on public funds for a modern and practical infrastructure as well as an attractive range of public art. Yet for a city to function effectively both are required in order to meet the needs of residents, visitors and businesses.

Conclusion B

To conclude, the success of a city depends on having cultural attractions to make it an attractive place to live or visit, but also on having an efficient infrastructure so that people want to remain living there and so that businesses can thrive. Hence, I believe that expenditure needs to be allocated to both public art and public services.

Conclusion C

Finally, it is important to consider the effect that not providing such facilities might have on the residents of the city. They may feel a lack of pride in their city which could lead to an increase in crime. This may well result in people moving away from the city no matter how good the infrastructure is. Therefore, I believe it is important that cities provide cultural facilities as well as good services.

9 Look at the Useful language box and add any other examples you know.

Useful language: Conclusions

Introducing the conclusion	Re-stating your opinion	Stating the final decision / conclusion or recommendation
To sum up, **In conclusion,** **To conclude,**	See Useful language: Expressing opinions in Unit 4, page 70	**Therefore,** **Hence,** **As a result,**

10 Choose a model answer from Unit 2 or 4 from the back of the book. Cover up the conclusion, read the essay and write your own conclusion using the language from the box and the self-check-questions above. Compare with the model.

Further practice

11 Write a complete answer to the question below using the ideas and language in this unit. You should spend about 40 minutes on this task.

Write about the following topic:

Does Art give our lives meaning and purpose or is it merely a distraction from real life?

How do you feel about this?

Give reasons for your answer and include any relevant examples from your own knowledge or experience.
Write at least 250 words.

12 Compare your essay with the model answers on pages 195–196. Note which of the two model answers uses a balanced argument essay approach and which uses an opinion essay approach?

TIP

Your real IELTS Task 2 question may look different from the ones you have practised – be flexible. Read the question carefully and respond accordingly. Keep calm if the question looks different from those you have seen in class – you will still be using the same writing and exam skills.

Study skills

Improving your spelling

1 Read these ideas for improving your spelling. Which of these spelling strategies would you use?

1 I find it really helps practising groups of words that follow a particular spelling rule, like 'fried, cried and tried.' All those words end in 'y' so that helps me remember the spelling.

2 I think it's important to learn how to spell correctly the words we often use in our writing, but unless I write these words down, I'd never remember them.

3 For me, using an English dictionary regularly is a good way of checking my spelling. When I'm writing and I'm not sure how to spell a word, I just look it up.

4 When I write words in my vocabulary book, I underline the silent letters (eg psychology).

2 Fill in the spaces to complete the following commonly misspelt words.

0 receive
1 accom_ _ _ _tion
2 qu_ _e
3 ps_ _ _ology
4 conside_ _ _ _e
5 geo_ _ _ _ _ical
6 lib_ _ _y
7 envir_ _ _ent
8 nec_ _ _ary
9 op_ _ _ _ _nity
10 mil_ _ _ _ium
11 ac_ _ _ding
12 ph_ _ _cal

Dictionary focus

1 Add vowels to complete the following words which name the Arts. Check the meaning of any you do not know in a dictionary and record them.

0 ph_t_gr_phy - *photography*
1 p_ _nt_ng
2 m_s_c
3 sc_lpt_r_
4 l_t_r_t_r_
5 th_ _tr_
6 d_nc_
7 p_ _try
8 c_n_m_

2 Find the following words in the unit and check the meaning of any you do not know in a dictionary.

individualistic p.120	expression p.122	facilities p.133
genius p.122	ambitious p.122	utilities p.194
form p.122	function p.133	reflect p.195

9 Tomorrow's world

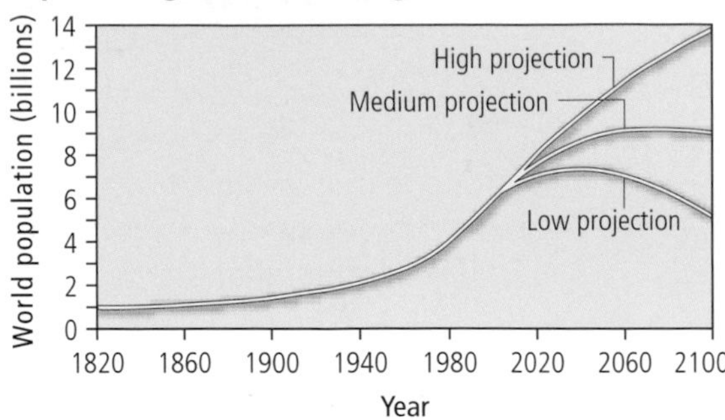

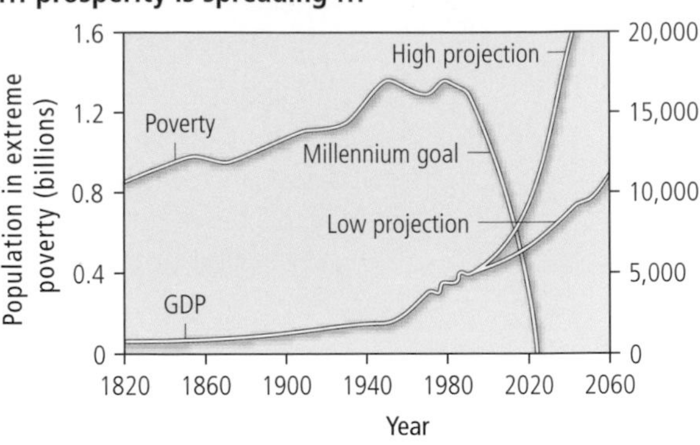

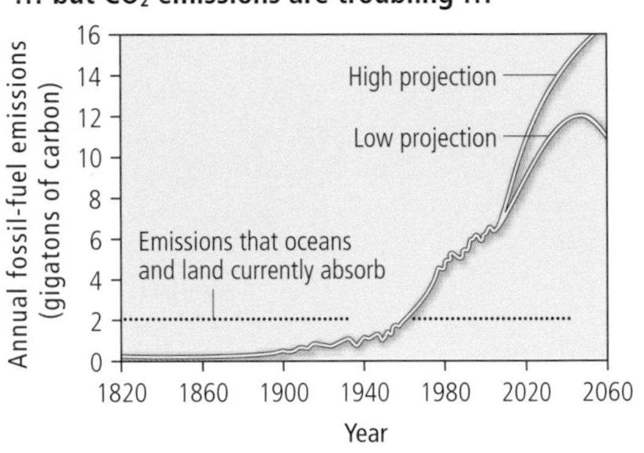

Three World-changing Transitions Based on a graph by Jen Christiansen (permission kindly granted for Macmillan to amend)

SOURCES: Angus Maddison University of Groningen (historical population and GDP); U.N. Population Division (population projections); Intergovernmental Panel on Climate Change (economic projections, scenarios A1 AIM and A2 ASF, rescaled; emissions projections, scenarios A2 ASF and B1 image); François Bourguignon École des Hautes Études en Sciences Sociales and Christian Morrisson University of Paris-I (historical poverty); WORLD BANK 2005 WORLD DEVELOPMENT INDICATORS (2001 poverty); U.N. MILLENNIUM PROJECT (poverty projection); G. Marland, T. A. Boden and R. J. Andres Oak Ridge National Laboratory (historical emissions); DREW SHINDELL NASA Goddard Institute for Space Studies (sustainable emissions level)

Work in pairs. Study the graphs and answer these questions.

Graph 1: Population growth is slowing

1 What happened to the size of the human population between 1950 and 2000?
2 What are the three predictions for population growth this century?
3 What factors do you think could contribute to a rise or fall in population growth?

Graph 2: Prosperity is spreading

4 According to the graph, what will probably have happened by 2020? By 2060?
5 Which countries do you think will benefit the most from these changes?

Graph 3: But CO_2 emissions are troubling

6 What important changes took place between (a) 1940 and 1980? (b) 1940 and 2000?
7 What is the main source of CO_2 emissions?
8 Why do you think CO_2 emissions are troubling for the environment? What can we do to reduce the problem?

Reading

Identifying the writer's purpose

A writer's purpose or reason for writing is something you find by reading and understanding the whole of a passage. However, it is possible to say what the purpose of individual paragraphs is.

The paragraphs below come from a passage about the growth of cities. Which paragraph (**A–D**)

1 makes a prediction?
2 makes a comparison?
3 describes change?
4 argues for a point?

A
From the beginning of the Christian era to about 1850, the urban population of the world never exceeded 7 percent. The Industrial Revolution quickly changed that – today 75 percent of people in the U.S. and other developed countries live in cities, according to the United Nations.

C
Urbanization in the developing countries (such as China and India) has long lagged behind that of the West and Japan. Early in the 20th century probably no more than 5 percent of the population in developing countries lived in cities. But since then, the proportion in these countries has increased twice as fast as that of the West.

B
An enduring myth is that the country is healthier than the city. Historically that was true, but no longer. Urban sanitary measures and access to good medical care have made the cities healthier. Another myth is that city people are isolated. But a study by the University of Washington found no difference in the strength of social ties.

D
The U.N. forecasts a continuing increase in world urbanization over the next quarter of a century to 61 percent. If the developing countries match the record of the West and Japan, the world will eventually reach a level of over 80 percent.

TIP

The topic sentence is the most important sentence in a paragraph because it gives the topic or main idea of the paragraph. It is often, but not always, the first sentence of the paragraph.

1 Skim read the passage on page 138 and answer question 1.

1 The writer's purpose is to

A argue for an opinion.
B present a problem and a solution.
C describe a cause and an effect.
D describe advantages and disadvantages.

Yes, No, Not Given

2 Read the passage and answer questions **2–7**.

Do the following statements agree with the views of the writer? Write:

YES if the statement agrees with the views of the writer.
NO if the statement contradicts the views of the writer.
NOT GIVEN if it is impossible to say what the writer thinks about this.

2 Scientific developments and religion will provide the answers to man's future needs.
3 In years to come, the land area on the planet will determine how much human life the Earth can support.
4 The Earth's capacity to support human life cannot be linked to the availability of any single resource.
5 Current estimates of the number of people the Earth can support are not completely accurate.
6 Science has addressed the question of how many humans the Earth can continue to support.
7 Humans in the future will be willing to settle for a lower standard of living than people today.

Remember

See Unit 7, page 106 for advice on how to approach this question type.

Human Population Grows Up

As we swell toward nine billion in the next half a century, humanity will undergo historic changes in the balance between young and old, rich and poor, urban and rural. Our choices now and in the years ahead will determine how well we cope with our coming of age.

1 In the short term our planet can provide room and food, at least at subsistence level, for 50 percent more people than are alive now because humans are already growing enough cereal grains to feed 10 billion people a vegetarian diet. But as demographer–sociologist Kingsley Davis observed in 1991, 'There is no country in the world in which people are satisfied with having barely enough to eat.' The question is whether 2050's billions of people can live with freedom of choice and material prosperity, however freedom and prosperity may be defined by those alive in 2050, and whether their children and their children's offspring will be able to continue to live with freedom and prosperity, however they may define them in the future. That is the question of sustainability.

2 This question is as old as recorded history. Cuneiform tablets from 1600 B.C. showed that the Babylonians feared the world was already too full of people. In 1798 Thomas Malthus renewed these concerns, as did Donella Meadows in her 1972 book The Limits to Growth. While some people have fretted about too many people, optimists have offered reassurance that deities or technology will provide for human-kind's well-being.

3 Early efforts to calculate Earth's human carrying capacity assumed that a necessary condition for a sustainable human society could be measured in units of land. In the first known quantitative reckoning, Antoni van Leeuwenhoek estimated in 1679 that the inhabited area of Earth was 13,385 times larger than Holland and that Holland's population then was about one million people. Assuming that 'the inhabited part of the earth is as densely populated as Holland, though it cannot well be so inhabited,' he wrote, 'the inhabited earth being 13,385 times larger than Holland yields … 13,385,000,000 human beings on earth,' or an upper limit of roughly 13.4 billion.

4 Continuing this tradition, in 2002 Mathis Wackernagel, an author of the 'ecological footprint' concept, and his colleagues sought to quantify the amount of land humans used to supply resources and to absorb wastes. Their preliminary assessment concluded that humanity used 70 percent of the global biosphere's capacity in 1961 and 120 percent in 1999. In other words, by 1999 people were exploiting the environment faster than it could regenerate itself, they claimed, a situation that is clearly unsustainable.

5 This approach has many problems. Perhaps the most serious is its attempt to establish a necessary condition for the sustainability of human society in terms of the single dimension of biologically productive land area. For instance, to translate energy into land units, Wackernagel and his colleagues calculated the area of forests that would be needed to absorb the carbon dioxide produced in generating the energy. This approach fails for energy generation technologies that do not emit carbon dioxide, such as solar panels, hydropower or nuclear plants. Converting all energy production to nuclear energy would change the dilemma from too much CO_2 to too much spent nuclear fuel. The problem of sustainability remains, but biologically productive land area is not a useful indicator of it.

6 Other one-dimensional quantities that have been proposed as ceilings on human carrying capacity include water, energy, food and various chemical elements required for food production. The difficulty with every single index of human carrying capacity is that its meaning depends on the value of other factors. If water is scarce and energy abundant, for example, it is easy to desalinate and transport water; if energy is expensive, desalination and transport may be impractical.

7 Attempts to quantify Earth's human carrying capacity or sustainable human population face the challenge of understanding the constraints imposed by nature, the choices faced by people and the interactions between them. Here I will draw attention to the questions of human choice involved in assessing sustainability.

8 What will humans desire and what will they accept as the average level of distribution and material well-being in 2050 and beyond? What technologies will be used? What domestic and international political institutions will be used to resolve conflicts? What economic arrangements will provide credit, regulate trade, set standards and fund investments? What social and demographic arrangements will influence birth, health, education, marriage, migration and death? What physical, chemical and biological environments will people want to live in? Finally, and significantly, what will people's values and tastes be in the future? As anthropologist Donald L. Hardesty noted in 1977, 'a plot of land may have a low carrying capacity, not because of low soil fertility but because it is sacred or inhabited by ghosts.'

9 Most published estimates of Earth's human carrying capacity uncritically assumed answers to one or more of these questions. Estimates made in the past half a century ranged from less than one billion to more than 1,000 billion. These estimated are political numbers, intended to persuade people, one way or another: either that too many humans are already on Earth or that there is no problem with continuing rapid population growth.

10 Scientific numbers are intended to describe reality. Because no estimates of human carrying capacity have explicitly addressed the questions raised above, taking into account the diversity of views about their answers in different societies and cultures, no scientific estimates of sustainable human population size can be said to exist.

11 Too often attention to long-term sustainability is a diversion from the immediate problem of making tomorrow better than today, a task that does offer much room for science and constructive action. No one knows the path to sustainability because no one knows the destination, if there is one. But we do know much that we could do today to make tomorrow better than it would be if we do not put our knowledge to work. As economist Robert Cassen remarked, 'Virtually everything that needs doing from a population point of view needs doing anyway.'

Matching: Identification of arguments

3 Answer questions **8–13**.

Match each statement with the correct person A–F. You may use any letter more than once.

> **Remember**
>
> You may not need to use all of the names in your answers. Some names you may need to use more than once.

8 Humans are using resources more quickly than the planet can replace them.
9 There is a direct relationship between land area and human population.
10 People want more than only the smallest amount they need to stay alive.
11 Cultural as well as scientific factors can affect the usability of an area of land.
12 The earth is already over-populated.
13 Waste absorption is an important factor in sustainable energy production.

A Kingsley Davis
B Donella Meadows
C Antoni van Leeuwenhoek
D Mathis Wackernagel
E Donald Hardesty
F Robert Cassen

4 Answer question **14**.

14 According to the passage, who has expressed views which the writer does **NOT** agree with?

A Kingsley Davis
B Mathis Wackernagel
C Donald Hardesty
D Robert Cassen

Vocabulary 1

Academic vocabulary

1 Find words in the Reading passage which mean the same as the expressions in 1–12 below. The words in the passage are all in the Academic Word List which was introduced in Unit 5 on page 87. Paragraph numbers are in brackets ().

> **TIP**
>
> The words in exercise 1 are all marked as high frequency words in the Academic Word List and the Macmillan Dictionary.

0 one part of a hundred (1) ...percent...
1 to say clearly what something is (1) ....
2 to believe something is true (3) ....
3 calculated or guessed (3) ....
4 an idea (4) ....
5 a judgement or opinion about something (4) ....
6 a way of thinking about or dealing with something (5) ....
7 to discover or prove that something is true (5) ....
8 something that shows information (5) ....
9 something that affects the way in which something else happens (6) ....

10 the way in which something is shared among people (8)

....

11 relating to business, industry and trade (8)

....

12 in a way which is important / importantly (8)

....

2 These are some of the words from exercise 1. Complete the table, using any other derived words as appropriate.

NOUN	VERB	ADJECTIVE	ADVERB
assessment	0 assess		
1	assume		
concept	2		
3	define	4	
distribution	5		
6	7	economic	8
9	establish	10	
indicator	11		
12	13	14	significantly

Language focus

TIP

You could be asked to speculate about the future in Writing Task 2 and Speaking Part 3.

Expressing the future: probability

See Grammar reference, page 177.

1 Look at statements **a–e** about life in the 21st century and answer the questions.

1 Which modal verbs and adverbs express certainty and which express probability or possibility?
2 Which of the expressions in italics could you replace with these expressions without changing the meaning of the sentence:

i are unlikely to
ii certainly won't
iii could
iv is likely to
v is / are certain to

a Domestic robots *will* be in common use in people's homes.
b There *will probably* be a major attack on the Internet.
c We *probably won't* discover new life forms on Earth.
d The Earth *may/might* be struck by an asteroid.
e We *definitely won't* communicate with life from other planets.

2 Look at statements **f–g** and answer the questions.

1 In which is the speaker / writer describing:

i an action or event in progress in the future
ii an action completed before a specified future time

2 What future tenses are used? How are they formed?
3 Which modal verbs could replace *will* to express probability or possibility?

f In 20 years' time, we *will be curing* many diseases using cloned organs.
g By the end of the century, human life *will have settled* on the moon.

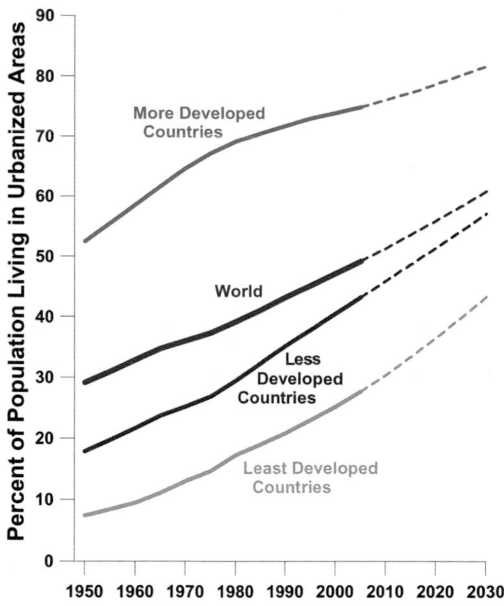

Source: United Nations, UN World Urbanization Prospects. The UN defintion of urban varies somewhat by country, although generally non-agricultural settlements as small as 3 to 5 thousand population are included. In addition, the definition within countries has varied from time-to-time. Nevertheless, the data are believed to more or less reflect the overall trend of urbanization. The largest countries in the "Less developed" category are China and India, while the largest in the "Least Developed" category are Ethiopia and the Congo (Kinsasha). Solid lines are estimated, dotted lines are projections.

3 Look at the graph on the left which describes population trends and complete the paragraph. Use the word(s) in brackets. Put the verb in an appropriate future form.

Since 1950 the percentage of the world's population living in cities has risen steadily. By 2010 it is estimated that about 75% of the population in developed countries **1** ________ (live) in urbanized areas and by 2030 the prediction is that the number **2** ________ (rise) to around 80%. This is higher than the world average, which is likely to be about 50% by 2010 and **3** ________ (reach) 60% by 2030. In less developed countries the number of people living in cities **4** ________ (probably / be) as high as those in developed countries, while in the least developed countries the numbers **5** ________ (probably / be) even lower than those for the less developed countries.

Population Living in Urbanized Areas
Rodger Doyle / Scientific American

4 Make predictions about the likelihood of these events happening by 2050.

a Life will have been discovered on other planets.
b People will be living longer.
c The world will have become over-populated.
d The world's climate will have changed dramatically.
e We'll be using environmentally friendly energy sources.

Use language like: I think we / they will (almost) certainly + verb … We / They're (un)likely to + verb … / It's (un)likely that + clause … We / They'll probably / possibly + infinitive + verb … / It's probable / possible that + clause … / There's a probability / possibility that + clause … / … is forecast / predicted / expected to + verb

5 Tell your partner. In 6 months', 1 years' and 5 years' time, what do you think you

a will be doing?
b will have done?

Listening 1

TIP

When you hear a number or a date, write it as a number not as words or you may lose marks for spelling.

Example: 16th of September 2007 – 16.09.07

Section 2: Listening for dates and numbers

1 How would you say these dates and numbers? Compare your answers with a partner.

1 February 9th 2009
2 18 December 2012
3 9/02/06
4 53 88 2017
5 54 999 420

2 2.11 Now listen and check your answers.

3 2.12 You may hear dates and numbers in the listening recordings. Listen to the following recording and write down the numbers and dates you hear.

1 ....
2 ....
3 ....
4 ....
5 ....
6 ....
7 ....
8 ....
9 ....
10 ....

TIP

Students often have problems distinguishing between numbers like 15 and 50. The syllable stress in smaller numbers is at the end (16 – sixteen) and in larger numbers, it is at the beginning (60 – sixty.)

4 2.13 Listen to the following sentences and write down only the numbers and dates you hear.

1 ....
2 ....
3 ....
4 ....
5 ....
6 ....
7 ....

5 2.14 You are going to hear a radio programme. Before you listen read questions **1–12**.

Questions 1–12

Sentence completion

Complete the sentences using no more than **TWO WORDS AND/OR A NUMBER**.

1 The survey had similar responses on the internet and telephone, both being around ....
2 The greatest invention of the past 200 years was the bicycle which had .... of the public vote.
3 The first bicycle was wooden and was invented in ....
4 The bicycle changed women's rights as from .... women began wearing trousers.

Note completion

Complete the notes using **NO MORE THAN TWO WORDS AND/OR A NUMBER**.

	% of Votes	Interesting fact	Uses mentioned
Computer	**5**	Defined first as a person who did mathematical calculations.	Home, business and **6** ....
Internet	12%	Originally used as part of **7**......................	Online shopping, entertainment **8** ....
Radio	**9**	Reginald Fessenden gave the first radio broadcast from a ship in **10**	Send ship signals.
Mobile		Children will first use **11** .... on a mobile.	Take photographs, be personal organizers and **12** ....

Writing 1

Task 1: Describing illustrations

1 You may be given an illustration of a device or machine and asked to explain how it works, or to make comparisons. Read the following description. What is being described?

0 It is an everyday object that has a simple design.
1 The outside is made of leather or plastic.
2 It is oblong-shaped.
3 It consists of a number of small pockets.
4 It is used for carrying money.

2 Add the underlined language to the correct place in the table below.

Useful language: Describing illustrations

A Position	B General words
at the top / bottom on the right / left side in the right / left hand corner in the middle the X is situated + around / above / below / inside / next to + the Y *The hard drive is situated inside the computer.* the X is covered with Y *The front of the speakers is covered with material.* the X + is constructed + of Y (and Z) *The keyboard is constructed of plastic.* the X contains Y (and Z) *The top section contains the control panel.* the X is joined together by a Y *The sound system is joined together by a series of cables.*	object (n) design (n + v) structure (n +v) material (n) function (n + v) versatile + ity (adj + n) capable +ity (adj + n) tool (n) machine (n) device (n) system (n)
C Purpose	**D Useful language presented in earlier units**
X is used to +inf *A fan is used to cool the system.* X is useful / necessary for + ing / n *Air is necessary for cooling.* The role of the X is to + inf *The role of the fan is to cool the system.* The X + prevents / stops / protects / avoids + the Y from +ing / n *The fan prevents the system from over-heating.* The X + allows Y to + inf *The fan allows the system to cool.*	Ordering (Unit 5) Comparison (Unit 3) Purpose and results (Unit 5) Process verbs (Unit 5) Passive verbs (Unit 5)

Question strategy

Writing tasks based on a diagram or illustration look different from graphs, charts or process questions, but the approach is similar. Which one of the following four tips is wrong?

1 describe the information you have been given
2 focus on the main features (not every detail)
3 give your opinion
4 make comparisons where appropriate

Remember

Task 1 answers are factual and do not include your opinion.

3 Complete these tasks with a partner using language from the table on page 143.

1 Choose an object that you and your partner both have with you. For example, a watch, music player, mobile, electronic dictionary, pen, etc. Don't let your partner see your object.
2 Now take turns to describe your object: describe what it's made of; what it looks like (how the different parts are arranged); and how it works.
3 Take turns to try to draw each other's objects from the verbal instructions.
4 Compare the drawings with the real object.
5 Now compare the objects. What differences are there?

4 Read the Task 1 question below and answer the questions.

1 What similarities are there between the two phones?
2 What are the most significant differences: size, weight, colour, materials, features?

The illustrations show two stages in the development of the mobile phone.

Summarize the information by selecting and reporting the main features and make comparisons where relevant.

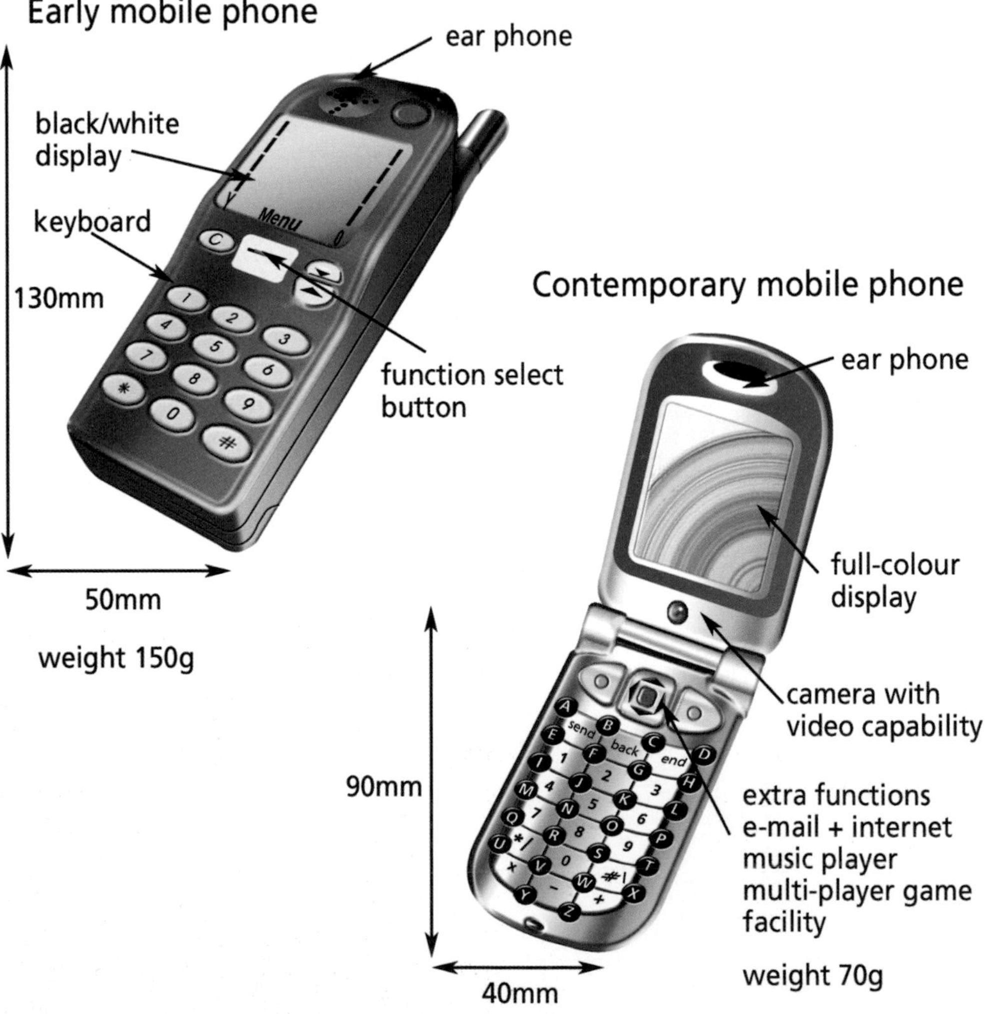

5 Read the model answer and complete the gaps with language from the Useful language table on page 143.

Remember

You will improve your score if you transform words from the illustration in your answer eg *music player* ⟶ *play music.*

Paragraph plan	Comparing illustrations model answer
Paragraph 1 Introduce the illustrations and describe the similarities (parts, position and purpose).	The illustrations show two mobile phones, an early model and a more recent design. Despite the many differences, both phones share the same basic design principle. The **(0)** main part of both phones is a keypad, which **(1)** __________ enter information. Above this are the control buttons for selecting different functions. The top section of the phones **(2)** __________ the display and earphone.
Paragraph 2 Describe the main differences.	However, there are several major differences, the most significant of which is that the contemporary model is hinged so that it folds in half. Its **(3)** __________ is reduced by 40mm and width by 10mm, compared to the earlier phone. It is also under half the **(4)** __________ of the later model (70g and 150g respectively). Another variation is that the contemporary mobile has greater **(5)** __________ and can access email and the internet, play music and has a multi-player game **(6)** __________ as well as a camera with video capability. The much larger colour display is clearly **(7)** __________ these extra functions.
Summarizing sentence Summarize the main differences and similarities.	Overall, it can be seen that both function as telephones, but the contemporary mobile is much more **(8)** __________ despite its reduced size. *184 words*

Further practice

Question strategy

If you feel that there is not enough information on an illustration to write 150 words, use the following techniques:

1 Follow a paragraph plan.

2 Use longer phrases where possible (eg *in the summer months* instead of *summer*).

3 Use each label of the diagram as the basis of a sentence.

6 Answer the question below using the language presented in this unit.

The diagram below shows some design principles for an energy-efficient house and how they work in different climates.

Summarize the information by selecting and reporting the main features and make comparisons where relevant.

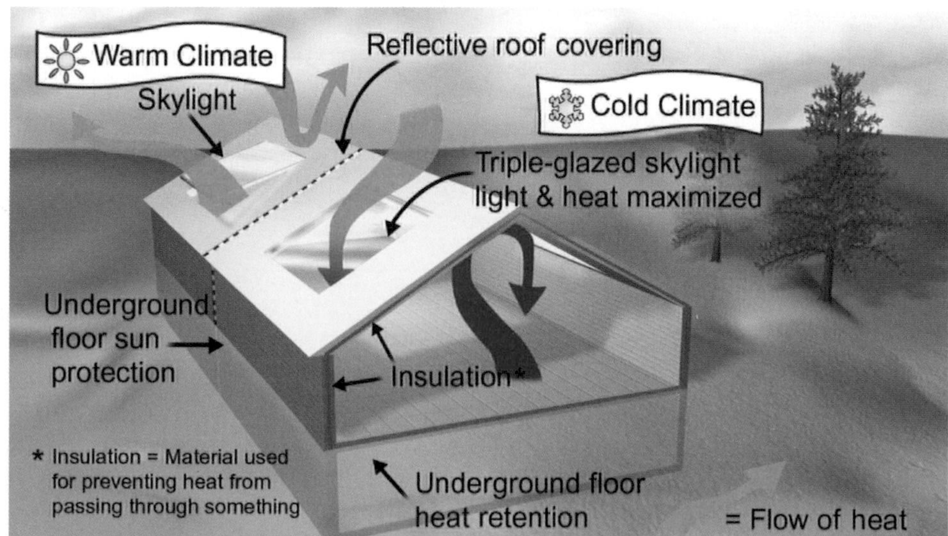

7 When you have finished, compare your answer and your paragraph plan with the model on page 195.

Speaking

Expressing likes and dislikes

1 Look at the following Part 1 topics and make your own questions about each one. Some questions have been done for you as examples. Now practise your questions with a partner. Take it in turns to be the candidate and the examiner.

Speaking Part 1 topics

1 Numbers
  1 What is your favourite number?
  2 Are numbers important in your culture?(Why/Why not?)
  3 Are you better at remembering names or numbers?

2 A business you would like to run
  1 What kind of business would you like to run?
  2 Do you think it's better to work for a small business or a multinational company?
  3 (Your idea) ....

3 An art or museum exhibition
  1 How often do you visit art galleries and museums?
  2 (Your idea) ....
  3 (Your idea) ....

4 A person you know who likes dangerous sports.

2 2.15 and 2.16 Listen to two candidates speaking about the Part 1 question below. Make a note of the expressions for describing likes and dislikes in the table below.

Topic: Shops
1 Do you prefer using local shops or big supermarkets?

Like	Dislike

3 Now turn to page 205 and check your answers.

4 Now practise using the expressions from exercise 2 by speaking about the following Part 2 topics and the related follow-up questions. Take it in turns to be the candidate and the examiner.

Exam information

For Part 2, you need to practise talking about a wide variety of topics. You should be ready to talk about a past, present or future situation.

1

Describe an electronic gadget you like to use.

You should say:
What it looks like
How often you use it
Why you like it
And you should also say what kinds of electronic gadgets you think will be popular in the future.

Follow-up questions:
1 Did this gadget cost a lot of money?
2 What kind of electronic gadgets do your friends own?

2

Describe what you hope to do in the future.

You should say:
What this is
Why you want to do it
Why you think you may be good at it
And you should also say if it is important to make plans for the future.

Follow-up questions:
1 Have you always wanted to do this?
2 Do you think you may do something different in the future?

Writing 2

Task 1: Maps

1 Occasionally, a Task 1 question may show two maps and ask you to compare them, or give you one map showing different locations for a proposed development such as an airport, school or hyper-market. Look at the map below which shows three possible locations for a leisure centre (A, B or C). Work in pairs.

1 Describe the main features of the map and their relative positions.
2 Describe and compare the advantages and disadvantages of each location. Consider space, transport and environmental issues.
3 State which location is best and explain why.

The map below shows three possible locations for a leisure centre. Summarize the information by selecting and reporting the main features and make comparisons where relevant.

Exam information

The map question may require you to discuss hypothetical situations for example, ***If** the leisure centre **was** located by the factories, it **would** ...* or *...This location **would be** more environmentally friendly*

2 Read the model answer and complete the gaps with phrases **a–h**.

Paragraph 1: *Describes the map and describes the advantages and disadvantages of A*

The diagram shows a map with three potential locations for a proposed leisure centre.

0 .... the leisure centre was located in between the factories **1** .... the map, at (A), the site would not be very attractive, but would be easily accessible to the workers. Also, **2** .... the river would benefit users interested in water sports.

Paragraph 2: *Discusses the advantages and disadvantages of B*

Location B is in the middle of a residential area **3** .... factories. It would give easier access for local residents, who **4** .... less car pollution as they would not need to drive there although **5** .... problems of congestion if people from out of town used the facilities.

Paragraph 3: *Discusses the advantages and disadvantages of C*

Turning to location C in **6** ...., it would have the most attractive setting due to being **7** .... forest. However, the environmental destruction **8** .... the construction of the centre, and the on-going pollution would be major disadvantages.

Summarizing sentence: *States which is the best location with reasons*

Overall, building the leisure centre in position B would combine the easiest access for users with low environmental impact.

180 words

0 If
a its proximity to
b surrounded by
c away from
d caused by
e one disadvantage could be
f to the right of
g the left part of the map
h would create

3 Note the paragraph structure of the answer to the Map question. What types of language are used in the answer?

Vocabulary 2

Prefixes

1 Which of these prefixes refer to numbers less than 1 (-) and which to numbers more than 1 (+)?

2 Match the prefixes **1–7** with the number which they represent (**a–g**).

1	centi	**a**	1 billionth or (1 / 1,000,000,000)
2	deca-	**b**	one millionth (1 / 1,000,000)
3	kilo	**c**	one thousandth (1 / 1,000)
4	mega-	**d**	one hundredth (1 / 100)
5	micro-	**e**	ten (10)
6	milli-	**f**	one thousand (1,000)
7	nano-	**g**	one million (1,000,000)

TIP

A prefix, like a word, can have more than one meaning. These meanings may be similar to one another.

3 In pairs, discuss the meaning of these words. Then use a dictionary to check your answers.

1 centimetre / centipede
2 decade / decathlon
3 megabyte / megalopolis
4 microsecond / microclimate
5 milligram / millennium
6 nanosecond / nanotechnology

Listening 2

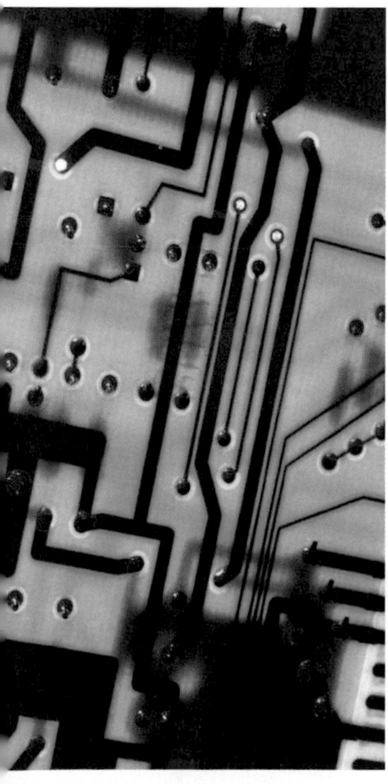

Section 4

Prediction

1 Work in pairs. How do you think nanotechnology might be used in:

1 medicine?
2 industry?

2 2.17 You are going to hear a lecture on the science of nanotechnology. Before you listen, read questions **1–13**.

Summary completion

Complete the summary on nanotechnology using **NO MORE THAN TWO WORDS AND/OR A NUMBER.**

Extremely small objects are created through the use of **1** .... and **2** .... Nanotechnology began in the realm of **3** .... which proved that what was small was in effect, better. The development of **4** .... after the Second World War meant that electronic circuits could be built in a smaller area, thus saving **5** .... and **6** .... In modern transistors, electrons can travel up to **7** .... nanometres. However, in the future, companies may not carry on **8** .... nanotechnology if it becomes too unaffordable.

Diagram completion

Label the diagram using **NO MORE THAN TWO WORDS AND/OR A NUMBER**.

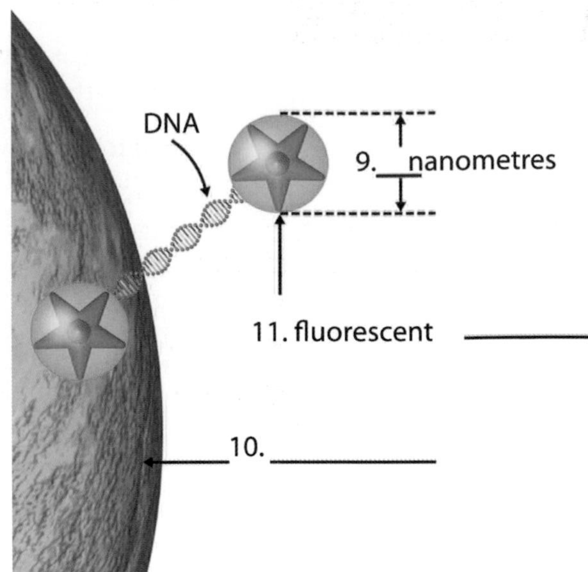

Sentence completion

Complete the sentences using **NO MORE THAN THREE WORDS**.

12 An assembler could be used to build a

....

13 Scientists are worried that these machines

....

Pronunciation

Sentence stress: Weak forms

1 Mark the stress in these sentences.

1 It's on the table.
2 Your phone is on the table.
3 Your mobile phone is on the table.
4 You haven't lost your phone – it's on the table.

2 2.18 Listen and check your answers.

3 These words are normally stressed in English: nouns, main verbs, adjectives, adverbs, negative auxiliaries.

Weak forms, or words which are not normally stressed, are: articles, prepositions, auxiliary verbs, conjunctions, the verb 'to be.'

4 Mark the stressed syllables on these sentences. Then take turns reading them to your partner.

1 The bicycle is a great way to get regular exercise and it's much better for the environment.
2 The Internet began as part of the United States military network, but it later began to be used by businesses and academic institutions.
3 Nanotechnology has crept into many areas of our lives.
4 Scientists are concerned that there's a real possibility that these machines could replicate themselves.
5 Next week I'll be looking at nanotechnology and recent developments in the field of molecular biology.

5 2.19 Listen and check.

> ***TIP***
>
> Unstressed words and syllables are said very quickly and may be difficult for you to hear. Weak forms and unstressed syllables often contain the schwa sound /ə/.

Study skills

Understanding question task words

1 It is important to understand the question task words to make you sure you do not move away from the topic.

Match the question words in the table to the given definitions. Check your answers using the Macmillan Advanced Learner Dictionary.

Question task word	Definition
1 Justify	A To carefully think about a situation or problem in order to make a judgement
2 Evaluate	B To offer an idea or suggestion
3 Analyse	C To explain how things / situations are different and how they are similar
4 Suggest	D To show that there is a good reason for something, particularly something that others believe is wrong
5 Summarize	E To examine something in detail in order to explain what it means
6 Describe	F To write about a topic in detail
7 Discuss	G To give details or an explanation about what something or a situation is like
8 Speculate	H To describe a situation and then give an opinion about its value or importance using evidence.
9 Assess	I To discuss and give reasons why something has happened
10 Compare	J To bring together all the important points, leaving out any specific details.

Dictionary focus

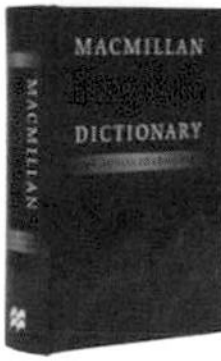

Revision of linking devices

1 These linking expressions have all been covered in this book. Put them under the heading which describes how they are normally used.

although as a result (of) because (of) consequently despite/in spite of due to for instance finally first of all furthermore however in addition in conclusion in the same way lastly moreover nevertheless next on the other hand provided (that) similarly so so as (not) to so that such as therefore to conclude to sum up unless whereas/while yet

Sequencing ideas	**Expressing conditions**	**Expressing contrast**
firstly, secondly	If	but
Adding further support	**Stating results**	**Expressing similarities**
besides	thus	likewise
Providing reasons	**Giving examples**	**Concluding statements**
(in order) to	for example	in summary

TIP

Learn how to use linking devices in a sentence and how to punctuate as well as learning their meaning.

10 From me to you

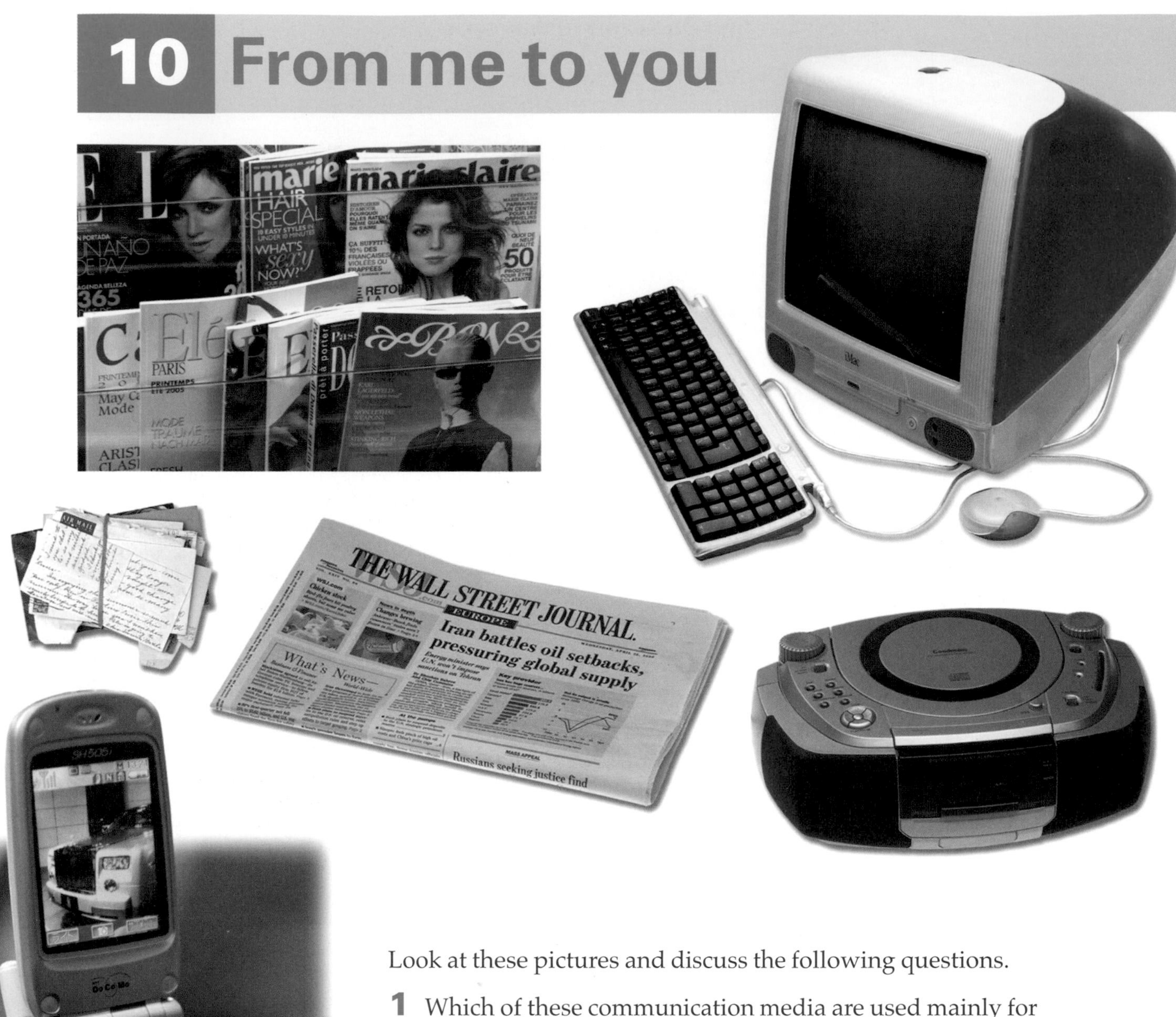

Look at these pictures and discuss the following questions.

1 Which of these communication media are used mainly for (a) interpersonal communication? (b) mass communication?

2 Which (a) are published information? (b) transmit, receive information electronically? (c) store information electronically?

3 What are the ways in which people in your country communicate with (a) family and friends and (b) business associates?

Reading

Identification of main idea and supporting information

1 Read the first paragraph from a chapter on mass media.

1 Which sentence contains the main idea of the paragraph? What does it tell you?
2 What early forms of mass media does the writer mention?

2 Which new media forms do you think the writer will mention in the remainder of the passage?

3 Now read the rest of the passage and check your answers to question **2**.

New Electronic Media

The term 'mass media' refers to the organized means for communicating openly and at a distance to many receivers within a short space of time. These criteria are relative, since the earliest forms of mass media (the printed book or pamphlet) were limited to the minority of a society that happened to be literate and relatively close to the place of publication. There has been a continuous development of technologies since the earliest forms of media (rock paintings) to the latest forms of new electronic media.

The expression 'new media' has been in use since the 1960s and has had to encompass an expanding and diversifying set of communication technologies. However, the foundations of the current 'communications revolution' rest on two main innovations. One is satellite communication and the other is the harnessing of the computer. The key to the immense power of the computer as a communication machine lies in the process of digitalization that allows information of all kinds in all formats to be carried with the same efficiency and also intermingled. In principle there is no longer any need for other forms of media, since all could be subsumed in the same computerized communication centre. In practice there is no sign of this happening. Alongside computer-based technologies there are other innovations that have in some degree changed some aspects of mass communication. New means of transmission by cable, satellite and radio have immensely increased the capacity to transmit. New means of storage and retrieval, including the personal video recorder, CD-ROM, compact disc, etc. have also expanded the range of possibilities, and even the remote control device has played a part. While not directly supporting mass communication, the many new possibilities for private 'media-making' (camcorders, PCs, printers, cameras, etc.) have expanded the world of media and forged bridges between public and private communication and between the spheres of professional and amateur.

The implications of all this for mass media are still far from clear, although it is certain that the 'traditional' media have benefited greatly from new media innovations as well as acquiring new competitors. Secondly, we can conclude that the communications revolution has generally shifted the 'balance of power' from the media to the audience, in so far as there are more options to choose from and more active uses of media available. Traditional mass communication was essentially one-directional, while the new forms of communication are essentially interactive. Mass communication has in several respects become less massive and less centralized. Beyond that, it is useful to distinguish between the effects of enhanced transmission and the emergence of any new medium of communication.

In respect of transmission, the main changes have been the installation of cable systems, the development of satellites for direct broadcasting or feeding into cables and the adaptation of telephone networks to carry many new kinds of traffic. The impact of these changes is still mainly limited to a relatively small proportion of the world population. The main results have been to expand the existing supply without yet fundamentally changing what is transmitted or what is consumed.

In respect of the emergence of any new medium, we can at least recognize the claim of the Internet to be considered as a medium in its own right. This is based on having a distinctive technology, manner of use, range of content and services, and distinct own image. Its recognition as a medium has been held back by the fact that the Internet is not owned, controlled or organized by any single body, but is simply a network of internationally interconnected computers operating according to agreed protocols. Numerous organizations, but especially service providers and telecommunication bodies, contribute to its operation. The Internet as such does not exist anywhere as a legal entity and is not subject to any single set of national laws or regulations. However, those who use the Internet can be accountable to the laws and regulations of the country in which they reside as well as to international law. Despite the plausibility of counting the Internet as a mass medium, its diffusion is limited and it has not yet acquired a clear definition of its function. It began primarily as a non-commercial means of intercommunication and data exchange between professionals, but its more recent rapid advance has been fuelled by its potential as a purveyor of goods and many profitable services and as an alternative means of interpersonal communication. It is still very marginal as a means of mass communication.

Multiple-choice questions

Question strategy

See Unit 3, page 42 for advice on how to approach this question type.

4 Answer questions **1–3**.
Choose the correct letter **A**, **B**, **C** or **D**.

1 The main topic discussed in the text is

A the ways in which communication takes place.
B the importance of the Internet as a means of mass communication.
C the history of mass media communication.
D the effect of technological change on communication.

2 According to the passage, which of the following is responsible for an increase in computer-based technologies?

A digital technology
B new ways of storing information
C better ways of retrieving information
D satellite communication

3 Which of these changes has **NOT** occurred as a result of media innovations?

A increased competition for 'traditional' media
B increased choice for consumers
C stricter laws for Internet users
D more audience interaction with the media

Remember

A summary completion question may only test a section of the passage. Read the summary first and then scan read the passage to find the relevant section.

Summary completion (from a list)

Question strategy

See Unit 2, page 30 for advice on how to approach this question type.

5 Answer questions **4–8**.
Complete the summary below using words from the box.

There is an argument that the Internet should be counted as a means of **4** ________ . This is despite the fact that it is not possible to say which **5** ________ owns and operates it, which **6** ________ regulates its use or what its true **7** ________ is. Although its uses in **8** ________ and communication have helped to increase its popularity, this still does not justify calling it a mass medium.

activity corporation country data exchange image individual interpersonal communication mass communication media organization nations purpose service provider telecommunications trade

Sentence completion

Question strategy

See Unit 6, page 93 for advice on how to approach this question type.

TIP

Scan read the passage for the words in italics to help you to locate the answers to the questions. Answers can be found both before and after the key words.

6 Answer questions **9–12**.
Complete the sentences below with words taken from the Reading passage.
Use **NO MORE THAN THREE WORDS** for each answer.

9 *Satellite communication* and *computer-based technologies* underlie the ....
10 Inventions like the *personal video recorder* and the *compact disc* have improved information ....
11 Changes to the way we communicate have given the *audience* ....
12 Information *supply* has increased as a result of changes to methods of ....

Yes, No, Not Given

7 Answer questions **13–15**.
Do the following statements agree with the views of the writer? Write

YES if the statement agrees with the views of the writer.
NO if the statement contradicts the views of the writer.
NOT GIVEN if it is impossible to say what the writer thinks about this.

13 Computer-based technologies are capable of meeting all of our communication needs.
14 The effects of changes to ways in which we transmit information have been felt globally.
15 The Internet will one day be recognized as a legitimate medium of mass communication.

Language focus

Articles

See Grammar reference, page 177.

1 Match the beginnings of the rules (**1–3**) with an appropriate ending (**a–c**).

1 We use the indefinite article (a / an) ____
2 We use the definite article (the) ____
3 We use zero (no) article ____

a when the reader / listener knows which person or thing we are talking about, eg Have you logged on to the computer yet?
b with plural or uncountable nouns when we talk about people or things in a general way, eg Computers are coming down in price.
c when the person or thing we are talking about is new to the reader or listener, eg I bought a new computer last week.

2 Match the rules (**0–7**) for the use of articles with the examples (**a–f**)

Indefinite article (a/an)	**Definite article (the)**
0 Use when you mean any example of a type or class. c	1 Use when you are referring to a specific example of a type or class. ____
2 Use when you say what type or group someone or something belongs to or what their job is. ____	3 Use when explaining which person or thing you're referring to. ____
4 Use with a singular countable noun when one example of a type or class represents all the examples of the type or class. ____	5 Use with a singular countable noun to make a general statement about a group of people or things. ____
6 Use in some expressions of quantity. ____	7 Use with superlative adjectives. ____

a He's *an* electronic engineer.
b *The* computer has revolutionized the way we use information.
c You need *a* dictionary for this exercise.
d *A* computer needs to be maintained regularly.
e One of *the* earliest forms of mass media was rock painting.
f Hand me *the* dictionary, please.
g Only *a* small proportion of the world's population has been affected.
h He's *the* engineer who repaired my television.

3 Complete the text. Use *a/an, the* or leave the space blank. Use the Grammar Summary on pages 177–178 to help you.

There was **1** ____ time when researching **2** ____ school or college term paper was much simpler. **3** ____ student writing about, for example, **4** ____ Wright brothers might have borrowed **5** ____ book on **6** ____ history of aviation from **7** ____ local library or looked through **8** ____ family's encyclopaedia. Today, **9** ____ students can identify these and thousands of other resources on **10** ____ Internet, but they are not always good at sorting **11** ____ valuable information from **12** ____ useless.

Listening 1

Section 1: Multiple-choice: Diagrams

1 2.20 You are going to hear a student getting information about the university learning resource centre. Before you listen, study the pictures and underline the keywords in the pictures. Read questions **1–7**.

Questions **1–2**
Look at the following pictures and choose the correct letter **A**, **B** or **C**.

A

B

C

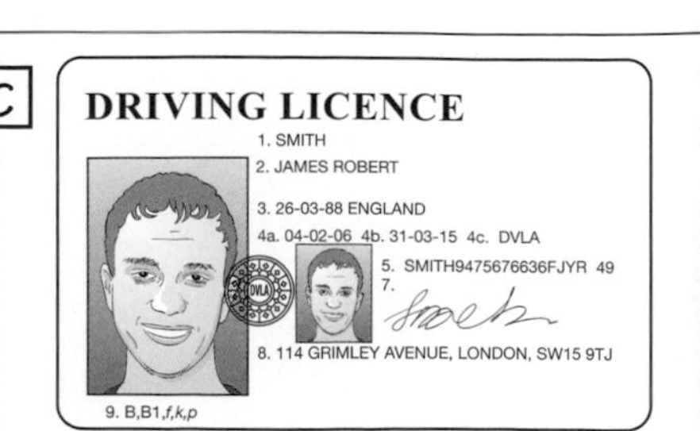

Which form of identification is preferred?

1 ....

A £1.00	B £1.50	C £1.75

What will the fine be for a two-day loan book returned one day late?

2 ....

Sentence completion

Questions **3–7**
Complete the sentences using **NO MORE THAN ONE WORD** for each answer.

Students find it easier to **3** .... internet passwords they have changed.
Students don't have to waste time finding books because the reading lists are **4** ....
The **5** .... library loan system provides links to other libraries.
Guest speakers' **6** .... and **7** .... are put on tape and CD.

2.21 Before you listen, read questions **8–11**.

Multiple choice

Questions **8–10**
Choose the appropriate letters **A–F.**

Which **THREE** ways can students find a book using a computer?

A By using subject keywords
B By keying in an author's first name
C By using words in a book title
D By typing in a book list
E By typing in an author's family name
F By using the information desk

8 ....
9 ....
10 ....

Question **11**
Choose the appropriate letters **A–C**

A computer ban lasts:

A 1 week
B 2 weeks
C 3 weeks

11 ....

Vocabulary

The media

1 Match the words associated with the media with the definitions **a–m**.

1 bias
2 a broadcast
3 a broadsheet
4 censorship
5 a channel
6 coverage
7 a commercial
8 journalism
9 the media
10 paparazzi
11 the press
12 a station
13 a tabloid

a newspapers and magazines, radio and television and the Internet
b newspapers and magazines
c news about something in the media
d the act of reporting the news for the media
e a programme that is received by radios or televisions
f not allowing news to be broadcast, usually for political or religious reasons
g a television station and its programmes
h an attitude which makes a person treat other people unfairly or differently
i a newspaper which contains more information about famous people than serious news
j a newspaper which contains mainly serious news
k photographers who follow famous people in order to take photographs of them for the press
l an advertisement on the television or radio
m a company that transmits radio or television programmes

2 Discuss these questions in groups.

1 Do you prefer reading a tabloid or a broadsheet? Why?
2 Should the press be free to report what it likes or should there be censorship by the government?
3 Do you think paparazzi ever act irresponsibly? If so, give an example.
4 Do newspapers in your country show political bias?

Listening 2

Section 3

1 Discuss the following questions with a partner

1 How is international news reported in your country?
2 What kind of news stories interest people in your country?

2 2.22 You are going to listen to two students talking to their tutor about their essays on news values. Before you listen, read questions **1–12**.

Questions **1–12**

Multiple options

Choose two letters from **A–E**

What are the main objectives of Gabriella's essay?

A To look at how news is shown on television
B To contrast presenters and broadcasters
C To analyse news values
D To describe the importance of the news
E To study newspapers

1 ....
2 ....

Choose one letter from **A–E**

Gabriella had problems with:

A Writing introductions
B Selecting information
C Finding newspapers
D Reading enough newspapers
E Choosing newspapers

3 ....

Table completion

Complete the following table using **NO MORE THAN TWO WORDS** for each answer.

PARAGRAPH	CONTENT	PROBLEMS
Gabriella **1**	• Negativity in news items • The preference of the general public for **4**	• Not enough reasons • Not enough examples (eg Compare **5** .... versus ....)
Gabriella **2**	• The importance of **6** .... in the news • Emphasizing why people **7** .... in the news.	None
Dong **3**	• Describing the **8** .... in the news.	• Not enough **9** .... (eg objective and subjective)

Summary completion

Complete the following summary using **NO MORE THAN THREE WORDS** for each answer.

Newspapers aim for **10** ...., namely news stories that have happened recently because this is what the public is interested in. Newspaper reporting has also been influenced by **11** .... which makes the news more immediate as we can **12** .... much faster than previously.

Speaking

Parts 1, 2 and 3

1 2.23 and 2.24 Listen to two candidates answering the Part 1 questions below. Write **Y** for Yes and **N** for No for questions **1–7** for each speaker.

Topic: Libraries

1 Do you often use a library? (Why / Why not?)
2 Are libraries popular in your country?
3 Do you think people will still visit libraries in 10 years' time? (Why / Why not?)

		Speaker 1	Speaker 2
1	Does the speaker keep going and speak for a long time without unnecessary hesitation?	☐	☐
2	Does the speaker use collocations and idiomatic expressions?	☐	☐
3	Does the speaker make many grammar mistakes?	☐	☐
4	Does the speaker use signpost language to introduce what they are saying?	☐	☐
5	Can you understand everything the speaker is saying or is their pronunciation sometimes unclear?	☐	☐
6	Does the speaker give reasons or examples to develop their answer?	☐	☐
7	Is the speaker's vocabulary repetitive?	☐	☐

2 Work in pairs. Ask each other the following Part 1 questions. Speak for 1–2 minutes about each topic.

Topic: Mobile phones

1 Are mobile phones popular in your country?
2 Is there anything you don't like about mobile phones? (Why?)

Topic: Emails

1 How often do you write emails?
2 Do you think emails are a good way to communicate with others? (Why / Why not?)

3 Look at the following Part 2 topics. Take it in turns to be the examiner and the candidate. Use the questions in exercise 1 to assess each other.

Examiner: I'd like you to speak about the following topic for 1–2 minutes. First, you have 1 minute to make notes and think about what you are going to say.

1

Describe your favourite TV programme.

You should say:
What this is about
How often you watch it
Why you like it

And you should also say what types of TV programmes are popular in your country.

2

Describe an advertisement you have seen or read that you liked.

You should say:
What it is
Where you first saw it
Why you liked it

And you should also say whether or not advertising is necessary and why.

Remember

Remember to expand your answers. You will get a higher mark for fluency if you give longer answers.

4 Now ask each other the following Part 3 questions that follow on from the topic you have spoken about in Part 2. Take it in turns to be the examiner and the candidate.

Examiner: Now I'd like to ask you a few general questions about the topic you've just been speaking about.

Topic: TV programmes

1 Compare the kind of TV programmes that children and adults usually enjoy watching.
2 Do you think that parents should control how much television their children watch?
3 Evaluate the effectiveness of television as a means of communicating the news compared with other media forms such as the internet and the radio.

Topic: Advertising

1 Should companies be targeting children in their advertising campaigns?
2 Compare the use of the internet in advertising with other media forms such as television and radio.
3 Do you think advertisements should be censored? (Why / Why not?)

Writing

Task 2

Keeping your focus

1 Re-order the words below to make sentences describing the two parts of a Task 2 question.

1 which part you the question introduces of the **TOPIC** you what subject should write The first tells about.
2 you this which the **TASK** is tells kind you what of essay should Following write.

2 Remembering the four criteria that examiners use to mark your writing will help to keep your writing focused. Match the four exam criteria to their corresponding focus (see pages 6 and 7 for review).

Exam criteria	Focus
1 Task response	A Vocabulary, collocation and spelling
2 Coherence and cohesion	B Simple / complex structures, punctuation and number of errors
3 Lexical resource	C Organization and linking
4 Grammatical range and accuracy	D Does the essay fully answer the question? Is the writer's view clear, and are the ideas relevant and well supported?

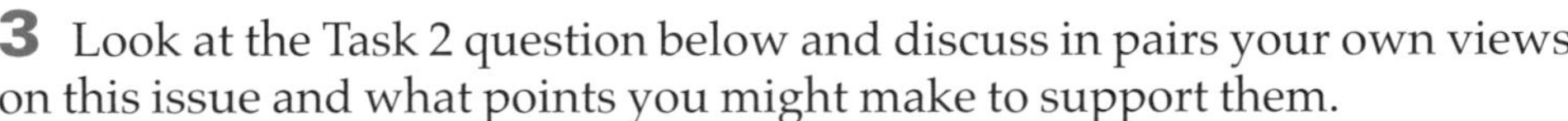

3 Look at the Task 2 question below and discuss in pairs your own views on this issue and what points you might make to support them.

An increasing number of products for children are advertised on TV. Such advertisements sometimes rely on 'pester power' to persuade parents to buy the products.*

Do you think children's products should not be advertised on television? Would this be unfair to manufacturers?

* the ability of children to make their parents buy things for them by continuing to ask for them until they agree to do it. Source: MED

Question strategy

It is important to keep looking back to the question as you write to make sure that every sentence you write is relevant to the question.

4 Read the three extracts from answers to the question above and assess them with a partner using the four exam criteria. Focus your assessment on how relevant the points are and if there are any language problems.

Student A: Extract from body paragraph 2

Also, many children already have too many toys and every year new toys are launched and children learn that by constantly asking their parents they can get them to buy more toys so it is my view that this can lead to children not being able to enjoy what they already have as they always ask for new toys. It is natural that parents want their children to have the best toys I feel it is important that they should also try to teach children to value things and to learn patience

Irrelevant point – doesn't link the ideas to the topic of advertising. First sentence too long. Punctuation mistakes.

Student B: Extract from body paragraph 1

A first point is to consider what the purpose of an advertisement is. It is to persuade consumers to buy something, and therefore it is in their nature to not mention weaknesses. For example, an advert for a luxury car may focus on the power, style and comfort rather than the high running costs. However, it could be argued that it might be useful if the public were reminded that adverts are not objective reports but highly subjective descriptions. Despite having some merits, I feel this idea is unnecessary except in the case of products aimed at children who are too young to make accurate judgements.

Student C: Extract from body paragraph 3

A problem is that if TV advertissing of childrens' produtcs was banned, then how would people learn new things? Such an idea will mean manufactories can only tell people about their things in magazines and so on. This would not be fair to those companies. I beleive that the anser is not a ban on advertissing childrens' products but for goverment to have more control over the content of adverts for childrens' produtcs.

5 Write two body paragraphs to the question using your own ideas, then swap with a partner and assess each other's writing using the four exam criteria.

Different question tasks: expecting the unexpected

Question strategy

Do not assume that the question will always be worded in the way you are familiar with – there are many different question tasks.

6 Look at the topic part of the question below and the different possible tasks.

1 Which tasks ask you to write about two aspects of the issue?
2 Which tasks ask for (a) a general focus on the topic as a whole, and (b) a specific focus on one aspect of the topic?

TOPIC STATEMENT
Newspapers should be under some governmental control to avoid the potential risks of a totally free press.*   * newspapers and news magazines. Source: MED
POSSIBLE TASKS
***0** What are the disadvantages of government control of the press?*   ***1** Write an essay giving your point of view.*   ***2** What do think are some of the problems of a free press? What measures could be taken to reduce them?*   ***3** Discuss the advantages and disadvantages of a free press.*   ***4** Do you agree or disagree? How important are newspapers in modern society?*   ***5** How do you think the internet affects issues of press freedom? Will the internet lead to an end to newspapers?*   ***6** To what extent do you agree with this statement?*

3 Match the tasks on page 163 to the sentences paraphrasing what each is asking you to do.

What the Task requires you to do

0 *Describe the possible problems of governmental control of the press.*
A Decide your view and support it. Include a discussion of the role and importance of newspapers in today's world.
B Explain both sides of the argument and give support. Conclude with your own view.
C Decide how much you agree / disagree and write an essay supporting your opinion.
D Decide your view and write an essay supporting it. Refute opposing views where relevant.
E Decide if you think the internet has an effect on the arguments surrounding press censorship. Then describe whether you think newspapers will eventually be overtaken by the internet.
F Describe some potential problems of having a free press and suggest possible solutions to these problems.

Remember

Look at Unit 6 to review the language and structure of Introductions and Unit 8 to review Conclusions.

Stating your view

7 It is important that your own view is clearly stated in your essay. Complete the table by adding the language below to show where the writer's opinion is given.

1 .... describes the problem. May state the writer's view on possible solutions. States that the essay will look at solutions.
2 .... a restatement of the writer's opinion.
3 .... states that the essay will look at both sides of the issue.
4 .... the writer's opinion.
5 .... states the writer's opinion.
6 .... the writer's opinion of the most suitable solution.

	Balanced argument essay	**Opinion essay**	**Problem & solution essay**
INTRODUCTION	Introduces the topic and .... **a.**	Introduces the topic and .... **b.**	Introduces the topic and .... **c.**
CONCLUSION	Summarizes main points and concludes with .... **d.**	Summarizes main points and concludes with .... **e.**	Summarizes main points and concludes with .... **f.**

8 A good introduction should paraphrase all the points raised in the question.

1 Read the introductory paragraph from the essay below. What do you think the question was?
2 Which essay type is it?

> **Remember**
> Avoid repeating words by using synonyms or paraphrases.

Some people argue that stronger regulations are required to censor the media from publishing stories about the private lives of famous people. This raises the question of whether privacy rules should be different for celebrities compared with members of the public. My own view is that there needs to be a distinction made between the degree of protection offered to ordinary people compared with those who have made a decision to live in the public eye.

Check your answer in the back of book, page 188.

9 Read the complete answer to the question on media censorship from exercise 8 on page 166 and complete the exercises.

1 Find synonyms for: (a) law, (b) celebrities, (c) non-celebrities in the introduction.
2 Notice how varying the word class avoids repetition eg *censorship (n) – censor (v)*. Find transformations for the question words *protect* and *privacy* in the introduction.
3 List all the media topic vocabulary including useful collocations eg *invasion of privacy*
4 Does the essay follow the structure suggested in Unit 4, page 69.
5 Do the body paragraphs follow the plan suggested in Unit 6, page 102.

Some people argue that stronger regulations are required to censor the media from publishing stories about the private lives of famous people. This raises the question of whether privacy rules should be different for celebrities compared with members of the public. My own view is that there needs to be a distinction made between the degree of protection offered to ordinary people compared with those who have made a decision to live in the public eye.

People who are not famous but who find themselves at the centre of a major news story may find the invasion of privacy extremely upsetting. Furthermore, they may lack awareness of the impact such publicity may bring, which might result in alienation from the communities in which they live. Some people would argue that the media have a right to publish any stories that are in the public interest but I feel strongly that censorship should be enforced if the individuals concerned do not agree to release the story.

In contrast, celebrities should be prepared for the attention of the media in all aspects of their lives. Indeed, many celebrities encourage the media to talk about them as this raises their profile. In such cases I do not believe that they should be able to use censorship regulations to protect themselves from negative publicity. Furthermore, I would argue that, as far as politicians and people in positions of power are concerned, it is probably a positive force to allow the media to monitor their behaviour. Whilst I would agree that having unwanted publicity must be an unpleasant experience, I firmly believe that it has to be an accepted risk of being famous.

To sum up, the issue of media censorship laws and how far these should be applied to famous people remains unresolved. My own opinion is that these laws should be strongly enforced to protect ordinary people, but more sparingly applied for celebrities who must accept that media scrutiny is part of the career they have chosen.

321 words

Further practice

10 Write a complete answer to the question below. Spend no more than 40 minutes.

Write about the following topic:

Many people believe that increasing levels of violence on television and in films is having a direct result on levels of violence in society. Others claim that violence in society is the result of more fundamental social problems such as unemployment.

How much do you think society is affected by violence in the media?

Give reasons for your answer and include any relevant examples from your own knowledge or experience.

Write at least 250 words.

Study skills

Using idiomatic expressions

REMEMBER

Idiomatic expressions are often more appropriate in speech than in writing.

1 Add the expressions in the box to the sentences. Use a dictionary to check the meaning of any you do not know. You may have to change the grammar.

a to be part and parcel	f to get the wrong end of the stick
b to be on the same wavelength	g get through the red tape
c in this day and age	h to go round in circles
d one thing that struck me about ...	i (start) from scratch
e in the long run	j to read between the lines

1 I think it's often easy to .... when you don't know someone very well. You can more easily misunderstand them because you don't really know what they're thinking.
2 I read the wrong books for my essay so even though I had already written 500 words, I had to .... and do the whole essay over again.
3 Charities sometimes find it difficult to get food aid to where it is most needed because they have to .... and deal with government regulations.
4 .... it's hard to imagine life without mobile phones.
5 Although recycling may initially cost a great deal of money, ... it will benefit the environment and could cut down on the detrimental effects caused by global warming.
6 Despite numerous meetings to solve the problem of traffic congestion, the debate kept .... and no solution was found because the local councillors could not agree.
7 We have been close friends for ages now and I can usually tell what my friend is thinking because we have so much in common and we ....
8 .... this whole issue of health is that the media influences women to have a negative body image.
9 Making mistakes .... of the learning process and it is only by correcting mistakes that learners can move to the next stage.
10 It is essential not to take situations at face value, but .... to find out what the truth is.

Dictionary focus

1 Find the words in the unit. They are all commonly found in the academic word list.

potential p.153	proportion p.153	persuade p.162
shift p.153	censorship p.158	role p.164

1 Guess their meaning from the context then check in a dictionary.
2 Which have multiple meanings or multiple word forms (eg noun and adj)?
3 Which often have dependent prepositions. What are they?

Grammar

Unit 1 Tense revision

Use

1 A verb phrase will give information about:
- time, or when something happened.
- aspect, eg whether an action is complete or incomplete, permanent or temporary.

See Unit 5 for information about active and passive uses of verbs.

2 The simple aspect is used for actions or events which we think are finished or permanent.
Present simple: used for facts, opinions and regularly occurring actions or events, eg There *are* many highly respected universities in America. I *live* in London and *travel* to work by train.
Past simple: used for regularly occurring or completed past actions or events, eg I *attended* university in London. I *travelled* on the Underground.

3 The continuous aspect (to be + present participle) is used for actions or events we think are incomplete, involve change or temporary.
Present continuous: used for temporary or incomplete present actions or events, eg The number of students attending university *is decreasing,* but we hope to see an improvement in numbers.
Past continuous: used for incomplete or interrupted past actions or events, eg The school *was preparing* its students for final exams when bad weather forced it to close.

4 The perfect aspect (to have + past participle) is used when we look back from one time to an earlier time.
Present perfect (simple or continuous): used for a present action or event which is connected to the past because it is still continuing or recently completed eg Numbers *have been falling* since last month. I'*ve* just *received* my exam results.
Past perfect (simple or continuous): used to describe a past action or event that happened before another past action or event, eg
The government *had predicted* that student numbers would improve, but instead they fell.
Universities *had been warning* the government for some time before it acted.

5 These are the main ways in which we refer to the future in English:

Future simple: used to refer to facts or to state beliefs about the future, eg I'*ll be* twenty years old on my next birthday. I don't think there *will be* an end to world conflict.

Going to: used for predictions where there is evidence for the prediction or to state intentions, eg I don't feel well – I think I'*m going to be* sick! I'*m going to study* Architecture at university.

Present continuous: used to describe arrangements, eg We'*re flying* to Paris tomorrow.

Future perfect: used for actions or events we believe will be completed by a point of time in the future, eg By the end of the year I'*ll have completed* university.

Future continuous: used to describe actions or events we believe will be in progress at a point of time in the future. Example: In five years' time fewer young people *will be studying* abroad.

See Unit 9 for more information on future tenses.

6 In academic English, verbs in the simple aspect are the most common and present simple is the most common tense.

Form

Regular and irregular verbs:
Present simple: increase; rise
Past simple: increased; rose
Future simple: will increase; will rise

Present continuous: am / is / are increasing; am / is / are rising
Past continuous: was / were increasing; was / were rising
Future continuous: will be increasing / will be rising

Present perfect: have / has increased; have / has risen
Past perfect: had increased; had risen
Future perfect: will have increased; will have risen

Present perfect continuous: have / has been increasing; have / has been rising
Past perfect continuous: had been increasing; had been rising

There is/was ...

Use

1 When we say that something 'is' or exists we can start the sentence with *There + be*. In these sentences, *there* the grammatical subject and the real subject, or what we are talking about, comes after the verb.

eg There are **many reasons** why I felt it necessary to ask you here today, eg Look! There's **snow** on the ground. (*many reasons* and *snow* are the real subjects of the sentences.)

2 *There + be* is usually used to introduce new information or topics. This new information is usually in the form of an indefinite noun or pronoun.

eg *There is* ***a lamp*** *on the table* (new information / indefinite) is more likely than *There is* ~~**the lamp**~~ *on the table* (known information / definite).
eg *There is* ***someone*** *at the door* is more likely than *There is* ~~***John***~~ *at the door*.

Form

1 We use a singular form of *to be* before a singular or countable noun, and a plural form before a plural noun. This remains true if there is more than one noun after the verb, eg ***There are some tools*** *and a bucket in the shed,* but ***There is a bucket*** *and some tools in the shed.*

2 We can use *there* as a grammatical subject with all tenses of the verb *to be*.

3 Be careful with the word order of *there + be* clauses when *to be* is followed by a participle. In these sentences the participle does **not** separate *to be* and the noun following it.

eg There **are 24 teams** competing in the tournament, NOT There ~~**are** competing **24 teams**~~ in the tournament.

There **has been an investigation** ordered into the death, NOT There ~~**has been** ordered **an investigation**~~ into the death.

4 *There* is often used with modal verbs and *seem*. In these sentences we use an infinitive form of *to be*.

eg **There must be/has to be** a reason for this. **There should be / ought to be** someone here to help you. **There seems to be** a mistake.

Practice

1 Complete the table.

Present simple	decrease	fall
Past simple	**1**	fell
Future simple	**2** will decrease	**3**
Present continuous	is decreasing	**4**
Past continuous	**5**	**6**
Future continuous	**7**	**8**
Present perfect	**9**	has fallen
Past perfect	**10**	**11**
Future perfect	**12**	**13**
Present perfect continuous	has been increasing	**14**
Past perfect continuous	**15**	**16**

2 For a Task 1 Writing question the tenses you use must match the times given in the diagram. Complete the following sentences by putting the verb in brackets into the most appropriate tense. Name each tense.

1 The number of students choosing Business __________ (increase) considerably throughout the 1980s.
2 If the trend continues, by 2025 the percentage of graduates ___________ (double).
3 For the last five years, on the job training ______ ______ (rise) steadily.
4 Figures for this year ____________ (reveal) a slight drop.
5 In the next decade, the ratio of males to females________________ (level off).
6 The table shows that retraining ______________ (grow) for the last 30 years.
7 The proportion of non-Asian students __________ (decline) gradually in 2000 but this year it ______________ (remain stable).
8 The cost of subsidies, which ____________ (fall) throughout the 1990s, __________ (begin) to rocket in 2000.

Unit 2 Sentences and their subjects

Sentences

Use

1 We use sentences to make statements, ask questions, or to make requests or give commands. A sentence can also be an exclamation.

2 We use conjunctions, eg *and, because, if, since* to show relationships between ideas in a sentence.
eg Many young people say that they smoke *because* they are unhappy.
Because links the reason for the action with the action.
eg Six out of ten boys *and* seven out of ten girls feel pressured by schoolwork.
We use *and* to add one piece of information to another.
Note: Conjunctions and other linking expressions are covered in Unit 8.

3 To use English effectively you need to know

- the meaning of conjunctions and other linking expressions in English
- how to use them grammatically in a sentence.

Form

1 A simple sentence contains one clause with a noun phrase (subject) and a verb phrase. The verb phrase must have a tense:
eg Many young people **feel** unhappy, but NOT ~~Many young people **feeling** unhappy~~

2 A compound or complex sentence contains two or more clauses joined by a conjunction. We often omit subjects and auxiliary verbs after *and, but* or *or*.
eg Many young people feel unhappy **but** (they) lack understanding of how to deal with their emotions. (The sentence has two clauses.)
eg **When** the children were asked about quality of life, England was in the bottom half of the league, **while** Dutch, Swedish and Greek young people were the happiest. (The sentence has three clauses.)

Sentence subjects

Use

1 Statements and questions in English must have a grammatical subject. See Unit 1 for sentences beginning with *There + to be …*

eg There is a book on the table, but NOT ~~Is a book on the table~~

It is raining, but NOT ~~Is raining~~

2 The sentence subject is often the agent, or person or thing responsible for an action.

eg **Alex** put the book on the table.

3 With verbs that describe states, eg *is, live, know* the subject is often the person or thing experiencing an action or state.

eg **Yun** is a doctor. **She** lives in China.

4 With a passive verb the subject is usually the person or thing affected by the action.

eg **The bank** was robbed yesterday.

Form

Subjects may take the following forms:

- Noun: **John** is a doctor.
- Pronoun: **He** is married to Alice.
- *-ing* clause: **Swimming** is his hobby.
- Infinitive clause: **To become a doctor** was John's childhood ambition.

Practice

Parts of speech 1: Revision

1 Match the parts of speech in A with their examples in B.

Example: 0–f

A	B
0 nouns	a can, must should
1 main verbs	b what, who, how
2 adjectives	c do, be, have
3 adverbs	d the, some, our
4 determiners	e and, however, nevertheless
5 pronouns	f London, book, beauty
6 auxiliary verbs	g she, her, myself
7 modal verbs	h live/ lived, swim/ swam/ swum
8 linking expressions	i heavy, quick, happy
9 question words	j heavily, quickly, hard

2 Match the expressions (1–7) with the sections of the text in italics (a–g).

1 adjective + noun
2 preposition + noun
3 determiner + noun
4 preposition + adjective + noun
5 modal verb + verb
6 linking expression
7 adjective + adjective + noun

(a) *The number* of overseas students who study (b) *at British universities* could rise to 850,000 by 2020. (c) *However*, British universities need to spend more (d) *on facilities* to continue to attract (e) *overseas students*, or they (f) *will find* (g) *many overseas students* turn to other countries, including the US Germany and France.

Parts of speech 2: Revision

1 Match the grammatical term in **A** with its definition in **B**.

A

1 infinitive
2 present participle
3 past participle
4 auxiliary verb
5 modal verb
6 phrase
7 clause
8 sentence

B

a the form of the verb ending in *-ing* ; used in progressive tenses and as an adjective, eg *living, doing*
b a verb used with another verb to show tense or to form questions, negatives or the passive, eg *do, be, have*
c a word or group of words which form a unit in a clause, eg *the boy* (noun), *is walking* (verb), *to school* (preposition)
d the basic form of the verb, eg *(to) live, (to) do*
e a group of words that expresses a statement, question or instruction; contains two or more clauses, eg *The boy is walking to school because the bus drivers have gone on strike.*
f an auxiliary verb used with a main verb to show certainty, permission or intention, eg *will, must*
g a group of words that contains a subject and a verb; is a sentence or a main part of one, eg *the boy is walking to school*
h the form of the verb ending in *-(e)d* for regular verbs; used in perfect tenses, the passive and as an adjective, eg *lived, done*

2 Match the terms (1–9) with the sections of the text in italics (a–h). For one of the terms there is no example.

1 infinitive	5 modal verb
2 present participle	6 subject / noun phrase
3 past participle	7 verb phrase
4 auxiliary verb	8 relative clause
	9 simple sentence / clause

(a) *Albert Einstein* was born in Ulm, Germany on March 14, 1879. From (b) *being* a shy child, (c) *whose parents feared his slow development*, he grew up (d) *to be* a first-rate scholar. When he left school, his record (e) *showed* the highest possible grade in geography, history, algebra, geometry and physics. In spite of this, there is a belief that he was a poor student. Perhaps this is due to the fact that he dropped out of school at the age of around 14 and rejoined his family who (f) *had* (g) *moved* to Italy. Then, during his higher education at the Zurich Polytechnic he skipped most of his classes, *hating* them because of the Polytechnic's regimented methods.
(h) *He continued his studies alone.*

Unit 3 Compound adjectives

Use

Compound adjectives are used to condense a lot of information in few words. They are more common in writing than in speech.

There are two main types of compound adjectives:

1 Compound adjectives which are original to the text in which they occur. These words will not usually be found in a dictionary.
Example: **oil-rich** shales; hydrogen **fuel-cell** activity

2 Compound adjectives which are used so commonly that they have become part of the vocabulary of the English language. These words will usually be found in a dictionary
Example: a **short-sighted** policy = a policy which shows little thought for what is likely to happen in the future

Form

1 The most commonly used compound adjectives are formed in the following ways:
   1 adverb + adjective, eg **environmentally friendly**
   2 adverb + participle, eg **highly strung; well-known**
   3 adjective + participle, eg **best-selling; hard-working; ready-made; short-sighted**
   4 noun + participle, eg **king-sized; man-eating; face-saving**
   5 adjective + noun, eg **full-time; high-speed**
   6 noun + adjective, eg **accident-prone; lead-free; sugar-coated; tax-free**

2 Compound adjectives usually come before the noun they describe. However, they can also come after certain verbs.

Example: He's a **well-known film star**.
He**'s** quite **well known.**

Practice

Replace the relative clause in italics. Use an appropriate compound adjective below.

environmentally friendly face-saving
hard-working high-speed lead-free
ready-made sugar-coated

0 Firms will compete to employ individuals with talent *who are willing to work hard.*
Firms will compete to employ hard-working individuals with talent.

1 There is an increased demand for products *which do not cause pollution*
2 Sales of petrol *which has no added lead* have soared in recent years.
3 Many doctors still prefer to prescribe tablets *which are covered in sugar* for children.
4 Many commuters now travel from London to Paris on trains *which travel very quickly.*
5 Foods *which have been prepared in advance* are a popular choice for working parents.
6 The government was forced to make a compromise *which would avoid further embarrassment.*

Unit 4 Defining and non-defining relative clauses

1 **Relative pronouns:** We form relative clauses using these relative pronouns: *which, who, whom, whose, that, where, when, why*. *Which, who* and *that* are used most frequently.

Example: Chocolate contains substances **which** are known to affect the hypothalamus.

Example: Men **who** eat modest amounts of chocolate live longer.

2 **Defining relative clauses**: these identify the person or thing we are talking about. They provide essential information in the sentence. In defining relative clauses we can use *that* in place of *who, whom* or *which.*

Example: Example: Chocolate contains substances **which/that** are known to affect the hypothalamus.

Example: Men **who/that** eat modest amounts of chocolate live longer.

Non-defining relative clauses: these add extra information or a second idea to the main idea. Non-defining relative clauses do not provide important or necessary information and are separated from the rest of the sentence with commas.

Example: Peter**, who/whom** I introduced you to last night**,** is the new Regional Manager.

We cannot replace the relative pronoun with *that.*

3 **Subject and object relative clauses**

The relative pronoun can replace the subject or the object of the relative clause.

Subject: Chocolate contains substances **which/that ~~(they)~~ are** known to affect the hypothalamus.

The subject relative pronoun is followed by a verb. We cannot leave out the pronoun.

Object: Chocolate is something **which/that/zero many people** feel guilty about eating **~~(it)~~.**

The object relative pronoun is followed by another noun or pronoun. If the clause is defining we can leave out the relative pronoun altogether.

I see an excellent doctor, **who/whom a colleague** recommended.

Whom is more formal then *who.*

4 **Participle clauses:** In academic writing it is common to replace a relative clause with a clause containing a past or present participle.

With an active verb we use a present participle. When the active verb is progressive we leave out the relative pronoun and the verb *to be*.

Active verb: The woman ~~who is~~ **sitting** next to the door has been looking at you. Do you know her?

When the verb is passive we keep the past participle and leave out the relative pronoun and the verb *to be*.

Passive verb: The article ~~which was~~ **published** in yesterday's *Times* could be useful.

Note: We cannot reduce the relative clause when the relative pronoun is the object of the clause.

eg The man who(m) I was telling you about is over there, NOT ~~The man I telling you about is over there~~.

Practice

Are these sentences right (R) or wrong (W)? Correct those which are wrong.

1 I was given a prescription for an acne medication which worked wonders for my complexion.

2 There are powerful forces, that are affecting the way doctors treat their patients.

3 Your doctor is not supposed to be an authority whom determines the course of action necessary.

4 Many drugs are available as over-the-counter remedies that consumers choose them themselves.

5 The patient has become like a customer ordering from a menu.

6 A sick patient is visiting a healthy care-giver will be entering into a one-sided relationship.

7 There is an inequality in the doctor–patient relationship that no amount of education can resolve it.

8 Governments, that are worried about the increasing cost of medication, are reluctant to pay for it.

9 Consumers, encouraged by drug companies, are becoming increasingly confident about their ability to make medical decisions.

Unit 5 The passive

Use

1 We use the passive when the person or thing responsible for the action, or the agent, is unknown, obvious or is less important than the action, event or process. The passive is commonly used in academic writing and in descriptions of processes.

2 In many passive sentences the agent is not mentioned.
Hurricanes **are named** to avoid confusion about which storm **is being described**. (No agent).

3 We do not mention the agent when the subject of the active sentence is a pronoun.
eg **We** name all tropical hurricanes. All tropical hurricanes are named ~~**by us**~~.

Form

We form the passive using the verb *to be* in the same tense as the active verb followed by the past participle of the active verb. When the agent is mentioned we use the preposition *by*.
eg The scale for measuring wind speed *was devised* **by** Sir Francis Beaufort.
The most commonly used active–passive transformations are:

	Active	Passive
Present simple	identify / identifies	am / is / are identified
Present continuous	am / is / are identifying	am / is / are being identified
Present perfect	has / have identified	has / have been identified
Past simple	identified	was / were identified
Past continuous	was / were identifying	was / were being identified
Past perfect	had identified	had been identified
Future simple	will identify	will be identified
Future perfect	will have identified	will have been identified
Modal verbs	will / may / could etc. identify	will / may / could etc. be identified

Practice

1 Put the verbs in brackets into an appropriate passive tense.

Did you know?

1 To meet the demand for hardwood, 4.5 million hectares of rainforest **1** ________ (log) each year. Hardwoods take hundreds of years to mature, so they **2** ________ (cannot/easily/ replace).

2 Topsoil can take 1000 years to develop, and yet it **3** ________ (can/destroy) in less than 10 years.

3 The rainforest contains such a density of plants that it **4** ________ (call) 'the lungs of the world'. The atmosphere on which life depends **5** ________ (create) by the exchange of oxygen and carbon dioxide which takes place when sunlight **6** ________ (convert) into energy.

4 Forests absorb solar energy. Now that they are disappearing, the 'shininess' of the earth's surface **7** ________ (alter). As a consequence, in the near future wind currents and rainfall **8** ________ (disrupt) and weather patterns worldwide **9** ________ (affect).

Unit 6 Conditional sentences

Use

1 We use **real** conditionals to talk about a possible situation and its result.
If/When you *boil* water, it *evaporates*. = The situation is always true.
If public awareness *is raised*, then real changes *will take* place. = The speaker believes that the change is likely if public awareness is raised.

2 We use **unreal** conditionals to talk about unlikely, hypothetical or imaginary situations.
If tourists *were* more considerate, there *would be* far less damage to the environment. = The speaker believes it is unlikely that tourists will be considerate.
If laws *had been enacted* earlier, there *would be* fewer issues to discuss today. = The past cannot be changed.

3 The modals used in conditionals are often *will* and *would*. However, other modals like *could*, *may* and *might* can be used to express less certainty about the result.

1 In first and second conditional main clauses we use *may*, *might* and *could* in similar ways to talk about possibility.
If X happens, then Y *could/may/might* happen.

2 *Could* ***not*** and *could* ***not*** *have done* can change the meaning of the main clause.
If tourism were banned, then many businesses *may/might not survive*. = It's possible that many businesses would not survive.
If tourism were banned, then many businesses *could not survive*. = It's certain that many businesses would be unable to survive.

3 Unless has the same meaning as If … not …
If X *doesn't happen*, Y will happen = *Unless* X happens, Y will happen.

4 *Provided (that)* and *unless* cannot be used in unreal conditionals.

Unless new laws are enacted, future generations will pay the price.
~~Unless new laws had been enacted, future generations would have paid the price.~~
Provided new laws are enacted, future generations will have fewer worries.
~~Provided new laws had been enacted, future generations would have had fewer worries.~~

Form

1 In real conditionals when the outcome is always true, we can use:

If/When + present tense, present simple
When *it snows/is snowing*, the children *love* to go outside to play.

When the outcome is likely to happen, we can use:
If + present, will/could/may/might
If you *tell/are telling* me the truth, I'*ll forgive* you.

2 In unreal conditionals when we talk about an unlikely or hypothetical situations in the future, we can use:
If + past simple/continuous, would/could/may/might + infinitive
If I *had* enough money, *I'd buy* a new car.

In more formal speech and writing we often use *were* in place of *was* after if:
eg If tourism *was/were* banned, businesses would be affected.

When we talk about an imaginary situation in the past, we can use:
If + past perfect, would/could/may/might have done/do
If you *had told* me the truth, I *could have forgiven/could forgive* you.

Practice

Re-write each sentence so that it contains the word in capitals.

0 Anyone who wishes to work in the tourist industry must speak English and one other language. IF
If you wish to work in the tourist industry, you must speak English and one other language.
1 The city was not chosen as the venue for the Olympics because the public transport system was inadequate. WOULD
2 Because governments don't invest enough money in protecting the environment, future generations will suffer the consequences. UNLESS
3 Assuming no delays, we should be at our destination by midday tomorrow. PROVIDED
4 Winning the lottery would allow me to travel the world. WON
5 The government ignored economic warnings and as a result the country is in recession. IF
6 Edward doesn't speak Spanish so he wasn't offered the job in South America. BEEN
7 Before the invention of the airplane travel to distant parts of the world was impossible for most people. WOULD
8 It's best not to apply for the job if you really don't want it. UNLESS

Unit 7 *That* - clauses

Use

1 *That* may be used as a conjunction which connects a clause to a larger sentence. *That* has no real meaning.

2 Clauses beginning with *that* may:

  1 report speech, thoughts, feelings or information
  eg The Prime Minister has **announced that** he will step down.
  eg Tests **show that** the drug is safe and effective.
  2 indicate an attitude towards a situation or event
  eg The Prime Minister is **certain/confident** that the war will be won.
  eg It is **unlikely that** he will prove to be correct.

Form

1 *That*-clauses can occur after verbs (*announced, show*) or adjectives (*certain, confident, unlikely*).
2 *That*-clauses may follow verbs or adjectives in sentences beginning with *It*.
eg It is **hoped/unlikely** that the situation will improve.
3 *That*-clauses which form the subject of a sentence may follow *The fact (that)...* or *In spite of/Despite the fact (that)...*
eg **The fact that unemployment has fallen** (sentence subject) does not necessarily mean that the economy is strong.
4 *That*-clauses should not be confused with defining relative clauses where the relative pronoun (*that, who, which,* etc.) replaces either the subject or object of the relative clause.
That - clause: It is clear *that immediate action must be taken.*
The clause following *that* contains all of its grammatical parts and could function independently as a sentence.
Relative clause: I have a number of ideas *that ~~(they)~~ could help to improve the situation.*
The relative pronoun *that* replaces the subject of the clause. The relative clause could not function independently as a sentence.

5 Some reporting verbs, eg *tell*, take a direct object before the *that*-clause.
eg Alex **said** that if I wanted the job I should apply for it.
eg Alex **told me** that if I wanted the job I should apply for it.

Practice

Put the verbs into the table. Use a dictionary to help you.

admit announce argue assume assure
claim convince deny estimate inform
insist persuade point out remind recognize

Verb + *that*-clause eg *say that*	Verb + Object + *that*-clause eg *tell someone that*

Unit 8 Linking expressions

Use

1 We use linking expressions to show:
  a the relationships between ideas in a sentence or paragraph
  b the structure of a text

2 We often use linking expressions in academic writing and argument to:
  a show that an action, event or conclusion is a result or consequence of something: *so, *therefore, *thus, as a result.
  b support (through an example) or restate information or arguments: *for example, **eg, that is, **ie, such as
  c show a contrast between two ideas or between less important information and the main point: *although, *however, despite, in spite of, nevertheless, on the other hand, whereas / while
  d list or add information or reasons to support an argument: first, second, lastly, *furthermore, in addition, as well as
  e explain purpose: *in order to; in order / so that, *so as to
  f to indicate a reason: because (of), since

3 Linking expressions are also used in academic writing to:
  a express time: *when, after, before, until, as, since
  b express a condition: *if, unless (See Unit 6)
  *These expressions are common in academic writing.
  **These expressions are not commonly used in academic writing.

Form

1 Conjunctions connect clauses to form a sentence.
  eg He left his parent's home **because** he wanted to live independently.
  Because he wanted to live independently, he left his parents' home.
  a Some prepositions also act in this way, but prepositions are followed by a noun, eg *despite, in spite of, because of* + noun.
  eg **Despite growing** up in a city, he preferred country living.
  Despite the fact that he grew up in a city, he preferred country living.

  b Some words can act as prepositions or conjunctions, eg *since.*
  eg He hasn't lived at his parents' home **since** last month. (preposition)
  Since he was no longer living at his parent's home, he was forced to spend less. (conjunction)
  c Some conjunctions can express more than one meaning, eg *as, since, while.*
  eg **Since** he's left, the house has felt empty. (time)
  Since he had to stop and change the tire, he was delayed. (reason)

2 Linking adverbials connect a sentence to another sentence or to a paragraph.
  eg Finding somewhere to live can be difficult. **However,** the more time and money you have to spend the easier it can be. **For example**, …
  a In academic writing, the most common place for the adverbial is at the front of the sentence. The next most common position is between the noun and the verb.
  eg **Therefore**, our work here is finished.
  Our work here, **therefore**, is finished.
  b Most, but not all, adverbials at the front of a sentence are followed by a comma.

Practice

Complete the first part of a Task 2 essay with an appropriate linking expression.

Some people argue that city officials should provide public works of art, **1** _____ others argue that they should put resources into efficient services and an effective infrastructure, **2** _____ communications and transport systems.

3 _____ putting a focus on infrastructure seems sensible, it does not necessarily mean that this would always be in the best interests of the city. In many cities, public art attracts people, **4**_____ making them popular locations to work and visit. **5** _____, the popularity of London is partly due to the famous buildings and statues, **6**_____ the city having some serious infrastructure problems with an aging underground and a congested road system.

7_____, I believe that public art is a major factor in a city retaining a skilled workforce and remaining an attractive destination for tourists.

Unit 9 Talking about the future

1 For some of the ways in which we refer to the future in English see Unit 1.

2 When we are talking about future events there is always a degree of certainty attached to what we say. We use *will* and *shall* to show that we are very certain that an event will take place. Other modals like *may, might* and *could* show that we are less certain about the likelihood of an event.
eg By 2050 the world's population **will have exceeded** 1 billion in number. (The speaker is certain.)
By 2050 the world's population **may have exceeded** 1 billion in number. (The speaker is less certain.)

3 We also use expressions like *certainly, (un)likely, probably* and *possibly* to show how certain we are about something happening.
eg They**'ll probably be** late, because they nearly always are, NOT ~~They may probably be late~~.

Form

1 We form the future perfect using *will have + past participle*.
eg By next year **I'll have finished** my College course.
2 We form the future continuous using *will be + present participle*.
eg By 2050 the majority of the world's population **will be living** in cities.
3 We say X ***will*** *probably/definitely/certainly* + **infinitive** ..., but X *probably/definitely/certainly* ***won't*** + **infinitive** ...
eg He **will probably be** late BUT
He **probably won't be** on time.

Complete these sentences. Use either the future perfect or the future continuous.

1 In the next century, people (live) on the moon.
2 By 2050, scientists (discover) how to turn lead into gold.
3 Twenty years from now, doctors (produce) the first human clone.
4 In the 21st century people (use) virtual technology for home entertainment, in place of television.
5 By 2010 all fuel-burning engines (replace) by 'greener' energy devices.
6 By 2100 humans (travel) to different galaxies to explore and colonize.

Unit 10 Articles

1 The indefinite article (a / an) is used with singular countable nouns. We use *a/an*
a when the person or thing is new to the reader / listener because the person or thing
- has not been mentioned before.
- is not already known to the reader / listener.

b when we mean any person or thing of a particular type.
eg You need **a dictionary** for this exercise.
c when we say what type, class or group something belongs to, or what job someone has.
eg My father is **a computer programmer**.
d with a singular countable noun when we use one example to make a generalization. Note that zero article with a plural noun has a similar meaning.
eg **A computer** needs to be checked occasionally for viruses. or **Computers** need to be checked regularly for viruses.
e with some expressions of quantity, eg *a few, a lot, a great deal*

2 The definite article (the) is used with countable and uncountable nouns. We use *the:*
a when the reader / listener knows which person or thing we are referring to because:
- the person or thing has been mentioned before.
- it is obvious because there is only one, eg *the sun, the earth, the beginning/end*
- it is clear from the context or situation.

eg Would you open **the window**, please?
b with singular countable nouns when we make a general statement about a class or group of people or things. Note that we can use the zero article in the same way.
eg **The car** is a popular means of transport, or **Cars** are a popular means of transport.
c when we refer to parts of a thing or parts of the body.
eg Using a computer can cause injury to **the wrists and arms**.
d before dates or periods of time, eg *the 12th of September, the 1980s.*
e when we explain which person or thing we are referring to by using a relative clause or a prepositional phrase,
eg **The school** which I attend specializes in Information Technology.

f before an adjective to form a noun which refers to a group or class.
eg **The rich** have better access to information than **the poor**.

g Other uses:
- before superlative adjectives, eg *the most efficient* system
- before the names of seas, deserts, rivers or groups of mountains, eg *the Pacific Ocean, the Thames, the Sahara, the Alps*
- before plural countries and republics, eg *the United States, the Republic of China*

3 Zero article (Ø) is used with uncountable and plural countable nouns when we are referring to people or things in a general way.
eg **Information** is widely available. (information in general)
The information they sent was misleading. (specific information)
Other uses:
- before institutions in general, eg She is in (Ø) hospital. He goes to (Ø) school.
- when talking about travelling by a particular form of transport, eg I travel to work by (Ø) car, bus, etc.
- before the names of individual mountains or lakes, eg the Himalayas but (Ø) Mount Everest; the Great Lakes but (Ø) Lake Superior
- before the names of streets, towns, countries, counties, states or continents, eg I come from (Ø) Canada.
- before the names of meals, eg What time is (Ø) dinner?

Practice

Complete the text. Use *a/an, the* or leave the space blank.

Research into mass communication research started at 1 ___ beginning of 2 ___ twentieth century. However, it was not until after 3 ___ Second World War in 4___ United States that 5 ___ possibility of 6 ___ communication science was first discussed. In fact, it was 7 ___ mathematician, Claude Shannon, who first provided the stimulus to 8 ___ social scientists to think about 9 ___ communication in model form.

Vocabulary

Unit 1 Word formation

1 Complete the table. Use your dictionary to help you.

	Subject	Person	Adjective
A	astronomy	**0** *astronomer*	**1**
B	**2**	biologist	**3**
C	chemistry	**4**	**5**
D	mathematics	**6**	**7**
E	**8**	neurologist / neuroscientist	**9**
F	physics	**10**	**11**
G	psychology	**12**	**13**
H	**14**	sociologist	**15**

2 Match each subject to the description of what it studies.

0 structure of substances and how they react with one another *chemistry*
1 stars and planets ____________
2 numbers and shapes ____________
3 the mind and behaviour ____________
4 living things ____________
5 society ____________
6 forms of energy, eg heat, light ____________

Unit 2 Collocation

It is important to learn which words often go together to make natural sounding English. This is called collocation.

1 Find adjectives from the box that commonly collocate with the abstract nouns below. You can use some adjectives more than once.

disruptive anti-social
expensive
violent healthy negative
relaxed stressful

1 (i) ____________ (ii) ____________ (iii) ____________ + **attitude**
2 (i) ____________ (ii) ____________ (iii) ____________ + **behaviour**
3 (i) ____________ (ii) ____________ (iii) ____________ + **lifestyle**

2 Look up the following words and answer the questions.

0 **disabled** Is the stress on the same syllable as *disability*?

No - dis'abled disa'bility (pronunciation)

1 **deal** What phrasal verbs can be made from this word and which one means *to act in order to solve a problem*? Does it require an object?
2 **deteriorate** What is the noun form and is it countable?
3 **pressure** What are the different meanings of this word and which one is being used in the following sentence? *There is now pressure on ministers to change the law.*
4 **social** What compounds and collocations are there for this word?
5 **employ** What other words can be made from this root word?
6 **government** Does this take a singular or plural verb?
7 **yob** Is this a frequently used word and would it be suitable for an IELTS essay?
8 **adolescent** Which silent letter might cause this word to be spelt incorrectly?
9 **change** What other ways can you find to say this?
10 **cause (v)** Find alternatives for this word that would be suitable for academic writing.

Unit 3 Dependent prepositions

1 Complete the paragraph with suitable dependent prepositions. Use a dictionary to help you.

If energy efficiency has so much potential, why isn't everyone pursuing it? One obstacle is that many people have confused efficiency **1** _____ discomfort. Another is that energy users do not recognize how much they can benefit **2** ____ improving efficiency because saved energy comes **3**____ millions **4** ____ invisibly small pieces rather than big chunks. Most people lack the time to learn **5** _____ modern efficiency techniques. And scores **6** _____ ingrained habits actually reward waste. Yet relatively simple changes can turn all these obstacles **7** ____ business opportunities. Enhancing efficiency is the most vital step **8** ____ creating a climate-safe energy system.

Adapted extract from Scientific American 2005.

2 Complete the table. Write in the missing parts of speech.

Verb	Noun	Adjective
1	consumption	**2**
3	**4**	derived (from)
5	**6**	renewable
7	shortage	**8**
9	**10**	refining / refined
X	detriment	**11**
12	speculator / speculation	**13**
14	**15**	alternative
expand	**16**	**17**
maintain	**18**	**19**
X	**20**	convenient

Unit 4 Vocabulary

1 1 Match these adjectives with the part of the body they refer to.

1 cardiac	a eyes
2 dental	b nose
3 gastric	c kidneys
4 nasal	d heart
5 optical	e ears
6 orthopaedic	f teeth
7 renal	g bones, muscles
8 auditory	h stomach

2 Use your dictionary to find one or two nouns which collocate with each word, eg *auditory nerve damage*, page 62.

2 Complete the word families below by looking up the given word in your dictionary. Where there is more than one form of the word note the difference in meaning.

Verb	Adjective(s)	Noun(s)
reduce		
		relaxant +
		stimulant +
	irritating	
confuse		
		reaction

The definitions below are for words made with the prefix *Counter-*.

1 What does this prefix mean?
2 Find the correct word in your dictionary to match each definition.

1 having the opposite result to the one intended
2 to reduce the negative effect of something by doing something that has an opposite effect
3 to have an effect that is equal and opposite to something else
4 actions taken to stop something else from happening or having a negative effect

Record the four words in your writing Task 2 vocabulary bank

Unit 5 Weather words: Adjective and noun collocations

1 Choose four adjectives which collocate with each noun and write them in the box.

blazing bright ~~changeable~~ fair gale-force
gusty hazy heavy light (x2) low mild
pouring scattered strong thick thunder
torrential unseasonable wintry

0 changeable	weather
	rain
	sunshine
	wind
	snow
	cloud

Unit 6 Dependent prepositions

Complete the sentences with a suitable preposition.

1 A major cause _____ accidents is drivers going too fast.
2 Any change _____ lifestyle can have an effect _____ your health.
3 The subject _____ cloning raises a number _____ ethical issues.
4 Traffic congestion causes serious problems _____ drivers.
5 Fuel-efficient cars have already gone _____ production.
6 The reasons _____ the present crisis are various.
7 The crash resulted _____ the deaths of all the passengers.
8 Solar energy offers a low cost solution _____ our fuel problems.
9 The figures indicate an upward trend _____ sales.

Unit 7

Complete each sentence with an appropriate reporting verb.

admit announce assure claim deny inform persuade remind

1 He __________ me that the report would be ready in time for the presentation as promised.
2 The CEO __________ the allegations that his company had acted illegally.
3 He __________ that no evidence had been found to support the allegations of illegal behaviour.
4 The company spokesman __________ that sales figures for this quarter would be lower than predicted.
5 They managed to __________ him that he was not to blame for the difficulties the firm was experiencing.
6 He __________ (already) the firm that he has made the decision to leave.
7 He __________ last week that regrettably he would be unable to continue to work for us.
8 She __________ me that we had met some years before at a conference.

Unit 8 Dependent prepositions

Complete each sentence. Use one word from List 1 as a noun or verb and one word from List 2. You can use any word more than once.

1 concern design make protect support take
2 about against as by for (x2) from in of up

0 The building was *made of* glass, marble and concrete.
1 The need for cities to expand must be balanced against a _____ _____ the environment.
2 The new art gallery was originally _____ _____ a stately home.
3 In warm weather, shutters will _____ a house _____ the effects of the sun.
4 Many people are justifiably _____ _____ the lack of housing and the rising property prices.
5 Many insurance policies will not _____ your home _____ flood damage.
6 The workforce is _____ _____ of a large proportion of women.
7 You can see from their size that these apartments were _____ _____ people with a physical disability.
8 The ceiling is _____ _____ high stone columns.
9 I promised to _____ him _____ his campaign to become mayor of the city.

Unit 9

1 1 Complete the table. Use different forms of the words.

Noun	Adjective	Adverb
1	probable	**2**
possibility	**3**	**4**
5	**6**	certainly
likelihood	**7**	X

2 Re-write each sentence, starting as shown, so that the meaning stays the same.

0 It's probable that scientists will discover a cure for cancer this century.

Scientists will probably discover a cure for cancer this century.

1 It's possible that a solution to world poverty will be found.
There's a …
2 People will almost certainly be taking holidays in space by the end of the century.
It's almost …
3 The likelihood of developing heart disease is increased in people who smoke.
People who smoke …

2

summarize	justify	analyse	discuss

Match the question task words in the box above to the sentences.

1 Although many educators believe that the internet could replace teachers in the future, closer inspection suggests that this is clearly not the case. The reason for this is that there will always be a need for learners to have more complex concepts explained to them face to face. As yet, this is something that a machine cannot do.
2 Overall, the major disadvantages of using email are the negative effects it may have on health and communication. Finally, while there can be no denying that emails have made global communication more efficient, they should not be allowed to replace personal communication.
3 One of the dangers of the internet as a communicative tool is that it is difficult to control the information that is stored on it. Some attempts have been made to do this, but the sheer volume of information makes this an almost impossible task.
4 Although it is certainly true that space travel has taught mankind a great deal about the universe, there is still the argument that too much money is being spent on this. I am convinced that governments need to focus their spending on concerns closer to home, like health care, education and the environment. These should be their primary targets because they affect the general public in a more direct way.

Unit 10

1 Complete the table with the missing noun or adjective form of the words. The missing words appear in the Reading passage on page 153. Use the paragraph numbers in brackets () to help you to locate them.

Adjective	Noun
0 organized	organization
social (1)	**1**
(1)	**2** literacy
published (1)	**3**
efficient (2)	**4**
fundamental (2)	**5**
innovative (2)	**6**
informative (2)	**7**
8	privacy (2)
9	tradition (2)
technological (5)	**10**
11	number (5)
12	commerce (5)

2 Check the meaning of the words in the box then read the text on mobile phones and fill the gaps. All the words are from Unit 10 and are included in the academic word list.

~~evaluation~~ distinctly design primarily conclude computer principles seek acquired impact range

The Mobile Revolution

Any (0) _evaluation_ of modern technology would (1) __________ that the growth of mobile phone ownership as well as innovations in (2) __________ have had a major (3) __________ on the world of communication. Through applying the (4) __________ of digital technology, mobiles have (5) __________ a (6) __________ of extra uses. Modern mobiles used to be (7) __________ devices for speaking to other people but now they are also capable of many (8) __________ different functions, including text messaging, email, internet, digital photography and video. As manufacturers (9) __________ to include more facilities, some designers believe that the mobile phone will eventually be capable of being your (10) __________, music & film player, TV, radio, games console and personal organizer.

Additional material

Unit 6

Speaking (page 100)

3

Describe the car you own or would like to buy **A**

You should say:
What type of car it is
What you use it for
Why you chose it

And you should also say why you prefer a car to any other form of transport

4

1 Do you think it's better to travel alone or in a group?
2 Does tourism only have a positive effect on a country?
3 Do you think long-distance travelling will still be popular in the future?
4 What is the most popular tourist attraction in your country and do you think it will still be popular in 10 years' time?
5 Will there be any changes in the way people choose to travel in the future?
6 Give possible reasons why people like to go travelling.

Unit 10

Speaking (page 161)

Look at the following Part 3 speaking questions on modern technology. Take it in turns to be the candidate and the examiner. Check that the 'candidate' has answered the question appropriately by using the table in exercise 1.

1 Assess the ways in which email and text messaging has affected the way children learn to read and write.
2 Speculate on how society might survive and function without modern technologies, like the internet and satellite communication.
3 Justify the use of the internet as an advertising tool.
4 Evaluate how technology has affected the way people communicate.
5 Describe how the internet has affected people's shopping habits.
6 Compare the speed of life now to what it was in the last century.

Unit 7 Editing your writing

1 It is a good idea to edit your writing to check that it is clear and accurate.

Read the following table and decide what kind of writer you are.

Poor writer	Average writer	Good writer
Band Scores : 2–4	Band Scores: 5–6	Band Scores: 7–9
1 Does not check if what they have written is accurate.	**1** Sometimes checks that what they have written is accurate.	**1** Makes sure that what they have written is accurate and that the facts are correct.
2 Does not control the length. Writes too little.	**2** Sometimes controls the length.	**2** Writes the correct amount and does not write more words than the question requires.
3 Has no clear sense of purpose in writing. Does not really know why they are writing and does not clearly understand the topic.	**3** Knows why they are writing, but does not clearly understand the topic.	**3** Defines the purpose clearly in their introduction. Knows exactly what they are writing about and has a good understanding of the topic and the question.
4 Works in any order and does not write a plan.	**4** Does not always write with a plan.	**4** Prepares and plans writing well.
5 Is unable to change the style of writing to suit different topics and questions.	**5** Can only slightly change the writing style.	**5** Has the flexibility to change the style of writing to suit different topics and questions.
6 The writing has too many grammar, spelling and punctuation mistakes which badly affect communication.	**6** The writing has many grammar, spelling and punctuation mistakes.	**6** Writes correctly and pays attention to grammar, spelling and punctuation. Checks work for mistakes before handing it in.
7 Has a limited vocabulary.	**7** Uses too much repetitive and memorized vocabulary.	**7** Has a wide vocabulary and is always developing their vocabulary by learning new words and expressions and then using this vocabulary in their writing.
8 Writes untidily. The handwriting is difficult to read.	**8** Writes neatly, but not everything is clear.	**8** Writes neatly.

Word missing	ʎ
Wrong word	WW
Tense	T
Article	art
Grammar / structure	g
Singular / plural	s/p
Spelling	Sp
Countable / uncountable	c/u
Punctuation	P
Your meaning is not clear or impossible to understand	M?
Wrong verb form	Vb
Your verb and subject do not agree	Ag
Start a new paragraph here	NP

1 Correct the following paragraph using the correction key provided.

These days increasing numbers of people choose to travel by plane. The main reason for this is convenient way to travel long distances. Travelling long distance are an essential part of many people's lives. It is certainly true that the time is money therefore air travel can save companies a substantial amount of money, also it can be seen that this factor. In certain parts of the world particularly in remote places like islands air travel is often the only option However, air companies have a responsibilities to ensure passengers is safe. To ensure passengers are safe means to have regular safety checks on planes to keep the planes in good working order.

Look at some of your own writing. Use the correction key to help you correct six grammar and punctuation mistakes.

Unit 6

Speaking (page 100)

3 **B**

Talk about a place you would really like to visit

You should say:
Where it is and when you went there
Why you want to go there
Who you would want to travel with
And you should also say whether or not travelling is important to you.

Unit 10

Writing (page 165)

8 *Tougher censorship is required to protect the privacy of celebrities from unwanted media attention. Privacy should be respected whether someone is famous or not.*

Do you agree or disagree?

Writing

Unit 1

Model answer for Writing on p22

The diagram shows staff training by four companies for the period 2003 to 2006. In 2003, companies A, B and C had similar levels (between 25% and 28%), with company D significantly lower at 20%. By 2006 all companies had increased their training with D rising substantially to become the second largest at 35% whilst A grew less, ending about 10% lower than the others.

A and B showed similar trends rising slightly in 2004, falling a little in 2005 then growing more steadily in 2006 with the gap between them gradually increasing. In contrast, C and D showed very different changes. In 2003 training by D fell to a low of about 17% whilst C rose steeply reaching a high of over 35%. After significant growth by D, and a steady decline by C in 2004, the two companies converged in 2005 with C peaking at around 37% and D at 35%.

Overall, it can be seen that staff training for all four companies increased, although following very different trends. (171 words)

Comments

The answer follows the plan given on page 22. Firstly, the diagram is introduced then there is a description of some of the main features supported by figures from the diagram. In the second paragraph, the other changes and differences are described. There is good use of language to describe changes over time. The answer ends by describing the overall pattern.

Unit 2

Model answer for Writing on p38

In modern society, violence in schools is rising and playground bullying seems to be increasing. The issue is whether or not parents should deal with this problem by teaching their children to fight back. The arguments on both sides of this debate need to be examined carefully.

Many people believe that violence only breeds further violence. Evidence for this is found in research which shows that children who grow up in violent families often grow up to be violent themselves. Furthermore, some children may enjoy the power associated with violence and develop into bullies. However, there are examples of bullying being stopped as a result of victims hitting back. This shows that there are occasions when violence may help to end bullying.

However, looking at the issue in the long term, there is a strong case for supporting parents who promote anti-violent behaviour. If children can learn that there are other ways of solving disagreement, then it is possible that when those children become adults they will behave similarly and try to resolve conflict through discussion and compromise rather than by force. In my view this is a powerful argument for encouraging a non-violent approach to school bullies.

Another aspect of this issue is the fact that bullying occurs in school time when parents are not present. Hence, it could be argued that it is better for schools to deal with this problem by promoting anti-bullying policies and offering support to victims. Although this makes practical sense, it ignores the fundamental effect that parents can have on their children.

In conclusion, despite there being circumstances when a violent response to bullying may be justified, it is my belief that teaching non-violent strategies is more productive in the long term. Also, although schools have a role to play, it is the parents who can have the most significant effect.

(303 words)

Comments

The essay follows a similar plan to the one on page 37 and states that the essay will take a 'balanced argument' approach. The three body paragraphs each have a clear point and are well supported. The essay considers arguments on both sides of the debate but also makes the writer's own opinion clear throughout. A good range of linking expressions are used to link ideas within as well as between sentences.

Unit 3

Model answer for Writing on p54

The table shows different sources of fuel for producing electricity and their percentage use in five European countries in 2001. Generally, the five countries showed a significant difference in their patterns of consumption. Taking nuclear fuel first, Belgium had the highest percentage at 58%, with Sweden second at 45%. In marked contrast, Italy used no nuclear power at all. Turning to Coal and Lignite, Germany and Britain used this to generate a large proportion of their electricity (50% and 34% respectively), a much higher percentage than the remaining countries.

Regarding Petroleum products, Italy produced 27% of its electricity from this source. In comparison, the other countries only generated 2% or less of their electricity from this fuel. However, Hydro and Wind reveal another pattern with Sweden producing almost half of its electricity (49%) this way (over twice as high as Italy which had the second highest percentage at 20%). Finally, a significant amount was produced from other sources with three countries (Britain, Italy and Sweden) generating around 40% of their electricity from other fuels.

Overall, it can be seen that there was a significant variation in which fuels countries used to generate their electricity. (195 words)

Comments

After briefly summarizing the main pattern, the writer describes the main differences and similarities in each of the fuel types. There is good use of language to make comparisons. The answer ends with a description of the overall pattern. Note that it would also be possible to describe the table by comparing countries.

Unit 4

Model answer for Writing 1 on p65

Recent advances in drug technology have resulted in doctors prescribing drugs more frequently. While this development has many benefits, it may promote a focus on treating symptoms at the cost of causes. I partly agree with this view although there are situations where making symptoms the priority is valid. This essay will seek to examine this complex issue.

It is my view that drugs are often prescribed for recurring ailments such as headaches with no attempt to discover the reasons why they may keep happening. For example, medicine may help a person with backache, but not investigating the cause may mean the backache keeps returning. Although there is a case for trying to simply cure the symptoms, I believe that ignoring the long term issues is ultimately counter-productive.

Similarly, regarding the treatment of mental illness, it is clear that pressures on the health service in countries such as the UK do encourage doctors to use drugs rather than spend time trying to uncover the deeper reasons for an illness. These drugs may only sedate a patient rather than cure them. Obviously, in cases where patients cannot function at all this may be the only alternative. However, in my opinion the routine use of drugs avoids addressing the psychological issues in the person's life that may be causing the illness.

On the other hand, for certain world-wide killers such as cancer and HIV the cause may be unknown, so drug treatment of the symptoms becomes the main focus. If drugs improve a patient's quality of life, this can only be positive until the causes are better understood.

To conclude, there are many situations in which I believe increasing drug use leads doctors to look at symptoms more than causes, which may result in the illness continuing. However, a flexible approach is recommended as some medical conditions are helped by the use of modern drugs. (312 words)

Comments

The writer has chosen an 'opinion' approach and uses a good range of topic vocabulary (health) throughout. Paragraphs 2 and 3 use the paragraph plan from page 65. They begin with a main idea supported by examples or further information. Then an opposing idea is mentioned which is refuted by returning to the view of the writer. The essay ends with a re-statement of the writer's view and their recommendation.

Model answer for Writing 2 on p70

As world population rises, it is becoming more evident that unless we find ways of producing more food, we could be faced with a serious food crisis. It is often claimed that the only solution to this crisis is through genetically modified food. Yet, in my opinion, there is no justification for developing farming methods that could harm human health and the environment.

Scientists may be convinced that GM foods provide a quick solution to feeding the world's population. Through science, plants can be made to grow faster and a wider variety of crops can also be created. Although this means more food is being produced, the quality of this food could ultimately be detrimental to human health because of the unknown, long-term risks of genetic modification. In my view, this is one of the major reasons more people are buying organic food. Surely scientific progress should not disregard the long-term effects GM foods could have on health.

However, it is also important to consider the issue of producing enough food, both at a local and global level. Many parts of the world, such as Africa, continue to experience famine and starvation. Therefore, there could be a case for saying that GM foods may help to reduce this food shortage. Certainly, in many parts of the world, people are forced to rely on international aid for food. Yet I would argue that GM foods are not the solution. This is something that needs to be tackled in the political arena and governments may have to put more money into alternative ways of producing foods.

In conclusion, while we need to meet the demands of an increasing world population, GM foods are not the solution. I am certain that unless governments look at alternative methods of food production, the harmful health and environmental effects caused by GM foods may prove irreversible. (310 words)

Comments

This writer here has also chosen an 'opinion' approach but this time there are only two body paragraphs – both quite long. The first looks at the issue from a personal perspective whilst the second adopts a local / global perspective. A good range of language is used to describe opinions throughout.

Unit 5

Model answer for Writing on p83

The diagram shows the different stages involved in the construction of a straw bale house. The process commences with the demolition of the previous building and the preparation of the ground in order to give a solid base for the new building. After this the bales are positioned and secured. At this point the roof is installed and the external finish completed.

Following that, work commences on the inside of the house with several steps happening simultaneously. Electrical and plumbing work is completed to provide heat, light and water, and the house is insulated to reduce energy loss. The next stage of the process is when the structure is inspected by the buildings officer to ensure safety requirements are met. Before the property can be furnished it must be decorated. This step involves painting and carpeting as well as putting up curtains and other decorative fittings.

Finally, the construction is finished and the new house is ready for sale. (160 words)

Comments

The answer is logically organized and correctly uses present simple passives to describe this man-made process. Few words have been copied from the diagram and many have been grammatically changed eg furnishing → furnished.

Model answer for Writing on p86

The diagram shows the different changes carbon goes through as it is transported from fossil fuel to atmospheric gas and back again. To begin with, carbon, in the form of coal and oil, is extracted from within the earth by mining. After this stage is complete, these fossil fuels are burnt, so as to provide energy for goods manufacturing, the production of electricity, and transport, in fuels such as petrol and diesel.

As a result of burning fossil fuels, CO_2 is released into the atmosphere, which causes pollution and contributes to global warming. The negative effects of this step in the cycle are balanced by the CO_2 being absorbed by trees. Any reduction in trees, caused by forest clearance, reduces CO_2 absorption and adds to global warming. The final stage of the process is when trees decay and gradually form back into coal and oil.

Once the final stage has been completed, the carbon returns to its original state as a fossil fuel and the cycle continues again. (167 words)

Comments

The answer follows the paragraph plan given on page 86 and has a good range of vocabulary. The summarizing sentence describes the situation after the final stage and explains that this process is cyclical.

Unit 6

Model answer for Writing on p99

In recent times, travelling by plane has become more affordable as airline prices have dropped dramatically. The issue is that these cheap air fares do not reflect the environmental cost of air travel: planes burn fossil fuels at a higher rate than any other form of transport. Governments and individuals need to take action to reduce the harm that low-cost airlines cause. This essay will offer some suggestions of how they could achieve this.

To avoid the situation becoming any worse, governments could restrict licences for any further low-cost routes and place a minimum price limit that would take into account the environmental damage caused. Furthermore, if they considered placing a tax on all low-cost airlines, it might discourage them from developing this market. Whilst these measures could be effective, they would probably be highly unpopular with the majority of travellers, so democratic governments might be wary of implementing such measures.

Although governments have a role to play, it is ultimately consumers who need to be persuaded to choose more sustainable forms of transport over air travel, even if the flight is inexpensive. It may be effective to educate people that although the cost of a flight is cheap, the environmental cost is high. I believe advertising campaigns could work to discourage people from taking unnecessary flights despite low ticket prices.

To sum up, low-cost airlines offer air travel at low prices which do not reflect the environmental damage caused. In spite of the legislative measures that governments could take to reduce this trade, it is my belief that the best answer would be to raise people's awareness of the environmental damage caused by air travel and to persuade them to only use it when necessary.

(294 words)

Comments

The introduction begins with a paraphrase of the question topic that uses a gerund subject ('…travelling by plane…'). The essay directly addresses the two aspects of the question by presenting two ideas: the role of government and the role of individuals. These ideas are developed by considering the results of the proposed solutions. A good range of language and grammar is used including modal verbs to avoid absolute statements ('… if they considered … it might … ', '… they would probably be …', 'It may be effective to …').

Model answer for Writing on p102

(Intro: Explain the problem)

In recent years, certain countries have adopted a policy of allowing private businesses to run transport systems which were previously publicly owned. However, many people are concerned about how transport safety standards would be upheld once a government gave up control. There are several potential solutions which I believe would be effective.

(Body 1: Govt. Laws)

One of the major roles of government is to make and enforce laws. If they made it against the law to endanger public safety, any company that did not comply with the regulations could be dealt with in a court. The advantage of this policy would be that the inevitable bad publicity from such a trial would certainly be a strong motivation for companies to maintain good standards.

(Body 2: Inspections & Fines)

Although the government would not be running the transport system, there is no reason that they could not control it by means of inspections and penalties if companies were not operating safely. If the government found dangerous practices resulting from an inspection, they could refuse to allow that company to continue trading. They might also consider financial penalties for lesser problems. The drawback of these ideas is that they would involve the government in running an inspection system which may well be expensive.

(Body 3: Don't allow private ownership)

A final solution would be to consider changing the law to stop private companies running any public transport. However, such a proposal might be highly unpopular with voters if they felt private companies had made improvements.

To summarize, the problem of balancing private profit with public safety on buses and trains is not easy to resolve. However, it is my view that if governments carried out regular inspections supported by a system of tough penalties, then public safety would be maintained. (285 words)

Comments

There is a clear introduction which shows the writer has understood the topic and task correctly. It describes what the problem is, gives the writer's view and explains the focus of the essay. In the body of the essay, three ideas are suggested and supported with further explanation. The third and fourth paragraph also include mention of opposing views ('The drawback of … ', 'However, such a … '). Synonyms for 'problem' and 'solution' are used (policy, drawback, ideas, proposal).

Unit 7

Model answer for Writing Task 1 on p116

The charts show world-wide manufacturing and exports as a percentage, from 1985 to 2005 in Germany, China, Japan and the US. The US had the largest share of global manufacturing and exports although its manufacturing percentage dropped significantly from around 36% in 1985 to under 24% in 2005. In contrast, China's manufacturing and exports represented the smallest share of the four countries. However, it was the country with the greatest growth, with manufacturing up from 5% to just under 15%, and exports up from about 3% to 7%.

Turning to Japan, it had the second largest percentage of manufacturing although by 2005 it was equalled by China. However, its exports experienced a steady fall ending as the lowest exporter of the group. Despite Germany's manufacturing being the lowest of the countries, it remained steady throughout the period. Its exports, however, represented the second largest percentage showing a slight increase from about 11% to 12%.

Overall, it can be seen that the US remained the largest manufacturer and exporter although the steady growth in China was significant.

(176 words)

Comments

The answer follows the plan given in Writing exercise 4 on page 117 and compares the two charts which is logical as the fixed parts (*country & percentage*) are the same in both. Language is used to describe change as well as make comparisons.

Model answer for Writing Task 1 on p118

The diagram shows the pattern of work for workers employed in four industries (catering, retail, transport and finance). Firstly looking at daytime work, the vast majority of finance staff work at this time (82%) whilst well under half of retail and transport workers follow this pattern (45% and 39% respectively). Conversely, only slightly over one fifth of catering employees work in the day with 35% working at the weekends, which is a similar proportion to retail staff at 30%.

For the catering, finance and retail sector, only a minority work at night (13%, 5% and 4% respectively).

In contrast, a third of transport staff are employed at night, which is almost equal to the numbers working in the day. Finally, for catering, transport and retail the numbers in evening work is approximately the same as those in weekend work. For the finance sector, evening work is equal in size to the combined total of night and weekend work.

To sum up, it can be seen that there is a wide variation in work patterns in the four sectors with only the finance sector employing the majority of workers in daytime work.

(191 words)

Comments

The answer focuses on comparisons (there are no changes over time) and chooses to approach the summary by comparing the differences in time of work. There is a good range of language to express the data (language for approximating figures and determiners) and the summarizing sentence gives a good summing up of the diagrams.

Model answer for Writing Task 1 on p118

The first diagram illustrates the reasons men and women chose to work at home in 2005. Overall, running their own business was the main reason for both males and females (69% and 65% respectively). In contrast, approximately a quarter of males put flexibility as a reason, which was twice as high as the female response (26% and 12% respectively). For childcare, the pattern was different again with almost a quarter of females giving this reason compared to very few males (5%).

The second diagram shows the hours men and women worked at home in 2005. The vast majority of males worked over 31 hours per week (82%) contrasting with a minority of females (5%) doing similar hours. This pattern is reversed when examining the under ten hours category with almost three quarters of females working this amount compared to only 2% of males. The 10–30 hours per week category shows fewer marked differences.

To sum up, it can be seen that men and women do not always give the same reasons for home working and, in general, men work longer hours at home. (184 words)

Comments

The answer describes each diagram separately because they are not measuring the same thing. Each point is introduced clearly and supported with figures from the diagram. The final sentence gives a summary of both diagrams.

Unit 8

Model answer for Writing Task 2 on p132

The issue of how to divide public funds in cities is one which many people feel strongly about. Some argue that providing facilities such as galleries and museums should be a priority for those in power. Others feel that the focus should be on practical things such as having effective telecommunications, good transport networks and well-run public utilities. This essay will discuss both these positions in turn.

Although putting a focus on infrastructure seems sensible, it does not necessarily mean that this would always be in the best interests of the city. In many cities, cultural facilities attract people thus making them popular locations to work and visit. For instance, the popularity of London is partly due to the famous galleries and museums, despite the city having some serious infrastructure problems with an ageing underground and congested road system. Therefore, I believe that cultural attractions are a major factor in a city retaining a skilled workforce and remaining an attractive destination for tourists.

On the other hand, the fact that a city provides good cultural amenities does not necessarily mean that it will be economically strong. Investors, businesses and entrepreneurs, who are a vital part of a thriving city, require a dependable infrastructure before they choose their location. In addition, if investment in infrastructure falls, a city may cease to function properly resulting in growing economic instability and social tension. It is my view that poor transport, faulty communications or unreliable services will all lead to the decline of a city.

To conclude, the success of a city depends on having cultural attractions to make it an attractive place to live or visit, but also on having an efficient infrastructure so that people want to remain living there and so that businesses can thrive. Hence, I believe that expenditure needs to be allocated to both public services and cultural facilities.

(315 words)

Comments

The question task tells the writer to 'Discuss both views …' and so a balanced argument approach has been used. The introduction makes it clear how the writer will organize their answer. In the body of the essay, language is used to refute opposing ideas and paragraphs 2 and 3 conclude with the writer's own view. The conclusion gives a clear summary and makes the views of the writer clear.

Model answer for Writing Task 2 on p134

In today's modern world, there is probably greater access to Art than ever before. Nevertheless, the function of Art remains an area of debate with some believing that it provides meaning and purpose to our lives, whilst others feel that it is only a momentary escape from more important issues. My own belief is that Art is fundamental to what makes us human.

A first point to consider is that the expression of our lives through Art is one of the few things that separates humans from animals. Man is the only creature who attempts to reflect his own life through Art forms such as painting. Furthermore, the fact that Art is often taken to mean the work of geniuses such as Picasso does not necessarily mean that Art is only a characteristic of modern man. Ancient cave paintings show that even in primitive times, the expression of the world around was important to humans. In my opinion this is a strong argument for showing how vital Art is to Man.

Some people believe that Art is just a brief distraction from normality. However, one of the major uses of Art is to lift people's spirits. The songs of slaves provide an example of how music can help people cope with pain. Similarly, paintings and sculptures are often used to remember historical events, keeping them alive in the culture. I believe this reflects a fundamental need to express our existence through Art.

To summarize, Art is something which has been a part of human history for thousands of years and helps people survive difficult times and express their existence. Thus, it is my view that Art is much more than just entertainment: it is one of the defining characteristics of being human.

(291 words)

Comments

This essay could be answered with either a balanced argument or an opinion essay approach. In this answer the writer adopts an opinion essay approach which is made clear from the final sentence of the introduction. The body of the essay provides ideas and examples to support the writer's view which is summarized in the conclusion. The third paragraph begins by mentioning an opposing view which is then refuted in order to support the writer's opinion.

Unit 9

Model answer for Writing 1 p145

Paragraph plan	***Describing an illustration model answer***
Paragraph 1 Introduce the illustration and describe the main features.	The illustration shows a house designed to use energy efficiently all year round. The house follows a conventional design but with a number of innovations. The first floor of the house is situated underground whilst the upper floor consists of a wide, low-angled roof. Along the length of this roof are a series of oblong-shaped skylights.
Paragraph 2 Describe how the house works in the summer.	In the summer, the skylights open fully, which allows heat to be released. The roof covering, which reflects heat, reduces heat penetration and helps to protect the house from becoming too hot in the summer. Similarly, the underground floor remains cool in the summer months as a result of being protected from the sun's rays.
Paragraph 3 Describe how the house works in the winter	In the winter, these features function differently and are used to retain heat. The skylights maximize the amount of light and heat entering the house and the wall insulation prevents this from escaping. The underground floor is less affected by cold weather as the surrounding earth helps to retain warmth.
Summarizing sentence	To summarize, it can be seen that the house uses design features which maximize heat retention in winter and heat loss in summer. (186 words)

Comments

The answer adopts a logical paragraph structure which describes the features of the house and their purpose. The illustration labels have been used as the basis of many sentences but the words from the labels have often been transformed (eg protection ⟶ protected).

Unit 10

Model answer for Writing on p166

There are different views on the causes of violence in the world today. Some argue that it is connected to people's exposure to violent scenes on television and in films, whilst others point to wider problems in society such as unemployment, poor housing and education as the root of anti-social behaviour. It is my belief that violence in the media plays a significant role in encouraging violent behaviour.

A first point is that as levels of violence in the media increase, so does young people's exposure to it. Even films aimed at children often contain violence and despite the difficulty of proving whether this directly affects society, it is hard not to be concerned. After all, children learn through modelling adult behaviour, so if the models they choose are violent then it is highly likely that they may be violent themselves.

Furthermore, the way violence is portrayed in the media is often stylized resulting in violence being seen as attractive. People who are easily impressed may then behave violently themselves. Although research has shown that aggressive behaviour is actually often the result of having aggressive parents, I still believe that the unrealistic way violence is shown in the media must have a negative result on society.

Finally, the media has become increasingly globalized which means that violence in programmes or films can be viewed all over the world. I would argue that the increasing quantity and level of violence seen around the world must be a negative force in society.

In conclusion, although it is difficult to prove beyond a doubt the effect of violence in the media on society, I believe that the result on the young, the unrealistic way it is shown and the global nature of media communications all have a significant and negative impact on society.

(299 words)

Comments

The answer is well-organized and remains focused on the question throughout. There is a clear introduction that states the writer's views which are supported by discussing different arguments in the body of the essay. The conclusion summarizes the main points and concludes with the writer's view re-stated.

Listening scripts

1 Learn to succeed

 **1.1**

(T=Tutor;S=Student)

T: Good morning, and how can I help you?

S: Good morning, my name is Sondra da Costa. I'm a first year student and I'm a bit confused about a few things. I was told by a lecturer to come here.

T: Okay then, take a seat Sandra and let me see how I can help you. Because this is your first year here, I'll need a few personal details. What did you say your name was again?

S: Sondra da Costa

T: Is that Sandra?

S: No, it's spelt with an 'O'.

T: So that's S-O-N-D-R-A. And can you spell your surname please?

S: It's D-A C-O-S-T-A

T: Is that all one word?

S: No, it's two words actually.

T: Fine, and are you living on campus or in other accommodation?

S: I'm living in university residences in Bramble House, the one on the main campus. Room number 13.

T: How are you finding it so far?

S: Much better than I expected. I have quite a large room and we have a shared kitchen and bathroom. The other students I've met seem really friendly.

T: That's good to hear. I think you've made a wise decision living on campus. Now just a few more details and then we can go on to discuss what's worrying you. Where are you from?

S: My mother is from South America, but I was born in the North of Spain.

T: That's interesting and ... er one more thing... Do you have a number we can contact you on in emergencies?

S: Yes. I have a mobile number. It's 07764543302

T: Let's just check that. Did you say ... 07764543332

S: No, it's 54-33-0-2

T: That's fine Sondra. Thank you. That's all the information I need for the moment.

 **1.2**

T: So how can I help you?

S: Well, I'm really worried about how I'm going to cope with university life ... I mean I feel like I don't know what's going on.

T: Don't worry Sondra. Most undergraduates feel like this in their first week.

S: Well, maybe if I knew the campus a bit better, that might help.

T: Do you have a map of the campus?

S: Yes. I was given one during orientation week, but to be honest I don't really understand it.

T: Well, let's look at it together. Okay, we are here now in Dalton House. Opposite this building is the Arts block where you'll find the computers. The computer rooms are open from 9.00am 'til 10.30pm weekdays, but closed on the weekends.

S: Are there no other computers on campus?

T: There are a few in the library that are available throughout the year, except Sundays. To get to the library you keep going down University Lane, past the Science Block on your left. Opposite the Science Block are the Chemistry Labs and the library is just on the right, next to Lab B.

S: Fine.

T: Another important building is the students' union. Turn left into Newton Drive. There are some trees and a little outside cafeteria. The students' union is just behind this.

One thing I must check ... have you sorted out your fees yet?

S: Well, I filled in a direct debit form so I suppose that means everything is fine.

T: Probably, but you should go to the Finance Office just to make sure. It's at the end of Newton Drive. You'll need some identification ... your passport or student ID.

S: And is there a bank on campus?

T: Yes, it's open normal banking hours and there is a 24 hour cash machine. The bank's in Isaacs Street which runs parallel to University Lane where we are now. Go past Lecture Hall B and the bank is opposite, just before you get to Lecture Hall A.

S: Great.

T: Probably the best thing to do is to walk around and familiarize yourself with everything. Don't worry, it won't take you long to settle in.

S: I'm sure you're right. I feel a lot better.

T: I also need you to fill in this form for the tutorial file. Take it away with you and then make an appointment to see me again and we'll go over it. My telephone number is on the form, here, at the bottom of the page. You can ring me anytime between 9.00am and 3.30pm from Monday to Friday ... er ... except on a Thursday when I'm only available in the morning.

2 Living together

 **1.3**

Good afternoon. Welcome to *Stop Smoking Now*. You're all here today because you've decided to stop smoking. However, making the decision to stop is just the first step. Yet if you follow these guidelines, no matter how tough it may be to begin with, rest assured, you will be on your way to becoming what you want to be, an ex-smoker. The first thing to remember is that there is not only one way. What I'll give you today are various methods you can choose from. They all work and they can all help.

The first method I would recommend is based on something we all have, but in different degrees, namely willpower.

Of course, just making the decision to stop, is an enormous act of willpower alone, but what exactly does this mean? It means having a strong mind, waking up every morning and telling yourself that you will not have that cigarette no matter how much you may want one. To do this successfully you really have to be determined to stay focussed. You need to be in the right frame of mind. But this isn't as easy as it may sound and it may mean doing other things to take your mind off having that cigarette, particularly when the urge is strong. I've found that different things can help you do this like taking up a hobby or having a smoking buddy – someone you can phone up when the going gets tough, a friend who can help you think about something else. Remember that each time you don't have a cigarette; you will feel better and stronger.

Of course, this method does not work for everyone, but there are other ways to help keep you on track.

Another way is to use smoking aids. There are many types so find one that suits you best. Take, for example, nicotine patches. You put one on every day and it gives you a controlled nicotine dose. Basically, you keep reducing the amount until your body stops craving nicotine. As your body gets used to less nicotine, you may experience withdrawal symptoms. Don't worry about feeling embarrassed people will notice because many nicotine patches are see-through. So where do you get them? Well, you can buy them from your local pharmacy or supermarket. You can also ask your GP for a prescription.

 **1.4**

Another method that is becoming more popular is alternative therapies. Giving up smoking is not only difficult for your body, but also your mind as the emotional stress can be really severe. One therapy that springs to mind is acupuncture. This can help you relax ... calm you down, making you much more likely to want to give up. Acupuncture usually lasts between 50 to 90 minutes. As your body and mind become stronger, you should need fewer sessions. The good thing about acupuncture is that it takes harmful toxins caused by smoking out of your body. And, I'm sure you'll all like this, it does not increase your appetite, so giving up smoking using this method means you won't put on weight! It can take as few as five acupuncture sessions to cure you, but of course, this depends on the type of person you are. I suppose one of the biggest advantages of using this method is that there are almost no withdrawal symptoms because it works from the inside. What I mean by this, is that acupuncture takes away your wanting to smoke and this feeling, on top of the feeling of calmness, stays with you after the treatment is over.

At the end of the day, it doesn't really matter which method you choose. What's important is that you make the decision and then stick to it no matter what. If you give up, think of the money you'll be saving! There is no better time to start than today. You can kick the habit for good!

1.5

(E=Examiner; S=Student)

E: Now I'm going to give you a topic and I want you to speak about it for one to two minutes. First you have one minute to think about what you are going to say and you can make some notes.

Here is your topic. I want you to describe an older person who has had an influence on your life. Okay?

S: Um … Well I think a person who had most influence is probably my grandfather. He is important for me. He always help me. I did not meet him really because he is my grandfather so actually he was always in my life. Really, we did many things together. He play with me always and sometimes read me story. Actually I like reading books because it can help me to relax. Um … I'm reading a good book now. It's about this woman and she remember her life … er … Actually it's a bit of a love story, but I'm liking it very much.

1.6

(J=Juliane;S=Sang Min;G=Gale)

J: Hi there, Sang Min. What have you been up to?

SM: I've just been to a tutorial. Weren't you two supposed to attend?

G: Yes, we were, but I had an essay to finish and Juliane offered to help.

J: Did we miss much?

SM: Well, I thought it was quite interesting. Er … It was all about spending habits among undergraduates. It was based on recent research done by a PhD student studying behavioural psychology.

J: Oh yes, I remember being interviewed by him about what I usually spend my money on.

SM: And what did you say?

J: Well, most of my money, probably around 75%, goes on basic living: paying rent, food costs and of course, university fees.

G: I'm the same, except my food bill is higher!

SM: We are all in the same boat here – virtually all my money goes on that too, but I also spend a lot of money on text books, between 100 and £120 a month, usually more. Realistically, it's closer to £150.

J: That explains why you get such good marks! Another aspect of the interview was students' use of credit cards, with a particular focus on how students manage these.

G: In my case, not very well! I always end up spending more than I planned to. It's too easy to use.

SM: Surely that must be the point … that students are given credit cards too easily before they've learnt how to use them. And the number of credit cards some students get, it's frightening. The average is about three cards.

J: Not only cards, students need to learn how to manage money too. And this is what the interview's meant to find out. By comparing and contrasting all the data, the root causes of student spending could be highlighted.

G: And the effects this has on students, I'd imagine would be more negative than positive.

J: Perhaps, but this was the other part of what the student was trying to achieve. You also need to study the effects to find answers.

1.7

J: But I think it all goes back to how we were taught to manage money when we were children.

G: That's true. Our behaviour now is closely related to the childhood environment and what we learnt from that.

SM: But how far back should we go? When do children really begin forming an understanding of what money means?

G: I've read that children between three and five can understand what's right and wrong. That's when they can learn concepts like sharing. At the age of six, most children can understand the value of money.

J: This suggests that if parents offered practical advice to their children at an early age, it could have a very positive impact on their spending habits in later life.

SM: It basically comes down to three areas. The first one is allowance. Parents should not try to focus on how much money they give their children, but rather on what they need.

G: Needs are difficult to define so parents need to resist the urge to give in when their children say, 'I want'.

J: For me, the only way to teach children the difference between needs and wants, is to give them a practical allowance. If my parents had not done that for me when I was younger, I don't think I would be able to handle the money they give me now.

SM: Mmm ... true. The second thing, I think is important, is saving.

G: Can you explain a bit more?

SM: Oh … Basically, parents need to introduce their children to personal finance. If we are expected to deal with money now, then we have to learn when we're younger.

G: I see what you mean. And it could be in quite simple ways like by helping them to open their own savings account.

J: There's one more area I think is vital.

SM: What's that?

J: It's buying. We spend excessively on credit cards because we don't know how to control money. We almost need to learn how and what to buy, which is why parents should allow their children to participate in this. If they want something expensive like a new pair of trainers, then they could be encouraged to save a bit of their allowance.

G: And parents could also promise to help by saying that they will pay the rest if the child at the end of their period of saving, still does not have enough.

1.8

1 appli'cation / ap'ply 2 associ'ation / as'sociate 3 communi'cation / com'municate 4 concen'tration / 'concentrate 5 di'rection / di'rect 6 edu'cation / 'educate 7 examin'ation / e'xamine 8 for'mation / form 9 infor'mation / in'form 10 in'struction / in'struct 11 oper'ation / 'operate 12 organi'zation / 'organize 13 popu'lation / 'populate 14 pro'duction / pro'duce 15 re'action / re'act 16 re'lation / re'late 17 situ'ation / 'situate 18 vari'ation / 'vary

3 Costing the earth

1.9

The Department of Energy denied claims that a change in its energy policy is being debated in light of fresh evidence of global warming. A government minister denied that a decision has been taken to back technologies for harnessing the power of renewable and sustainable sources of energy such as wind and solar power. The Department claims that renewables are unable to generate enough power to meet growing energy requirements economically. Campaigners for the environment point out that given the predicted steep rise in energy consumption it is more important than ever that the Government takes steps to reduce demands for conventional sources of energy, like fossil fuels, which are damaging to the environment.

1.10

(Dr D=Dr Dartford;M=Miranda)

Dr D: Good afternoon, Dr Dartford speaking.

M: Good afternoon Dr. Dartford. It's Miranda Smith here.

Dr D: Oh hello Miranda, how can I help you?

M: I'm really sorry, but I couldn't come to your lecture on the government's waste strategy yesterday because I was feeling ill. My essay has to be handed in in two weeks' time and I'm worried I might have missed something important. I really don't like it when I miss lectures, especially when I need the information for an essay.

Dr D: Well try not to worry, you can't help being sick. How about if I give you a quick summary of the main points.

M: That'd be great thanks. Just let me get a pen. Right I'm ready.

Dr D: To begin with, I stressed the importance of us re-using and recycling waste in the future. I made particular reference to the UK, which at the moment only recycles about eight per cent of household waste. The levels of industrial and commercial waste are much higher. It's frightening how much waste factories produce on a daily basis, but that's not all. The fact is that not only is this rate of recycling well below government targets, but it's at a much lower rate than many other European countries, which means Britain is just not keeping pace with the rate of growth in household waste.

M: That's pretty worrying, isn't it?

Dr D: It certainly is. What is more, we need to understand that if we are to achieve a more rational and sustainable use of our resources in this country, then we have to develop a fundamental change in the way we think about waste.

M: That won't be easy. What suggestions did you propose?

Dr D: Just give me a second, let me check my notes. OK, got it. Basically, there are a couple of ways this could be achieved. One of these is for more household waste to be separated.

M: You mean separated into things like newspapers, tins and stuff like that?

Dr D: Yes, that's the idea … then this separated waste would obviously need different forms of collection by local councils, but most importantly, it will require an expansion in the market for collected materials, which is one of the major barriers to increased recycling. New government targets have also been set for recycling or composting 30 percent of household waste by 2010.

M: But that's almost a fourfold increase, isn't it?

Dr D: It is indeed. Rather a frightening figure, whichever way you look at it.

1.11

Dr D: As you say, it's a fourfold increase, but my guess is it won't stop there. You must remember the previous government found that setting targets is one thing, but if the practical policies are not in place, nothing will happen.

M: So what is the government planning to do about all this waste?

Dr D: Well, apparently they're going to publish a final strategy setting out a range of policies to start and sustain the necessary changes. But the interesting part for me was that it's not only up to the government. To say we need more recycling is a simple message, but, and here is the crux of the matter, there's another one that isn't getting enough attention.

M: Really? What's that?

Dr D: It's quite obvious really, it's us, the general public. We have to reduce the amount of waste we make. It's our responsibility. Did you know that every hour, enough waste is produced to fill the Sydney Opera House? And the rate is increasing.

M: Actually, now you mention it, I remember reading somewhere that the reason for all this waste is our increasing wealth and the changes to our lifestyles. I guess it's quite obvious when you really think about it, I mean it's things like shops and supermarkets selling more pre-packaged foods and ready-made meals.

Dr D: Convenience is the key. People simply want their lives to be more convenient and there's also technological change that brings pressure to make people change their domestic appliances for newer models.

M: I never thought about that, but you're right. And I'm just as guilty. I threw out my old stereo so I could have a better model even though there wasn't really anything wrong with the old one.

Dr D: You see, you're a classic example that changing our present 'throw-away' culture is going to be an enormous challenge. At the end of the day, consumers will have an important role to play. It could all boil down to their choices and their willingness to support recycling by sorting their waste and accepting more recycled products.

1.12

See page 48, exercise 1.

1.13

See page 48, exercise 2.

4 Healthy body, healthy mind

1.14

Good morning. As part of our lecture series on everyday health issues, today's talk is on tiredness. We shall look at the main issues in turn, as well as some of the main research that has been carried out in this field.

Firstly, it is clear that tiredness is on the rise. No official data exists on the rate of people reporting to doctors with recurring tiredness but it's a very common complaint. Research suggests that people are not relaxing properly and often work when they do not have enough energy. Furthermore, products to boost energy are also on the rise – sales of so-called 'energy' drinks loaded with caffeine and sugar have grown by 23% over the last year. And this is not the only instance of an increase in products claiming to boost energy. Guarana, a herbal stimulant, can now be found in everything from chocolate bars to tea bags.

Now let's examine what it is that's making people so tired. Dr Liebhold, a Sydney GP, has done extensive research into this and he believes that financial pressures, not taking holidays, and not having time off when you become ill due to fear of losing your job, are all common causes. Some of the other suggested causes are low oxygen levels in offices, poor diet, or illness. The problem is that tiredness is a symptom of just about every kind of illness which makes tracking down the cause all the more difficult.

The next question to ask is are people getting enough sleep? Dr Mansfield from Melbourne's Epworth Sleep Centre, who specializes in sleep disorders, says insomnia often arises when people are going through a stressful period. Mansfield often needs to re-educate people in how to get off to sleep. He recommends keeping your body clock regular by going to bed and rising at similar times every day, and not drinking too much caffeine. And there is some truth in the old story about having a glass of hot milk before bed. Milk contains the amino acid, tryptophan which has been shown to help induce sleepiness.

Turning to the question of why we need sleep, researchers are still trying to answer this fundamental question. Sleep deprivation experiments have shown that after 14 days without sleep, rats will lie down and die. And after only three days' sleep loss humans get confused, forgetful and start having hallucinations, so whatever sleep does, it is important.

1.15

Let's now look at the medical aspect of the problem. If on-going tiredness is present, a diagnosis of chronic fatigue syndrome might be considered. University of NSW expert Professor Lloyd says that by a process of elimination, researchers have tracked the site of this problem to the brain, and Lloyd believes it is a problem with the proper functioning of the brain, rather than any structural abnormality. The good news, however, is that most chronic fatigue sufferers make a full recovery within six months of being diagnosed.

The final area to examine is diet. Sydney-based naturopath Leonie McMahon, believes inadequate breakfast is a common cause of tiredness and recommends increasing the consumption of protein at breakfast.

1.16

However, not all researchers feel the same way. Trent Watson, of the Dietitians Association, is not convinced by McMahon's theory explaining that our bodies don't really like to burn protein as a fuel so it doesn't really contribute to energy levels. Carbohydrates, however, found in fruit, breads and pastas are a more common fuel. 'Anyone following a rigidly high-protein diet with low carbohydrates, even if they are operating at low intensity during the day, could subject themselves to fatigue because they just don't have the carbohydrate stores,' Watson says. In general, a good way to stay energized from a dietary point of view is to eat red meat, green leafy vegetables and whole grains. These foods give red blood cells the building blocks for optimum performance in their role of delivering oxygen to muscles.

To sum up, tiredness is a health problem on the increase and there continues to be much debate surrounding its causes and remedies. Now, if there are any questions I'd be happy to answer them.

5 The world we live in

1.17

This week's 'Our World' programme comes from Canada where Usha Lee McFarling sends this report on how global warming is affecting the behaviour of Polar Bears and creating problems for the town of Churchill which depends on the bears for tourism.

Usha: The Hudson Bay polar bears are an unusual group. They spend half their year living on the frozen sea ice. And in a normal year, around springtime, when the weather gets warmer, the bears move onto land as the sea ice begins to melt. Once they have done this their lives enter a new phase which involves a change in their metabolism. They don't hibernate, but their bodies slow down because they won't eat for the next six months. During this half of the year they lose hundreds of pounds in weight.

Each autumn, as the temperature falls, the bears migrate past the small town of Churchill waiting for the Hudson Bay to freeze over again. When it has, the bears go back onto the sea ice. Now they can build up their fat reserves by feeding on seals. They survive because the surface of the Hudson Bay is normally frozen from mid-October through to mid-April. During these months, the bears sleep on ice floes and swim in the frigid waters.

Normally, that means millions of dollars for the town of Churchill, which earns money by taking tourists into the tundra to see the bears as they pass by the town. However, recently the weather has been warmer and the bears' behaviour has changed. The warm weather prevents the sea from freezing and so the hungry bears come into town looking for food.

1.18

Having spent six months without food the bears are at their most hungry and dangerous. Starving bears often lose their natural wariness and wander into town. If a town resident spots a bear they call the Bear Alert Programme on 675-BEAR day or night, to report a bear in town. Officer Richard Romaniuk and his crew will then shoot the bear with a sleeping dart. It will then be taken to polar bear prison.

Sometimes the officers capture four bears in a day. To keep the animals from associating humans with food, they are not fed in prison. The bears are kept locked up until the sea freezes. Once the sea has frozen again the bears are airlifted by helicopter and flown back to return to their natural winter habitat.

The program has two objectives. The first is to protect people from the bears. The second is to protect the bears from the people.

1.19

The town of Churchill has good reason to look after the bears. Rough estimates indicate the province of Manitoba earns in the region of $300 million each year from bear tourism. 'Bears are the backbone of our economy,' said town manager Darren Ottaway.
While Ottaway is concerned about an abundance of hungry bears coming to town in the short term, he is even more worried that global warming may mean no bears here at all one day.

For three weeks during bear season, sleepy Churchill blooms as about 15,000 tourists stream through town hoping to get close-up views of the animals from caravans of heated Tundra Buggies.Several chartered jets unload bear-gazers at the Churchill airport each day. Hotels and restaurants closed during the bleak winter fill to capacity.
Polar bears are not currently an endangered species. Their total population is estimated to be from 22,000 to 27,000. But the 1,200 Hudson Bay bears could face what scientists call a 'local extinction' – they could produce fewer cubs and eventually die out.

Officials and business leaders in Churchill have already begun planning for alternative ways of generating income. Ottaway is promoting whale watching and is delighted that Japanese tourists are willing to brave the bone-chilling cold of winter to view the Northern Lights. 'It's super news for us,' Ottaway said of the potential Japanese tourist boom.

Warmer weather, Ottaway said, could also extend the shipping season on Hudson Bay and attract more filmmakers. The science-fiction classic 'Iceman' was filmed nearby as well as an upcoming film, 'The Snow Walker.' 'When people talk about climate change, you have to look at the benefits too,' Ottaway said.

Others, however, feel differently. 'The bears have been in our community for years ,' said one resident. 'They're like neighbours and everybody ought to be helping to make sure their natural life cycle can be maintained.'

1.20

See page 80, exercise 2.

1.21

See page 80, exercise 4.

1.22

My favourite animal is a camel. It is quite a large animal and one thing about it that makes it easy to recognize is that it has a hump, either one or two, depending on the type. I think I saw my first camel when I went to visit my uncle. Er … He lives in a town where camel racing is really popular so you see camels everywhere, sometimes just walking in the streets. I really like camels because, for me, they move so gracefully when they walk and I've always found it fascinating that they can survive for long periods without water. I feel the camel is an important symbol of my country because I guess many people associate camels with my country. Er … It's also an important animal for food … I mean we drink camel milk. And of course, racing camels make lots of money for their owners, so there's an economic aspect as well.

1.23

Um … I think there is a dual responsibility for protecting animals. Firstly, it is the responsibility of governments to make sure this happens. There should be laws to ensure, for example, that whales and dolphins are protected. I remember reading somewhere that quite a few dolphins get killed because they get caught in fishing nets. Of course, we, the general public, also have an important part to play in this. As far as dolphins are concerned, we can make sure we only buy tinned fish that is dolphin-friendly and what I mean by this is that the correct fishing methods have been used. I feel quite strongly that animals like dolphins must be protected because if we don't do this, dolphins could be in danger of becoming extinct and that would be a real shame. There would be other effects too, like to the tourist industry. I mean, if you think about it, in many countries, like New Zealand and Australia, tourists pay to go and look at the dolphins and even swim with them, which must be quite an unforgettable experience.

1.24

Good morning and welcome to this series of lectures on man interfering with nature. This morning we are going to look at the issue of cloning. I'd like to begin by looking at some examples of animals that have been cloned before moving on to looking at how cloning is defined.

The first example I'd like to talk about is Idaho Gem, who was the very first mule to be cloned. Mules are a combination of horse and donkey. Idaho Gem is an identical copy of his brother Taz, who is a racing champion, thus we can make the conclusion here that he was cloned to follow in his brother's footsteps. The next example I'd like to refer to is CC, which stands for CopyCat. Like her name suggests, she was the first cloned kitten. Interestingly, CC was created in a laboratory in the state of Texas by the very same scientists who made Dolly the sheep in Scotland. CC is physically identical to her mother, Rainbow, and what is important about this is that it has opened the doors for people to clone their pets in the future. Now the last animal example I'd like to look at today is the pig. In 2001, five piglets were born – all female. They were created by a firm who claim that their birth is an important step for medicine. The idea is that pig organs and cells could be used in human transplants because the pigs have been cloned without a certain cell. This cell is a vital link because it is the one in human beings that is responsible for making the body reject donor organs. This means that not only is the transplant operation unsuccessful, but the patient's life could be at risk.

Now I'd like to discuss some of the current definitions of cloning.

1.25

One kind of cloning, the kind commonly found in plants, occurs when plants reproduce themselves around the original plants known as the parent plants. New plants can then grow. This is quite a natural process by which plants can form more of the same type of plant. Though you may not be aware of it, another type of cloning happens quite naturally in your body when old cells need to be replaced . Cells in your body split into two and make new chromosomes and it is the chromosomes that contain our genes. Embryo splitting is another form of cloning which can happen quite naturally when cells split to form two identical twins. You may then be asking yourself what all the fuss is about, if cloning does in fact happen naturally because sometimes man can interfere with nature and it can work. Take embryo splitting as an example. Now this type of cloning is quite common in farming and it is used to breed new bulls and cows. Embryos are placed into foster mother cows and these then grow into calves. And though some may consider this to be artificial, it has been going on for the last 10 years with relatively few problems.

Now the last type of cloning I'd like to mention is perhaps the most controversial. This type of cloning is called nuclear transfer and it is when the nucleus of a cell is put into an egg of another animal that is genetically the same. This is done in a laboratory and after about 5 or 6 days, the embryo is implanted into a donor mother,which is how Dolly the sheep was made. One argument in favour of cloning is that it can help in medicine as in the case of pigs being used in transplant operations. It is true that many people can wait for up to a year for a new kidney, and then still run the risk of their bodies rejecting the donor kidney; but will using pig organs really be the solution?

To answer this question, I'd like to take a look at some responses to the whole idea of using pig organs in humans. Neil Blackwood, who works for the company that cloned the five piglets, described it as a major medical advance that could solve the global problem of a lack of organs to use in transplant operations. This could lead in the future to saving human lives. Sheila Halliday, a leading transplant surgeon, does not share his view. She believes that although it is possible to use pig organs in humans, there are very real dangers. Halliday points out that diseases and infections could be passed from pig to human. Of course she does not yet know this for certain, which is why Halliday strongly advocates that more scientific research be done. She firmly believes pig organs should not be used in human operations until these findings are made public.

6 Going places

 1.26

(TA=Travel Agent; S=Student)

TA: Good morning. How can I help you?

S: I'm thinking of taking a year off university next year and I'd like to travel around Europe.

TA: Okay then. Do you have any idea where you'd like to go?

S: Well, I was thinking of starting in France and then working my way up to Eastern Europe, possibly going as far as Slovakia.

TA: Well there are a number of ways you can do this and we have various options available. It really depends on your budget and how you'd like to travel.

S: That's just the thing really. Um … I mean I've just finished my second year at university so obviously I'd like to do it in as cheap a way as possible.

TA: That's fine. Could you give me a rough idea of the price range you're looking at?

S: Realistically speaking, I'm hoping to pay between about 700 and 900 pounds. I could stretch to £1100, but that's really my limit.

TA: How long are you thinking of going for?

S: About ten months.

TA: To be honest, you'd be better off travelling for about seven months if that's your budget.

S: Okay, that's not too bad. So how would you suggest I travel?

TA: Well, because of the time limit, I don't think walking is a viable option. Of course in this day and age, the most convenient way to get around is by flying, particularly if you've got quite a bit you want to see in a short space of time. Saying that, I still think the best way to get around Europe is by train. As a student, you can also get a student railcard, which means cheaper fares.

S: That sounds brilliant. How do I go about getting a railcard?

TA: Well, if you decide that's what you want to do, then we can organize that all for you. You'll need to fill in a form and provide us with two passport photos and we'll do the rest. It costs about £36 plus about £10 administration costs.

S: Great, that's really not expensive at all. And what about buses? I was just thinking if I decide to go to places which are a bit more remote.

TA: There are always local buses, but these are not always a good idea. They can be quite unreliable and in some areas quite dangerous because the buses tend to be overcrowded and some of the drivers drive way too fast. So I would suggest you don't do this.

S: That sounds quite frightening! So what are my options then?

TA: You could hire a car, but it can be expensive. Still I do think if you're thinking about going to smaller towns and places which are off the beaten track, then hiring a car is by far the better way to do it. You can also look at sharing the costs by hiring a car with someone else.

S: That's a good idea. I guess I could put a message on the internet.

TA: You could do that, but don't forget that you meet people when you're travelling and you'll probably find someone who's going to the same place as you are.

S: That's true. I want to stay in youth hostels so I'm sure I'll find people who are interested in going to the same places. One last thing, what about taxis? I was thinking about if I go out at night. I use taxis all the time here.

TA: Ah, but taxis abroad are a different story. In certain countries, they're no problem, but by and large, taxi fares are high. If you do go out at night try walking home, but make sure you don't do this alone. Try and find people to go out with at night or come home at a reasonable time. But if you're staying in youth hostels, you should find plenty of young people to go out with at night.

S: I'm sure I will.

 1.27

TA: Now have you thought about how you'd like to travel to France?

S: Not really no.

TA: There are basically three ways. You can go by ferry, which leaves every day and night, or there's the hovercraft which is more pricey, but will get you there quicker and of course, you could fly.

S: Well, I don't think flying is an option for me as it'll be too expensive so I suppose I'll choose one of the other two. It's a pity really as I don't fancy the idea of travelling by sea. Last time I did that I got terribly seasick.

TA: Well, you're in luck then as at the moment there's a special deal on flights to France. In fact a plane ticket is now half the price of a ferry ticket which is usually the cheapest option.

S: That's great, I'll do that then. I much prefer flying anyway.

TA: I'll need to get some details off you then. Firstly, how will you be paying? Cash, cheque or credit card. If you pay by cheque, you'll need a cheque guarantee card.

S: I don't have my cheque book with me so it'll have to be by credit card.

TA: Fine, that's no problem. If you could just sign over here and then we'll have a look at flight times and I can sort out a youth travel card for you.

S: Fine. Can I use your pen please?

TA: No problem. Now let's look at times. There is a flight leaving at 9.00am and one that leaves half an hour later. Or you can choose a later flight at 11.30.

S: No I think 11.30 is too late so I think I'd prefer the flight that leaves after 9.00. I'm not very good at getting up in the morning!

TA: No problem, just give me a moment. Right, that's booked for you. Please remember that if you want to change this, you must give 24 hours' notice or you will lose your place.

 1.28

Good morning and welcome to this morning's lecture on transport. What I'll be doing today is comparing forms of transport in different countries to see how forms of transport are affected by factors such as geographical landscape and economic development. My focus will be on countries in South America, Europe and Asia.

The first country I'd like to look at is Colombia, which is in South America This is a country where geography plays an important role. Due to the huge amount of mountains and forests in this country, travelling by air is crucial. I don't know if many of you realize this fact, but Colombia was the first country to establish a commercial airline and in so doing they made aviation history. Today there are more than 400 airports in Colombia for domestic flights which highlights the point I made earlier that air travel is a vital means of transport in this country. Colombia also has a road network of about 48, 000km linking Colombia to Venezuela and Ecuador. Transport by road is important for trade as well as tourism. Apart from this, there is also a railway system, but it is in need of modernization. The other means of transport is by steamers with the *Magdalena* being the main waterway. Now let's turn to Colombia's neighbour Venezuela. Once again we see that internal flights are an important means of transport as, like Colombia, Venezuela has remote areas where flying is the easiest means of travelling from A to B. Trains are not popular and most of the railway lines are in the Highlands as this is where the iron ore mines are. Trains are an efficient means of transporting the iron ore from the mines to the factories. Thus we can see how transport and the economy are interrelated. Ships are also used extensively in this country and there are many ports, the main seaports being Puerto Cabello and Guanta.

Turning now to Europe. Belgium is a country that boasts one of the most compact railway systems worldwide. Inland waterways, or canals, are also an important means of transport, transporting both freight and people. Belgium also has the third largest seaport in the world, namely Antwerpen. Air travel is also important, although this is not linked to geographical terrain, as is the case in the South American countries we've already looked at. Next I'd like to look at the United Kingdom. Like Belgium, the UK has inland waterways, around 4000km, yet only about 17% of these are used for commercial transport.

The main inland port is Manchester and the chief seaport is London with Southampton taking second place. Air travel is extensive in this country and there are around 150 airports, the most famous being Heathrow. However, about 90% of passengers in the UK travel by road.

 1.29

Finally, I'd like to look at two Asian countries. China is a country which reveals how geographical size affects transport development. Roads and railways are widely used and this has led to a huge amount of bridges being built such as the Yangtse Bridge which is probably the most widely known. The Yangtse Bridge is 1.6km long and is built on two levels. The upper tier is for cars and pedestrians while the lower is for trains. Railways are especially important and over 80% of freight and passengers are transported by rail. With such a high proportion of people using trains, it is not surprising that governments in countries, like China are prepared to invest in the railway system. Obviously, a fast and effective train service will encourage businesses and the general public to continue using it. The last country I'm going to mention is Japan which has one of the most advanced transport systems in the world. The railway system is highly developed and the Tokaido railway, connecting Tokyo and Osaka has trains that can travel up to 250km per hour. Ships are also a vital means of transport, in both international and domestic areas.

To summarize, we can see that transport varies throughout the world, yet the importance of transport networks, be they air, sea, rail or road cannot be underestimated.

7 The world of work

 2.1

Well, I think it is highly likely that young people, particularly in my country, will still be buying brand names like Nike and Adidas. Of course I cannot definitely say whether or not this will be the case in other countries. Having said that, it's quite possible that brand names will still be popular amongst young people in Western countries because, if the present is anything to go by, then they will most probably still be trying to follow the latest fashions in the future.

 2.2

Hello and thanks everyone for coming here today. I know it's always a bit stressful going for a job interview, but it's best to be prepared. For any of you who may not know me, my name is Fiona Ogilvy and my job is to offer guidance and support for students with special needs. Now you wouldn't be here today if you weren't interested in finding a job in the holidays so let's get down to it and see what things you need to be looking out for. Most of you, I hope, will be applying for jobs with the companies that have been recommended by the university. The reason for this is that we here at the university, already know these companies and have established good working relationships with them. I've also been to visit all of them and checked out the facilities they have to offer. You really need to make informed choices when you're looking for a job and make sure you know before you even get to the interview stage, that your needs will be met. But I know that some of you are applying for jobs independently and have looked at companies outside the university recommended list, so for you it's best to plan ahead and be aware of what it is you may need while you're working. Things that you need to check when you go for an interview are: are there enough toilet facilities and are these easily accessible? Also, you want to check that all the public areas inside the building are barrier free so you can get direct access to these public spaces whenever you need to. And ask about ramps into the building so you know how many there are and where they are located. These kinds of things are so much more difficult to sort out when you've started work as they take time. But ramps are an absolute must so please make sure you know where they are. Another thing you must make sure of is that the lifts have the correct lowered control panels. Ask if all the lifts have this facility or if it's only certain ones. Now something I think that is often overlooked is working hours. What you want to make sure of is that you get flexitime. This basically means that your working hours are flexible and you can clock on and clock off at times that suit you – within reason of course! Most companies do recognize that it takes much longer for someone in a wheelchair to get on and off buses and trains – public transport can take that much longer so you need to be organized and prepared. And for those of you lucky enough to own a car, check how many disability parking spaces are available. Remember that it's your right to have a disabled parking space. These also need to be near enough to a wheelchair accessible entrance or ramp. OK, are there any questions before we move on?

 2.3

Right, let's move on then. Now I want to talk you through the series of visits to companies which we've got planned for next week. On Monday morning we will be visiting the Lowland Hotel. They have various summer jobs available working as a receptionist or conference organizer in their busy conference centre organizing and setting up conferences. You need to be prepared for working in an office environment and spending quite a bit of time talking on the telephone. The bus leaves for the hotel at 9.00am so make sure you leave yourself plenty of time to get there. When you arrive at the hotel, please gather in the reception area and wait for someone to take you to your first session, which will be a talk. The talk at the hotel will begin at 10am and then there will be a short tour of the hotel. There will be a light lunch provided which is usually salads and sandwiches. The next place we'll be visiting will be on Tuesday afternoon. We'll be going to visit a little local company that makes handmade paper and cards. For those of you studying art, this may be just what you're looking for. We'll be taken on a tour of the company which lasts 3 hours. The tour will start at 3.30 pm and after that you'll have a chance to meet some of the staff. Tea and coffee will also be provided. We have no trips planned for Wednesday, but on Thursday morning we'll be going to Tobago Travel Agency. This is a very popular choice amongst our students because you can get student discounts on holidays. We've booked a coach for this and it'll leave from outside the refectory at 8.00 am. You will need to bring a packed lunch for this so please don't forget. There is a little canteen where you can buy hot and cold food, but this is closed on Thursdays. Friday we'll be having representatives from all the companies visiting us so you will have a chance to ask any questions and, of course, put your name down on the list if you're interested in working for them over the summer. This event will take place in the main hall next to the library and it'll run from 10.30 until 4.00.

I really hope you make the most of this excellent opportunity to not only earn yourself some extra money, but also to gain experience of what it's like to work. And if you'd like to find out more, then please ask some of the students who worked last year. They're all wearing green badges and will be happy to speak to you afterwards.

 2.4

See page 116, exercise 3.

8 Art and the city

 2.5

Well, I think research is important for us as individual researchers. We need to know that our ideas and suggestions are valid. But more importantly, it's for others. We cannot prove our ideas effectively, unless we look back at the past, to research that has been done before. We then check past evidence with present day evidence to see if it correlates. So without research being done, ideas will not be made valid.

2.6

(M=Miwako; E=Enrique)

M: So Enrique, have you started your research project on cities yet?

E: I've done a bit of reading around the topic and made a few notes, but if I'm honest about it, I really haven't done as much as I'd have liked to because I'm finding it a bit difficult.

M: You don't know how relieved I am to hear you say that! I feel the same way. I think the key is to be able to make valid research questions.

E: You're probably right about that. Didn't we have some lectures on how to write research questions? I think it was towards the beginning of the term.

M: Yes we did. I've got my notes somewhere in this file. I tell you what, why don't we look at the notes together and then try and come up with some research questions. At least that would be a good starting point, give us some sense of where we're going with this.

E: Brilliant idea. Let's get started. OK, from what I remember, a good research question is all about knowing from the outset what it is you're trying to find out.

M: Yes, and now that I'm looking at my notes again, I see I've written here that it's to do with understanding and evaluation. So understanding a particular issue and evaluating any problems around it. And of course, a very important part is not overlooking any research that has already been done. Past research is just as important as what is being done now.

E: It's a bit, I suppose, like looking at the research that's already been done and seeing if it agrees or disagrees with your own ideas.

M: Mmmm … sure, I hear what you're saying, but to do that properly you have to have a clear idea in your head what your own research question is and by that I mean … specific areas you want to focus on. Let's face it, there's so much information out there and we can't possibly include it all in 2000 words.

E: Don't remind me ! The thought of writing 2000 words at the moment seems like a huge mountain to climb.

M: I know, but let's try to make a start. I think we're meant to be identifying what makes a successful city and also try to explain why there has been such a steady population movement of people from rural to urban areas. But I'm a bit confused because I don't think this is meant to be the main focus of our research.

E: Mmm ... perhaps that's why the lecturer said we need to write questions and that must be our starting point.

M: Okay … well what we're investigating is more than simply what elements make a city successful, but we're also trying to offer possible explanations so we have two questions:why do people want to move to cities and why do people choose to live in them?

2.7

E: Okay then, I think the first issue concerning successful cities must be the economy. People move to cities for better job prospects and successful cities are cities that have thriving economies.

M: That's true enough, it does mean that cities can offer good job opportunities, which seems to me to suggest that a city will only be successful if it attracts the right kind of people to work there.

E: What kind of person are you talking about?

M: Well, I suppose I'm referring to the skilled labour force. You know, the idea that up and coming young people will move to cities, settle there, maybe buy property and so that city will get the most talented, creative minds. But if a city doesn't offer this, then obviously it will lose out as university leavers will choose elsewhere.

E: You could be right there, but I also think that when cities encourage businesses to develop then you obviously have money pouring into the city, which can raise the general standard of living.

M: So we've definitely got a question worth investigating, but apart from the economic factor, I think another point worth mentioning is the environment.

E: Sure, we can research areas like the quality of the air, how clean it is and then there's traffic ... um … is there too much traffic, how is it controlled and also the issues of noise pollution and how the city manages its waste. Um … oh and I nearly forgot … the environment includes green spaces, like parks.

M: Those are all valid points, but I think you've overlooked the whole issue of beauty.

E: Beauty? Are you sure? What's beauty got to do with the environment?

M: Well don't you think if you were deciding whether or not you would live in a city, your first impressions would be made with your eyes. So the buildings in a city are really important. If the entire city looks like a concrete jungle, then it's unlikely to make people want to live there, is it? I think successful cities are those which have managed to strike a balance between old buildings and new ones. So of course, you'd have some buildings reflecting more modern architecture, but others that haven't lost their character and still represent the past.

E: You're right actually. I've often thought that buildings tell a story … I mean you can tell the history of a place by looking at the buildings.

M: I know exactly what you mean and let's not forget that the environment includes cultural aspects so for example, what's the cultural life like? For me, a successful city will be attractive because it will have lots to offer, like a good night life and a wide variety of places to visit in the day like museums and galleries, places like that.

E: True, true. My own view is that some cities have an energy about them … they're exciting to be in.

M: And other cities are the opposite! Well, we've covered so much ground here, but I think there's one final aspect we should research.

E: What's that then?

M: The social aspect because let's face it, cities are made up of people.

E: They are and surely a successful city would be one where there is a sense of community, a place where people would feel safe and want to raise families in.

M: This topic is limitless …

2.8

Welcome to this series of lectures on interpreting contemporary art. This morning I'd like to look at the whole issue of contemporary art, what it is, how do we interpret it, what are its uses and does art, in effect, have any advantages or disadvantages for society. I think at this point, it's important for me to clarify that I am looking at art from two main perspectives. Firstly, art as something made by and appreciated by individuals and secondly, art's relationship with society as it is society that supports, protects and encourages art. And I'm hoping that this lecture will act as a springboard for you to revisit your own artistic experiences and question your own ideas of what contemporary art means. Throughout this series of lectures, I'll be looking at various examples of art to illustrate my points.

However, if at any point, I show you an example which is unfamiliar, then please tell me as it is imperative that you be able to use your past experiences so that you can check to see if your ideas agree with mine. So if you have not seen a particular work of art before, then this will not work and let me remind you now, that at the end of these lectures, you will be given a written assignment which will consist of a 2500 word critical essay. This is not an art review, but an analysis of what you think this kind of art means.

Okay, so what is contemporary art? Well, my view is that contemporary art reflects a particular time in history. In terms of Western civilization, this is the period that became known as the Renaissance, which began roughly in 1450.

2.9

(See above for opening part of lecture.) But this becomes confusing as the modern era is also considered to be from 1789, from the time of the French revolution. Added to this are modern ideas and modern art that developed from 1890. This period has also been called the 'turn of the century.' To try and somehow bring all these periods together, I shall define contemporary art as any art created from 1920 up until the present day.

Turning now to the question of whether or not art is useful for society ... er ... well … when we look back at the history of the West, we can see that there has been a tradition, especially in Western Europe, of art that was official. This meant that the government sponsored or subsidized the art. It could be said, therefore, that art has a cultural use in that it can represent both the culture and history of a country … and ... um … let's remember what I said earlier, that this is both the history and culture of a particular time. Now the disadvantage of this kind of official art is that it tends to be academic and, by that I mean it is art that requires the person looking at it to be educated in art, at least to some extent. So it seems to me that this restricts this type of art to a particular social group and whether you agree with this concept or not will depend on if you believe that art should be accessible to everyone.

Of course, with the rapid developments in technology and advertising, the television, computer and various forms of digital media, art has changed and although there will always be a need for art to be subsidized by governments, we see today art forms that are surviving on individual subsidy. Sometimes this is through the support of wealthy patrons such as business men or famous people. But it also operates on a more simple level. Er ... I refer here to the art that is done on walls and in streets, sometimes called amateur art, but it is the art of graffiti and it is now accepted as an art form in itself. So here we come to what I see as another advantage for society in that art is a means by which people can express their ideas, their feelings. Of course, in the case of graffiti, there is much debate as to whether the advantages outweigh the more negative side which is when graffiti artists paint on public buildings. This creates unnecessary expense and also damages these buildings which are meant for public use. We will be looking at some examples of this later on.

Now many critics of contemporary art have pointed to art that is often violent and ... er ... even obscene. But I would like to suggest that such art is not meant to only shock us, it also has the element of exposure so it can teach us about the violence in society. This then brings us to another advantage of art: it can raise awareness, help us see things in a different light. The disadvantage of this is that art can be dangerous ... um ... what I'm saying here is that if we accept that contemporary art has the power to influence our feelings and attitudes, then we have to accept that art can evoke negative feelings like anger as much as it can give us feelings of hope and peace.

But art is, after all, about us so it can be about our beliefs and our behaviour and, as human beings, we possess both positive and negative traits. I'd like to show you some slides now to illustrate what I've been talking about ...

 2.10

Um … the best example I can think of is the *Mona Lisa*. It's really a famous painting, but that's not why I like it. I saw it in the Louvre Museum when I was on holiday last year. Uh … Of course, every tourist likes to go and see famous art, but I must admit that I was surprised the effect the painting had on me. There was something about the way her face was painted. Um … She seems to be smiling, but in quite a sad way. And I couldn't decide if she was looking at me or not! I remember standing there for a long time just staring at that face. Er … I believe that art is quite important because of the way it changes your perspective on things. For me this means that it helps me see things in a different way. Um … Ultimately I feel that art not only preserves our history and culture, but can also broaden our horizons and make us see life from a different angle.

9 Tomorrow's world

 2.11

1 February the 9th 2009
2 The 18th of December 2012
3 The 9th of February 2006
4 53 88 2017
5 54 999 420

 2.12

1 1760
2 763 0029
3 30
4 50
5 1860
6 15
7 1550
8 80
9 13
10 2016

 2.13

1 Some of the first more advanced mobile phones were introduced into high street shops in December 2006, just before Christmas.
2 It would not be true to say that he rode a bicycle from the age of 4 to 40, because when he was 14 he broke his leg, which meant he didn't ride for at least 12 months.
3 The company forecast that by 2014 there will be at least 120 billion children buying their computer game, an increase of about 19%, which is not as much as they had hoped for.
4 The first satellite was launched in 1958 and there are probably now over 150 still in operation.
5 He graduated from university in the 1960s and never dreamt that his invention would still be used 16 years later.
6 On the 18th November, 98,217 people visited the website and voted for the movie 'Titanic', first released in 1997.
7 I'd love you to give me a call sometime. I know you've got my old number, 237 5550, but I've got a new mobile now so my number's changed to 344 4533.

 2.14

Good morning. This is Jane Frost with this morning's edition of 'Wake up with Frost'. As you all know, for the last week we've been running a survey trying to find out what you, the listeners, think is the greatest invention of the last 200 years. The response has been amazing, double the amount we had last year, so thanks to all of you for taking part. We've had about 2000 responses online and about the same on our phone lines. The lines are now closed and this morning I can announce what the results were. So here it is … you the listeners have chosen as the greatest technological invention of the past 200 years, and let me not forget to mention that 65% of you voted for this ... it's the bicycle! Yes, the bicycle, first invented in 1818 and, would you believe it, the first bicycle was made of wood. The second bicycle had iron wheels … I cannot imagine what that must have been like to ride. It would have kept you fit at any rate. But for me, the best thing about the bicycle was what it did for women's rights. Yes, in the 1890s it was the bicycle that meant women could change their clothing, start wearing trousers or pantaloons as they were known. Before then women's clothes had been really uncomfortable and, I'd imagine, quite difficult to breathe in. So thanks to the ordinary bicycle, it was not only the man who wore the trousers in a home. Instead women could now feel far more equal to their male contemporaries. And I'm sure you'll agree, the bicycle is a great way to get regular exercise and of course, it's much better for the environment. And today over one billion people all over the world ride bicycles and for some, it's their only means of getting around from A to B. So to all you bicycle riders out there … keep up the good work! Coming in a close second, with 42% is the computer. I found out something interesting about the computer which is that really, this word first meant someone who did mathematical calculations. Of course, today with the development of the personal computer, computers are being used for everything from home use, to business and even digital photography. I don't know about you, but I can't imagine life without a computer now. I guess, closely related to the computer is the internet and this got 12% of your votes. Maybe like myself, many of you might think of the internet as being the World-Wide Web, but actually the web is only one part of the internet. The internet began as part of the United States military network, but it later began to be used by businesses and academic institutions. Of course today, the internet has so many uses. We use it for shopping online and entertainment as well as to find information and send emails. But sadly, there is a darker side to the internet and some of you have sent me emails about this.

Finally, with 5% of your votes, is the radio. We think the radio was invented by Marconi in 1896 and he opened his first radio or 'wireless' factory in the United Kingdom in 1898. In 1906, a man called Reginald Fessenden gave the first radio broadcast from Massachusetts. Ships could hear him at sea and apparently he played the violin. As yet, listeners, I've spared you from having to listen to my guitar playing. But certainly radio is still important. Let's not forget that it was by radio that the Titanic sent signals to other ships. And with the popularity of TV today, I was secretly pleased so many of you had still placed importance on the radio. So there you have it … the results of our survey. I think there are still important inventions that were not chosen but deserve a mention … nuclear power and, of course, communications satellite, something which I am certain will continue to change the face of how we communicate with each other over both long and short distances. In fact, for me, the mobile phone is one of the greatest inventions of the last 200 years. If I think back to my first phone and then I look at what is happening now. Children born today will probably be more likely to have their first experience of the internet on a mobile phone screen rather than a computer monitor. Some of the new mobiles that are now being sold make it just as easy and as quick to find information on the web as on a computer.

And let's not forget that mobiles now have digital cameras, word processing facilities, so you can type all your documents, and even personal organizers. I think it's quite possible that the mobile may even replace computers one day.

2.15

Candidate 1: I really love my little local corner shop. I simply adore being able to shop there, just because it's so convenient. I mean … it's got all the basics, bread, milk, washing up liquid and other things like that.

One of my favourite things is being able to pop down on a Sunday and buy the papers and some fresh bread. I know some of my friends think it's too expensive, but I think it's worth every penny. And I think little shops are such an important part of local life and so we should support them.

I feel really passionately about this because I've seen many small businesses being forced to close because they can't compete with larger chainstores. Anyway, my local store is totally amazing. I certainly couldn't live without it!

2.16

Candidate 2: Mmm … well, I usually try and shop at smaller shops as much as possible. If I'm perfectly honest, I just can't stand big supermarkets. They are so impersonal and I really hate the long queues. There's nothing worse than having to wait in a queue, especially when you're in a hurry. It's such a complete waste of time. I'm also totally disgusted by the way in which larger supermarket chains are taking business away from smaller shops. I'm all for supporting local traders because I think they're incredibly important for the community.

2.17

Good afternoon and welcome to this special seminar on what I believe is one of the most exciting ways in which science and technology have merged, namely through what has become known as nanotechnology. While it may be true to say that many inventions in the world of technology have been large-scale, nanotechnology proves that it's possible that what is bigger will not necessarily be best. For nanotechnology involves the science and ability to create something extremely small using computer and electronic technology. If we look back at the past, we see the pocket watch as an example of this. And in its day, this watch was much admired: something small, that could fit into a pocket and yet still function as well as a larger-sized watch or clock. Of course, to find a more recognizable starting point for nanotechnology, we need to look at the world of electronics. Certainly, electronics clearly showed that smaller was better. In fact, the smaller the electronic gadget, the more effective and useful it is. Now those of you who attended my lecture on electronics last week, will remember that I spoke about how earlier radio technology was quite awkward and difficult to operate. Then after World War Two, the transistor was developed which changed the face of radio. This involved a series of electronic switches that could be placed on a board no bigger than a postage stamp. This meant that an entire electronic circuit could be built in a much smaller area. Naturally, this was not only faster, but it also saved space and more importantly, energy. For those of you who are interested in the transistor, come speak to me afterwards and I'll give you a copy of my handouts from last week.

But moving on with the subject of today's talk, the development of the electronic chip meant that we began to use terms like microchip, and in doing so place importance on its size being vastly smaller. But as this form of microtechnology developed and literally became smaller, the word 'micro' meaning one millionth, was replaced with the word 'nano' which literally means one billionth. There were pessimists who doubted whether a transistor that small would actually work properly, but they were proved wrong and in a modern transistor, what is known as the gate length, or distance the electrons have to travel is only about 40 nanometres … um … I'm sure you will agree, this is unbelievably tiny and not only that, the electrons can travel incredibly fast. And as scientists continue to develop these transistors, there is every chance that they may become even smaller. Of course, one of the problems with developments and designs in technology is that they must not only be practical, but also affordable so it might be that companies will not continue supporting nanotechnology, if it turns out to be too expensive to produce in the long-term.

But one area where there has been major improvements is medicine where nanotechnology is being used to fight life-threatening diseases like cancer. Recently, an American university discovered that nanotechnology can be used to help make systems that supply drugs to the body. A quick way to make sure drugs enter the body is by making artificial molecules. These are in the shape of a star and are small enough to go into cells and release the drugs. In this new system, the molecule is made of two star-shapes, connected by a strand of DNA. Each shape is roughly 3–4 nanometres long. At one end, the star molecule will enter the diseased cell, while at the other end there is a tracking device, which is fluorescent so that it can light up when it has reached a diseased cell. It is hoped that this will be … um ... a more effective way to fight diseases. But we must not forget that dangers will always exist in the world of technological changes. One I'd like to focus on is as yet unproven and is still the subject of much speculation. It involves the idea that a molecular machine could be built using something called an 'assembler'. This means one machine would make another machine, but of course, these machines would be operated by people. However, some scientists are concerned that there is a real future possibility these machines could replicate themselves and so no longer be controlled by human beings. But while anything in the world of chemistry is probable, I think it's highly unlikely that we could ever develop a machine capable of replicating itself. Still, if anything, it shows that nanoparticles, like any technology should be carefully and constantly monitored. Next week I will be looking at nanotechnology and recent developments in the field of molecular biology. I hope that you will be able to join me then.

2.18

1 it's on the TAble.

2 your PHONE is on the TAble.

3 your MObile PHONE is on the TAble.

4 you HAVEn't LOST your PHONE – it's on the TAble.

[NB Capital letters indicate stressed syllables.]

2.19

1 The bicycle is a great way to get regular exercise and it's much better for the environment.

2 The Internet began as part of the United States' military network, but it later began to be used by businesses and academic institutions.

3 Nanotechnology has crept into many areas of our lives.

4 Scientists are concerned that there's a real possibility that these machines could replicate themselves.

5 Next week I'll be looking at nanotechnology and recent developments in the field of molecular biology.

10 From me to you

2.20

(R=Receptionist;S=Student)

R: Good morning. Language Resource Centre. How can I help you?

S: Hi, I've just registered to do a post-graduate degree and I was wondering how I go about joining the resource centre.

R: Okay, the first thing you need to do is come in and bring some form of identification with you.

S: You mean like my driving license.

R: Actually we prefer you to bring in something from your university registration. Students have in the past used their passports, but we really do prefer you to bring in your student card with your ID number. This should be on the front of the card and begins with the letters BNP followed by a number.

S: Okay, that's no problem. And could you tell me what facilities you offer in the centre?

R: Certainly. We have a range of books, although not as extensive as the library of course. Still, you'll find that we do stock some of the books on your reading list, particularly for post-graduate level. The undergraduate students usually find that the main library caters better for their needs.

S: That's good to hear because I was worried about not being able to find the books on the reading list, especially if more than one student wants to use the same book. I find that really frustrating.

R: We are aware of this and it's precisely because of this that we've got a special system whereby you can borrow books, but only on a short loan basis.

S: And how long is that?

R: There are two types of short loan books.

One is a two day loan, but the other one is for a single day and must be brought back the next day. We have to be really strict with this kind of loan so there is quite a heavy fine if you don't bring it back.

S: Of course, I hope I'm not going to be in that situation, but can you tell me anyway how much it is?

R: Sure, it's £1.75 for a one day loan and £1.00 for a two day loan ... then it's 50 pence a day on top of that.

S: 50 pence for each extra day!

R: Yes, until you return the book. It sounds steep, but it's really for the students' benefit. You said yourself that it can be annoying not being able to find books you need.

S: Okay fair enough. I presume you also have journals?

R: Oh yes, we have a wide range of academic journals and many of these are available online.

S: Fantastic! Can I access these from outside the college?

R: Yes, you can, but you need to register for this. Er ... You can do this when you come in. Basically you need your student ID again and we give you an internet password, which you can then change if you like. Most students do because it's easier for them to memorize.

S: I'll definitely do that. I'm hopeless at remembering passwords so the only way I can remember one is if I make it up myself.

R: You will also find reading lists online as well as where to find the books, so this means you won't have to waste time trying to find books you need.

S: That's really good to know. Knowing exactly where to go to find a book is such a time saver.

R: Mmm ... We also have a special page, which gives you links to other university libraries so if we don't have the book, er ... we can help you get it.

S: Is that any other university library?

R: No, it's just the ones that have joined. It's known as the inter-university library loan system. But you'll find when you go to the web page that quite a few universities have joined and it's growing all the time.

S: What a great idea. I mean, not only to be able to get books, but just to be given the opportunity to exchange ideas with students on other campuses.

R: I quite agree. Oh ... and you'll also see when you come in, that we have a wide selection of videos you can borrow. These range from films to actual lectures and seminars that have been videoed so students have the opportunity to watch them again if they need to or if for some reason, they were not able to attend. And it's pretty much standard that we video visiting lecturers.

S: And are these also available on tape?

R: Yes they are. And also on CD. Actually, having said that, we don't put all our lectures and seminars on CD, except visiting speakers. Their talks are always put on both so you can choose either.

S: This all sounds fantastic. I never realized there was so much on offer.

R: Yes, we're very proud of our Learning Resource Centre and the university has given extra funding to make sure we can keep all our resources up to date.

2.21

S: I know you mentioned online books and journals ... um ... how many computers does the resource centre have?

R: Oh we have a lot of computers. Basically there are three floors and we have computers on each one, but these are only for searching for the books or articles you may need. They cannot be used for anything else.

S: Oh I see. So they're really just search engines. And how do you use them?

R: Well, there are a number of ways you can do this. You can use the author's name, but I'm not talking about the first name. Only the surname will work so you need to know the correct spelling.

S: That sounds quite straightforward. And what are the other ways?

R: Well, you can also do a keyword search, which means typing in a keyword from the title of the book, that's for when you're not sure of the title. But when you do this, you will obviously get a list of books that have this word in the title.

S: In a way, getting a book list like this is really an advantage because it can give you ideas about what other books to read.

R: That's true, but just bear in mind that it takes a little bit longer. Of course, you can also type in a subject keyword and then you'll be given a list of authors and titles around that subject. The final way is of course by keying in the name of the book.

And don't forget, there's an information desk so you can always ask someone if you need help.

S: Where is that?

R: You'll find the help desk on the ground floor.

S: Great, and are there any other computers to use generally for checking emails and things like that?

R: Yes, there is a computer centre in the basement, but we prefer students to use these computers more for study purposes so please don't spend all your time doing things like checking your emails and you most definitely cannot use it to play computer games. If you are caught doing this, you will be banned from using our computers for 2 weeks. No, sorry, because of all the problems we had with this last year, this has now been increased to three.

S: One week without a computer would be too much for me!

R: Mmm ... But please don't worry, because when you first come, we'll give you a tour of the library and show you how everything works. Do you know where we are?

2.22

(G=Gabriella; D=Dong; T=Tutor)

G: Thanks for seeing me today. I've been really worried about my media assignment.

D: Yes, me too. I feel much the same way as Gabriella does.

T: Yes, I realized that. Um ... And thanks for sending me your first drafts. I've had a look at them and there are a few things that need revisiting.

D: I guessed you'd probably say that.

T: Right, let's start at the beginning. Um ... You both had different problems so I'll speak to each of you in turn. Let's start with you Gabriella. Tell me, what did you hope to achieve with this assignment?

G: Okay, erm ... well I suppose my main idea was really to look at the news.

T: Can you be more specific?

G: Well ... er ... my main focus was really news values, I mean how do presenters and broadcasters, people like that, actually decide what is newsworthy? And as much as I'd have liked to have studied TV news, I had to make the choice between television and newspapers, and I chose the latter.

T: Fine. Er ... Now that did come across in your introduction. But I wonder if the scope of your essay was too wide? You did try and include an awful lot.

G: I was afraid of that. I spent ages reading newspapers and trying to choose the right items. But it's really difficult to know what to include and what to leave out.

T: Well ... shall we look at it together and see if we can make the focus of your essay more specific? Many students find it hard to know what information to select, especially when they read a lot.

G: It would really help me to see where I've gone wrong so I don't repeat this mistake again.

T: Okay. Now here in paragraph one, you focus on the negativity in the news.

G: Yes ... um ... I was trying to highlight the fact that really, the general public will usually choose bad news above good. They seem to like it more because bad news sells ... it makes headlines. We like reading about disasters and tragedy.

T: That's true, but I think what you did not explain enough was why this is the case. Is it something in human nature or is it just that this is how we've become accustomed to receiving news? I thought maybe you could have given some examples here, maybe compared two newspapers, a broadsheet and a tabloid perhaps, to look at how they presented a particular negative piece of news. Er ... Was it dramatized for example? Which one was more sensationalistic?

G: Ah yes ... I can think of so many examples of that. I mean ... you can really see the dramatic effect in an item of news in the pictures that go with the story.

T: Right, now you're getting the idea.

G: Do you think I did the same thing in the second paragraph?

T: Actually, I thought you'd organized this much better. It was clearer. I liked the way you mentioned the value of continuity in the news. Er … Continuity is important because quite obviously, the longer an item of news lasts, the more people will buy the newspaper because they are interested in what is happening. Your example of war was a good one because … er ... most wars last a while so the story will stay in the news.

G: But I also wanted to explain how readers can lose interest in a news story and that was really my main emphasis.

T: Yes, I really liked that part of your paragraph. It showed you'd really thought about what you'd read and had the confidence to add your own ideas. The rest of your essay, apart from a few minor grammar mistakes, was fine.

D: And what about mine?

T: Well, the first few paragraphs were really good, clearly constructed and easy to follow. But er … I don't think you did this as well in the third paragraph. What were you trying to get across?

D: I was trying to explain about celebrities. What is defined in news terms as the personality angle. The fact that we are … er ... you know, interested in stories about famous people.

T: Sure, but I think you need to focus on what this means for the news. What about looking at how newspapers often publish popular news stories and how this might go against the news attempting to be neutral?

D: So what you are saying is the news is meant to be objective, but actually it isn't really?

T: Certainly … I'm saying you should try and make more comparisons between the objectivity and subjectivity and see which way the news usually tends to go.

D: Mmm … would you suggest I take a particular news item and compare the way two newspapers report on it?

T: That would be an excellent idea. In fact you could even use some of the ideas from your first paragraph – maybe take a so-called bad news story.

D: That's a good idea and I could use the same newspapers.

T: Yes, but you could also look at two other newspapers with similar styles … Um maybe another tabloid and broadsheet.

D: I like that idea.

T: I also felt maybe you could have included the idea of recent news because this links in with what you've already said.

D: I don't quite understand.

T: Well … I'm referring to the idea that newspapers try and get scoops, any big story that has recently happened. You could link this to your first paragraph and even your second.

D: The public is really interested in what is happening now rather than what is old news.

T: And you could bring in the effect of technology on the news at this point. It has affected news reporting and publishing tremendously. If you think about it, the internet has meant that news can be much more immediate than before so for example, as something is happening, it could be reported and published in a paper.

D: Oh yes, I remember reading once about an earthquake and just before the building collapsed, someone at the top sent an email to a newspaper. I mean this just proves that at the click of a button, we can communicate so much more quickly than before.

T: Yes, that's the kind of thing I'm talking about, but just make sure that you have evidence to support what you say.

2.23

Examiner: Do you often use a library?

Speaker 1: Er ... um ... I … I … I think I try to use library about … um … well … maybe once or twice a week.

Examiner: Okay, and are libraries popular in your country?

Speaker 1: Um ... um … Yes, yes … Libraries are very popular … yes, they have always been popular in my country.

Examiner: Do you think people will still visit libraries in ten years' time?

Speaker 1: Mmmmm … no … no … I think this probably won't happen … um … I … I can't say for certain, but I think probably not.

2.24

Examiner: Do you often use a library?

Speaker 2: Oh yes, I using library all the time. No-one can really live without a library because we needing it for many things, like education and also to broaden our minds.

Examiner: Right and are libraries popular in your country?

Speaker 2: Oh yes. I can definitely say that library is extremely important for many people in my country. We have long history of books and … yes, I think, it's true to say, that people in my country likes reading. In fact, they probably very much likes to reading.

Examiner: Do you think people will still visit libraries in say ten years' time?

Speaker 2: Well, no-one can really say what the future holds, but I think, yes, we will still go. Even though some people, they say internet will stopping people from reading. But I think there will always be people who prefer the books.

Macmillan Education
Between Towns Road, Oxford OX4 3PP
A division of Macmillan Publishers Limited
Companies and representatives throughout the world

ISBN 978-1-4050-8075-0

Text © Mark Allen, Debra Powell and Dickie Dolby 2007
Design and illustration © Macmillan Publishers Limited 2007

First published 2007

All rights reserved; no part of this publication may be reproduced, stored in a retrieval system, transmitted in any form, or by any means, electronic, mechanical, photocopying, recording, or otherwise, without the prior written permission of the publishers.

Designed by eMC Design; www.emcdesign.org.uk
Illustrated by Peter Cornwell, Stephen Dew, Stephen Elford (Lemonade Illustration), Roger Goode (Beehive Illustration), Martin Sanders (Beehive Illustration), Mark Turner (Beehive Illustration), Laszlo Veres (Beehive Illustration).
Cover design by Andrew Oliver.
Cover photograph supplied by Alamy.

The authors would like to thank Nicolette, Rosa and Luc Allen for their love, patience and cups of tea; Christopher Lewis for his patience and support; Keith Aleandri for inspiration and Christopher and Amanzi Dolby for much-needed background support; Pam Lynch, John Ward, and Suzanne Malin; Tom Wood, the IELTS team and all our colleagues at Sussex Downs College for their constant support; Sarah Curtis; Amanda Anderson for her tireless editing and sound advice.

The publishers would like to thank Paulette Dooler, Mary Jane Hogan, Nicola Joseph, Charlie Martineau, Graham Rogers and Jane Short.

The authors and publishers would like to thank the following for permission to reproduce their material:
Extract from 'Battle of Sexes Whirls Above Science Gap' by Natalie Angier and Kenneth Chang copyright © The New York Times Co 2005, first published in *The New York Times* 24.01.05, reprinted by permission of the publisher. Extract from 'Unhealthy, unhappy and with no self-esteem: British teenagers lag behind world's young' by Maxine Frith copyright © The Independent 2004, first published in *The Independent* 04.06.04, reprinted by permission of the publisher. Extract from article about 'Albert Einstein' from *Mensa* Magazine February 2005, reprinted by permission of the publisher. Extract from 'The End of the Oil Age?' by Andrew English copyright © The Telegraph 2004, first published in *The Telegraph* 29.05.04, reprinted by permission of the publisher. Adapted extract from 'More Profit with Less Carbon' by Amory Lovins copyright © Scientific American, Inc. 2005, first published in *Scientific American* September 2005, reprinted by permission of the publisher. Extract from 'Why eating chocolate is good for you' first published in *The Daily Mail* 28.03.00, reprinted by permission of Solo Syndication Ltd. Extract from '20 things you never knew about colds' first published in *The Daily Mail* 10.11.98, reprinted by permission of Solo Syndication Ltd. Extract from 'Your own medicine' by Shereen El Feki copyright © The Economist Newspaper Limited, London 2005, first published in *Intelligent Life* Summer 2005, reprinted by permission of the publisher. Extract from 'Tired all the time?' by Sara Phillips copyright © Sara Phillips 2004 taken from *www.abc.net.au/health*, reprinted by permission of the author.
Extract from 'Four hurricanes in five weeks' by Michael McCarthy copyright © The Independent 2004, first published in *The Independent* 21.09.04, reprinted by permission of the publisher. Extract from *Weatherwatch* by Valerie Wyatt and illustrated by Pat Cupples (Kids Can Press Ltd, Toronto, 1990), text copyright © Valerie Wyatt 1990, reprinted by permission of the publisher. Extract from 'A Lot of Bad News for Bears' by Usha Lee McFarling copyright © Los Angeles Times 2002, first published in *Los Angeles Times* 28.11.02, reprinted by permission of the publisher. Extract from 'Save the Rainforest' taken from *Wildlife Fact File* copyright © WWF-UK 2004, reprinted by permission of the publisher. Article about Disney, reprinted by permission of Euro Disney Associes S.C.A. Extract from 'The town that tired of life in the shadows' by Cahal Milmo copyright © The Independent 2005, first published in *The Independent* 26.03.05, reprinted by permission of the publisher. Extract from 'Ecotourism – Is it Really Worth It?' by Chad Crandell, Julie Curtis and Shannon Ingalls taken from *Social Issues and Psychology: Psychology & The Environment (www.users.muohio.edu),* Fall 1997, reprinted by permission of the publisher. Extract from 'You Want Any Fruit With That Big Mac?' by Melanie Warner copyright © The New York Times 2005, first published in *The New York Times* 20.02.05, reprinted by permission of the publisher. Extract from *Assertiveness for Managers* by Terry Gillen (Gower Publishing, 1992), copyright © Terry Gillen 1992, reprinted by permission of the author. Extract from *Twentieth Century Architecture* by Jonathan Glancey (Carlton Books, 1998), reprinted by permission of the publisher.Extract from 'Myths of the City' by Rodger Doyle copyright © Rodger Doyle 2005, first published in *Scientific American* September 2005. Extract from 'Human Population Grows Up' by Joel E Cohen copyright © Scientific American 2005, first published in *Scientific American* September 2005, reprinted by permission of the publisher. Extract from *Mass Communication Theory* 4th edition by Denis McQuail (SAGE Publications, 2000), copyright © Denis McQuail 2000, reprinted by permission of the publisher and author. Extract from *Macmillan English Dictionary For Advanced Learners* (Macmillan Publishers Limited, 2002), text © Bloomsbury Publishing Plc 2002, reprinted by permission of the publishers.

The authors and publishers would like to thank the following for permission to reproduce their photographs:
Alamy/Andre Jenny p114, Alamy/Charles Bowman (tl) p121,Alamy/Chuck Pefley (cl), p56, Alamy/David Crausby (tl) p56, Alamy/Diondia Images (t) p72, Alamy/Esa Hiltula (c) p104, Alamy/Eye 35.com (tr) p121, Alamy/Garry Gay (r) p72, Alamy/Iain Masterton (bl) p152, Alamy/Image State (bl) p8, Alamy/Image State, p121, Alamy/Jon Arnold (tl) p121, Alamy/PCL (tr) p152, Alamy/Jerome Yeats p152 (tl) Alamy/Phil Talbot (b & tr) p40, Alamy/Photolibrary Wales (tr) p8, Alamy/Skyscan Photolibrary (c) p120, Alamy/Worldfoto (r) p24.
Banana stock RF (tr, cr, b) p56.
Brand X pp44/45, 16, 52, 64, 111, 128, 142.
Corbis/Disney/EPA p94,Corbis/Murat Taner/Zefa (tl) p40, Corbis/Reuters (l) p165, Corbis/Richard Klune p88, Corbis/Simon Marcus (tl) p24.
Corbis (RF) pp129, 133.
Creatas P61.
Digital Vision pp76, 85.
Getty Images pp (c) p24, (tl & tr) p104, (r) p165.
Getty/Stone pp(br) p8, (tr) p24.
Getty/Taxi (l) p72, (tr) p120.
Martyn Chillmaid (tl) p8.
PhotoDisc pp13, 38, 80, 149, (tc) 152, 154, 162.
ThinkStock p35.

Commissioned photography by Chris Honeywell (cr & c) p152.

Picture research by Alison Prior

The authors and publishers would like to thank the following for permission to reproduce their photographic material:
Unit 2
Life satisfaction/Smoking Charts
The Independent
Unit 7
The New York Times

Although we have tried to trace and contact copyright holders before publication, in some cases this has not been possible. If contacted we will be pleased to rectify any errors or omissions at the earliest opportunity.

Printed and bound in Thailand

2012 2011 2010 2009 2008
10 9 8 7 6 5 4 3